THE MAGNIFICENT SEVEN

THE MAGNIFICENT SEVEN

College Basketball's Blue Bloods

MARK MEHLER AND JEFF TIBERII

Essex, Connecticut

An imprint of the Globe Pequot Publishing Group, Inc.
64 South Main Street
Essex, CT 06426
www.lyonspress.com

Distributed by NATIONAL BOOK NETWORK

British Library Cataloguing in Publication Information available

Library of Congress Cataloging-in-Publication Data

Names: Mehler, Mark (Journalist), author. | Tiberii, Jeff, author.
Title: The magnificent seven : college basketball's blue bloods / Mark
   Mehler and Jeff Tiberii.
Description: Essex, CT : Lyons Press, 2025. | Includes index.
Identifiers: LCCN 2024038630 (print) | LCCN 2024038631 (ebook) | ISBN
   9781493084470 (paperback) | ISBN 9781493084487 (epub)
Subjects: LCSH: National Collegiate Athletic Association. | Basketball
   teams—United States. | College sports—United States.
Classification: LCC GV885.415.N38 M45 2025 (print) | LCC GV885.415.N38
   (ebook) | DDC 796.323/630973—dc23/eng/20241208
LC record available at https://lccn.loc.gov/2024038630
LC ebook record available at https://lccn.loc.gov/2024038631

Contents

INTRODUCTION

Meet the Magnificent

ON JANUARY 17, 1998, WILT CHAMBERLAIN CAME ALL THE WAY HOME to Allen Fieldhouse just to say I'm sorry.

Sorry for letting down his team, the University of Kansas, and, at least in Wilt's worried mind, the entire sovereign state of Kansas, by not delivering them a championship in an excruciating 54–53, triple-OT loss to North Carolina in the 1957 NCAA title game.

In truth, the Big Dipper had nothing—NOTHING—for which to apologize. He played exceedingly well that evening, to the tune of twenty-three points and fourteen boards. Had his six teammates who saw action in that game managed to score more than thirty combined points, on horrendous 26 percent shooting, Allen Fieldhouse would be displaying five, rather than four, championship banners.

"I'm afraid they're going to boo me," Wilt confided to a reporter before taking center court at halftime to have his jersey retired.

Wrong again, big fella.

Wilt had neglected to consider that Kansas basketball fans tend to have a more sweeping view of their legends than can be defined by a single one-point loss. Wilt walked out on the court that night to rapturous, sustained applause, befitting a man of his accomplishments and fundamental human kindness and decency. Their welcome had the seven-foot-one colossus battling back the tears.

That loss forty-one years ago was "devastating to me," Wilt told the crowd, "because I felt I had let you all down."

"But then I come out here today and realize how many people have shown me so much appreciation, love and warmth . . . I learned one thing over the years, and that is that you have to take the bitter with the sweet. And how sweet this is right here!"

You'll be reading more about Wilt Chamberlain and his time at KU in this book, which is all about the evolution of seven legendary Division I basketball programs—their histories, their cultures, their triumphs (and occasional travails), and all the legends who made those seven stories worth telling.

Here's how we chose our subjects:

SUCCESS

Our "seven beauties"—Indiana, Kentucky, Duke, North Carolina, UCLA, Kansas, and UConn (the University of Connecticut)—to this date have collectively garnered forty-five of the eighty-five NCAA championships contested since the tournament commenced in 1939. That's a 53 percent win rate. Push the clock forward to 1950, and the win rate rises to 57 percent.

Each of the seven has won at least four titles (eleven for UCLA; eight for Kentucky; six each for UConn and UNC; five each for Indiana and Duke; and four for Kansas). Add to these dozens and dozens of Final Four and Elite Eight appearances.

Not to belittle the sheer delights of March Madness, but the ongoing success of these seven programs highlights an oft-neglected aspect of the NCAA tournament. Indeed, one might term it the obverse of madness. Beneath all the unpredictable zaniness of mid-March, there lies an equally thick layer of normality and sanity that fully reveals itself in early April.

LONGEVITY AND CONSISTENCY

None of our elite seven is a one- or two-decade wonder. All have earned their spurs over a period of at least three decades. Kentucky, for its part, started winning championships way back in 1948. It won again the following season, then twice in the '50s, once in the '70s, twice more in the

'90s, and a last one in 2012. That's five decades' worth of titles, under five different head coaches.

North Carolina has also hoisted NCAA tournament banners in five different decades, the first in 1957 and the most recent in 2017. Duke and Indiana each copped five titles over a span of four decades.

And then, there are the UConn Huskies, who were very late to this party but have more than made up for it. They didn't grab their first brass ring until 1999, but since then, they've been on quite a roll. A second title in 2004, two more in the following decade, a fifth in 2023, and a sixth in '24. In total, six championships in twenty-five years over the course of four decades, the most of any school during this period.

Of course, when it comes to miraculous rolls, we have the poster child in UCLA, which has won eleven championships in three decades— ten of them in one twelve-year stretch. That's a roll that will almost certainly never be approached, let alone duplicated, and qualifies UCLA for inclusion in this book regardless of its relatively brief longevity.

Moreover, as consistent as our seven have been on the winning side, they've been even more dependable when it comes to keeping the losing streaks to a bare minimum. Kentucky, for example, had its last back-to-back losing seasons more than one hundred years ago. Carolina hasn't gone back-to-back on the minus side in seventy-two years (1952), and Duke and Kansas haven't posted two losing records in a row in more than forty years. Regularity up and down the line.

All our blue bloods have been playing the long game.

Copious Legends

A basketball program cannot reach these kinds of heights without the benefit of legendary figures. All our programs have had the great good fortune to be associated at various times with the finest coaches and players in the college game. Men whose contributions to the game would have survived the ages, even without the banners.

Take James Naismith, who had the bright idea of stitching together some leather panels around a rubber bladder and making a healthy, fun game out of putting that ball in a peach basket. Naismith brought his marvelous invention to Kansas University in the late 1890s and established the first collegiate basketball program there. Naismith was soon followed as head coach by Phog Allen. All Allen did during the first half of the twentieth century was cement the notion that coaching mattered. Hence, the human coaching highlight reel that has defined KU basketball since its inception—Naismith, Allen, Dean Smith, Larry Brown, Roy Williams, Bill Self, Gregg Popovich, Ted Owens, John Calipari—all have left their imprints in Lawrence.

Michael Jordan, John Wooden, Kareem Abdul-Jabbar, Mike Krzyzewski, Bobby Knight, Bill Walton, Danny Manning, Frank McGuire, Jim Calhoun, and Isiah Thomas are just a few of the many Hall of Fame names contributing to those forty-five championships.

RIVALRIES

As Bette Davis had her Joan Crawford, the Yankees their Red Sox, and Bugs Bunny his Elmer Fudd, blue-blood basketball programs are energized by their fierce, ardent rivalries.

Where would Duke and UNC be without each other? Or Kentucky without Louisville, and UConn absent Georgetown and Syracuse? Similarly, Indiana wouldn't be quite the same without Purdue, or would Kansas without its in-state nemesis, Kansas State, or its old "border war" foe, Missouri.

UCLA, however, is the outlier in this regard. As the reigning king back when it was snatching up titles like violets in spring, UCLA was the primary target of every big-time college basketball program. For a brief period in the late '60s, Bob Boyd's USC Trojans, with their stifling stall tactics, befuddled the Bruins. Notre Dame and Houston also had their moments versus the Wizard of Westwood. Even now, with the afterglow of the ten Wooden championships long dimmed, the Bruins still seem to be standing alone on a hill and everyone else consumed with knocking them off it.

FOCUS, FOCUS, FOCUS

In 2006, a sexual abuse scandal surrounding the Duke University lacrosse team roiled the entire campus; the town of Durham, North Carolina; and a large chunk of America. But not so much the basketball team.

Asked many years later how the team managed to keep its eyes on the ball, so to speak, amid all that noise and discord, assistant coach Steve Wojciechowski nailed it concisely:

"Whatever was going on outside our little world, our main concern was about basketball, putting out the best team we could."

That kind of mind-set is essential in the achievement of long-term success and is a chief characteristic of all our seven blue bloods.

It can be glimpsed in John Wooden's meticulously mapped-out daily practice routine, executed with an attention to detail unmatched in the history of college basketball. Or in the demand of the fiery Indiana coach Bob Knight that his players put aside all else and adhere to the highest levels of discipline and self-control on the court. Unfortunately, Coach Knight didn't always apply the same level of discipline to his personal behavior, something you'll read about in some depth in the Indiana chapter.

THE LIMELIGHT TO THEMSELVES

It is no coincidence that none of our seven beauties has an accompanying big-time football program to hog the media attention, capture the loyalty of a large fan base, and gobble up all the sorely needed athletic department resources.

Although a few basketball teams (Michigan, Ohio State, Florida) have managed to share in the reflected glory of their powerhouse football programs, there appears to be a strong correlation between basketball success and pigskin failure.

UCLA, once again, is somewhat of an exception, as its football team, under the legendary Red Sanders, was the dominant sports program on campus during the early Wooden years. Sanders's 1954 team won UCLA's only football title, and his program won about 77 percent of its games overall. But once Wooden started piling up the titles, UCLA football faded into the thick LA haze and has not fully emerged since.

ROLLING WITH THE PUNCHES

There are no saints in college basketball. There never were.

But today, the stakes are higher, and the rules of the game have changed, muddying the waters regarding the differentiation between saints and sinners, or perhaps taking us to a place where concepts of saintliness and sinfulness are outmoded.

Be that as it may, big-time D1 basketball has been a cutthroat, dollar-driven business for quite some time, and any semi-successful team that has avoided disciplinary sanctions—major or minor—over the past decades has likely done so only by virtue of dumb luck. The only things the righteous had to gain in this hothouse environment were a clean conscience and a 2–14 conference record.

Grade-fixing, pay-for-play schemes and other recruiting excesses, drugs, hazing, bullying, sexual abuse, racism have long been commonplace crimes and misdemeanors in the college game. Not to mention the concentration of power as major basketball programs continue to switch conferences in search of the almighty buck, and lots of NIL (name, image, likeness) money begins to flow through an already corrupted system.

Kansas, North Carolina, Kentucky, UConn, and Indiana have all faced weighty sanctions in recent years. UCLA skirted accountability for decades regarding the actions of a booster named Sam Gilbert, whose beneficence toward UCLA players earned him the nickname "Papa Sam." But a mild stench of the Gilbert scandal still clings to the program.

And Duke, despite its relatively pristine image, has seen it smudged, with a number of reputed booster payoffs to recruits over the past several years and a minor violation on the part of Coach K himself in late 2019.

But like the blue bloods they are, these seven programs have weathered the worst of it and generally come out much healthier than their brethren.

For example, a bloody but unbowed Kansas demonstrated its resilience with a national championship in 2022. And a year later, UConn bid farewell to the infamy of a two-year NCAA probation by winning the grand prize.

A new dawn in college sports is surely going to turn most of the old ways of doing business upside down.

But whatever may pass for improper behavior going forward will just as surely be papered over by a lot of winning.

Rabid Fans

Rich Favreau, a Kansas University basketball fan for nearly sixty years, described the experience of walking into the Rules Gallery at Allen Fieldhouse and encountering the original copy of James Naismith's thirteen rules of basketball, enshrined in a glass case along with a portrait of the founder.

"The best way I can put it is that you feel like you're looking at the Ark of the Covenant," said Favreau.

That, my friends, is a basketball fan.

And Kansas has many tens of thousands of reverential rooters like Mr. Favreau, whose fandom is a kind of secular religion.

The same can be said of the other six blue bloods and their huge nationwide (verging on worldwide) fan bases.

The evidence lies in the warmth inside Cameron Indoor Stadium on cold January nights, and the smell of a bonfire raging on Franklin Street in Chapel Hill after a big Tar Heel win. Or the deafening roar of the invading horde of Huskie faithful at a Big East Conference Tourney final, rocking Madison Square Garden with endless chants of "UCONN, UCONN, UCONN!"

Although there is no concrete proof that this kind of religious fervor yields championships, it does recognize and celebrate the remarkable achievements of our seven beauties.

And, finally, *Quaquaversal* (shout-out here to Word Guru).

Loosely translated, this delightful adjective denotes something that, by its very nature, is all-encompassing. Which is what we mean when we talk about program "culture" and its utmost importance in the determination of success or failure.

These days, culture is primarily deployed as a buzzword, especially when it comes from the mouths of corporate executives and head basketball coaches, who tend to define it in its narrowest, most simplistic terms: a "good" team culture, one hears over and over, is characterized by trust among players and coaches, mutual respect, discipline, and a shared commitment to a one-for-all-and-all-for-one vision of the enterprise.

All of which is very well and good, as far as it goes. But a more accurate—and inclusive—view incorporates all the behaviors, philosophies, and feelings of everyone and everything that touches the program: the university, its athletic department, alumni/boosters, fans, legacy and social media, and the myriad benefits and blemishes of the society in which we live. And of course, once again, there's the money. Lots and lots of money, which is probably the single most transformative agent within this vast mélange.

Another crucial element of a program culture is constant change, as the coaching carousel keeps spinning, the portals open wide, and the one-and-dones or two-and-dones come and go in the wink of a young girl's eye. For example, it is not possible to replicate John Wooden's culture because the Lord made only one John Wooden. Likewise, Dean Smith, Adolph Rupp, Bobby Knight, Phog Allen, and all the singular talents who have helmed our blue bloods over the years.

These are powerful forces that converge to create the intense pressure-filled environments that all major D1 basketball programs must confront every hour of every day.

All this can take an enormous mental and physical toll on coaches, who are on the cutting edge of these ever-changing cultures and must bear the brunt of the disappointment when things don't work out according to plan.

To take just one stress-filled example: In this age of the portal, coaches now must expand their scope of recruiting beyond high schools, to encompass players from other college programs as well as their own valuable players, who now need to be re-recruited every year to keep them from seeking greener pastures elsewhere. And that's not to mention raising the NIL money that it takes to do all that.

Dr. Jim Taylor, a sports psychologist in northern California who counsels D1 coaches on how to create "winning" cultures that match their own personalities and skills, has seen up close what this type of stress can do to his patients.

"There are so many aspects to coaching at this level," he says. "Recruiting, teaching, [game] management, creating core values, dealing with the media and the boosters, getting players to buy in to a system that emphasizes common goals at a moment in time when everything they see and hear on the outside tells them otherwise."

So, given all this complexity and the underlying fissures, what cultural advantages do our blue-blood basketball programs possess that give them an edge over the competition?

Dr. Taylor suggests at least one big one: It's something that may seem as flimsy as gossamer but is, in actuality, as powerful a statement of purpose as a slam dunk—"institutional memory."

Very simply stated, it's the history of a program, embedded in all that has been written and observed over the decades. It's lodged in the memories and experiences of former players and coaches who remain lifelong program fixtures and living symbols of what was once great and could be again.

It's John Wooden and Roy Williams on game nights, assuming their regular seats under all those championship banners and spreading those positive vibes all over the arena. Encountering these monuments to success on a frequent basis, it becomes easier for players and fans to imagine the glories of the past and future as one.

Blue bloods do much better in preserving and harnessing those memories for maximum impact, either concretely (Kansas's Rules Gallery, the memorabilia at the entrance to Cameron Indoor), in song ("Indiana, Our Indiana") or event (Kentucky's "Big Blue Madness").

"You can call institutional memory a form of zeitgeist [a German word for 'time spirit']," concludes Dr. Taylor. "It's everywhere you look and to everyone involved in the program, it says 'remember.'"

So, consider the following a rekindling of those time spirits, as well as a celebration of what was and will most likely continue to be.

We hope you enjoy the tour.

CHAPTER 1

UConn

Quiet No More

NCAA titles (6)—1999, 2004, 2011, 2014, 2023, 2024
Final Fours (7)—1999, 2004, 2009, 2011, 2014, 2023, 2024
Elite Eights (13)—1964, 1990, 1995, 1998, 1999, 2002, 2004, 2006, 2009, 2011, 2014, 2023, 2024
NCAA tournament appearances—37* (1996 vacated)
Conference regular season titles—11 Big East, 20 Yankee
Conference tournament championships—2 ECAC, 8 Big East, 1 AAC

NESTLED SERENELY INTO THE FAR NORTHEAST TIP OF CONNECTICUT are a string of rustic hamlets known collectively as the "Quiet Corner." Once bustling communities powered by large watermills set on fast rivers, these early-nineteenth-century towns—Pomfret, Putnam, Woodstock, Thompson—haven't bustled in nearly a century. Today, the Quiet Corner appeals mostly to tourists drawn to its historic inns, antique shops, and pleasant hikes along the Quinebaug River, home to pickerel frogs, great blue herons, and spotted salamanders. More adventurous souls can hike the "hogback," a ridge line of exposed bedrock that marks the western boundary of the Quinebaug Woods, a hemlock forest resplendent in silvery white, dark green, and reddish browns.

Located a mere stone's throw to the west of the QC—about 8.6 miles as the crow flies—is the village of Storrs, home to the University of Connecticut and its men's and women's basketball teams. Apart from college basketball, Storrs, with a population of roughly sixteen thousand, was most famous not all that long ago for being "America's Best Place to Avoid Death Due to Natural Disaster."

Peter Tork of the Monkees went to high school there, as did the lead singer from Weezer. Wendy O. Williams of the Plasmatics moved into town in 1991 and died there in 1998.

"Well, we had a general store, a grocery, and one dairy bar," recalls Dom Perno Jr., a UConn graduate, former basketball team manager, and son of Dom Sr., who started at guard for UConn in the 1960s and went on to become head coach and an early catalyst in the program's transition from preeminent New England stalwart to national powerhouse.

In short, although Storrs may be geographically situated outside the immediate perimeter of the Quiet Corner, it remains as quiescent and uneventful as any redoubt whose primary purpose is being a good place to stay out of the path of a tornado. Or as many have termed it, a "cow pasture with a college."

Except, that is, on game nights at Gampel Pavilion. Then, like a basketball-inspired Brigadoon, sleepy Storrs stirs from its reverie, breaking loose in a cacophony of ear-shattering cheers and emotional outbursts. Every home game is a party (as is every road game, for that matter), and everyone in Storrs is invited.

It seemed to happen so fast. Back in 1995, the year the UConn women won their first NCAA title and four years before the elite men's squad won its first of six (and counting), Dick Vitale, the effusive-bordering-on-unhinged TV commentator, knighted Storrs as the "capital of the basketball world." In Vitale-speak, that was, at most, minor hyperbole.

But the change didn't happen overnight. The six NCAA championships, the internationally renowned brand name, and the hotels, commercial businesses, and upscale restaurants that currently abut the campus are all the outgrowth of many years of hard work and perseverance. Storrs's 125-year journey from collegiate cow pasture to Title Town USA, the first bona fide dynasty of this brave new NIL/portal world, is a compelling one.

The No-Coach Approach

Referring to its inaugural 1900–1901 campaign as a "season" seems a stretch, as UConn—then known as Connecticut Agricultural College—played only one game, and that was against the unformidable youngsters from Windham High School. Nevertheless, the Aggies did manage to win the game, making that ephemeral season the only undefeated one in the program's storied history.

Those early, formative years yielded a few interesting tidbits. For example, on the long list of men's head coaches, the 1900 to 1915 period reads "No Coach." Undoubtedly, this notation would have pleased James Naismith, the inventor of basketball, who didn't think coaches were in any way necessary to playing the game effectively (more on this in the Kansas chapter).

What stands out here is UConn's record under No Coach, which was slightly above .500. Suffice it to say that a lot of multimillionaire D1 head coaches today haven't achieved No Coach's long-term success.

On a much less breezy note, there were the events of 1933–1934, which presaged those that led to the integration of college basketball in the South in the late 1960s. On January 27, 1934, UConn was scheduled to take on the U.S. Coast Guard Academy on its home court in New London, Connecticut. Harrison "Honey" Fitch, one of seven sons of a New Haven postal worker and UConn's first African American basketball recruit, was a sophomore on that team (then called Connecticut State College).

By this point in our nation's history, blacks had already distinguished themselves in multiple domestic and foreign wars. Some thirty-one won Medals of Honor in the nineteenth century, and two hundred thousand black men saw combat in Europe in World War I. This would be followed years later by the 1.2 million blacks who served honorably during World War II. Nevertheless, the Coast Guard Academy apparently hadn't received the memo.

The Connecticut State players, after arriving in New London, went into the visitors' locker room, changed into their uniforms, and took the court. But the service academy officials refused to allow the game to be played if Fitch participated, and for an hour or so, the two sides argued heatedly about how to proceed. In the end, the game went on (State won), but coach John Heldman, without any explanation, kept Fitch, one of his best players, on the bench.

Many more discussions, lame excuses (a joint team statement termed it all "a very unfortunate misunderstanding"), and various protests ensued. The incident also received national media attention. Connecticut State students, for their part, rallied strongly around Fitch, and the student body voted overwhelmingly to have the coach fired. Heldman did the right thing and resigned the following year, but it's likely that four straight losing seasons had more to do with his inglorious exit.

And that's pretty much how the program's first forty-five years progressed. Quiet, unassuming, with a soupçon of racism. No fewer than ten coaches succeeded No Coach over that time, none to any significant effect, although a few of their names can be found on various buildings around campus.

A REAL LEAGUE, A REAL COACH

The year 1946 was, by comparison to its immediate predecessor (the end of a world war, the start of a cold one, the dawning of the nuclear age), rather placid. Nevertheless, it did have its moments, such as the first meeting of the UN General Assembly and the introduction of the modern bikini, named after a U.S. nuclear test site in the Marshall Islands.

But in the annals of UConn basketball history, 1946 was, indeed, a big year. For openers, it saw the founding of the Yankee Conference, consisting of the flagship public universities of the six New England states. It may not have been what later came to be known as a "power conference," but it was stable and made geographical and historical sense (Maryland, UCLA, and USC in the Big Ten? Stanford, California, and SMU in the ACC?). It also helped give the still-fledgling UConn program an identity.

But to take full advantage of that opportunity, Connecticut needed a coach who could take the program to the next level. This they found in a scrappy UConn player from the 1920s named Hugh Greer, who assumed the job during the 1946–1947 season and led the school to some 286 victories, a .719 winning percentage, and twelve conference championships (ten of them consecutively) over a sixteen-year period.

The undisputed highlight of the Greer years was UConn's improbable upset of Holy Cross on February 27, 1954, ending the Crusaders' forty-seven-game winning streak at home. Huskie captain Worthy Patterson, who later became the first UConn player to make it to the NBA (as the first African American on the then-St. Louis Hawks), hit the winning layup with two seconds left. Holy Cross, which had gone to the NCAA Elite Eight the year before, went on to win the NIT (back then as prestigious as the NCAA) in '54.

Patterson was one of only a dozen or so blacks on the UConn campus, but in a 2012 interview with the *Hartford Courant* (he died ten years later at ninety-one), Patterson recalled his time in Storrs as being joyfully free of racial animus.

"Nobody noticed color," he said. "If you were a student, you were a student. If you were a basketball player, you were a basketball player."

His time in St. Louis was considerably less pleasant.

"I couldn't eat with the team or stay in the same hotel," lamented Patterson. "I had to stay on the colored side of town . . . it was serious Jim Crow."

Dom Perno Sr., one of the few living souls who played under coach Greer in his final years, remembers his first college coach as a consummate gentleman, possessed of a calm demeanor, but one who had no compunctions at all about getting after one's ass if the situation warranted.

"There was no BS with him . . . he was a quiet man, but he had his words, and he would do whatever had to be done to get you to do what was expected of you. He saw something in me as a sophomore and gave me the chance to start, and for that alone, I'll always be grateful."

Perno says the entire team "took it very hard" when their esteemed coach died of a massive heart attack ten games into the 1962–1963 season. What kept their low morale from sending the rest of the season spiraling down the toilet was the respect the players had for their interim head coach, George Wigton, Greer's assistant. Wigton, a classy individual in his own right, guided the team to an 11–4 record and a trip to the NCAAs, where they lost a close first-round game to West Virginia. Wigton was not a candidate for permanent UConn coach, and he departed

Storrs for a new career coaching numerous sports at Bates College in Maine.

UConn, meanwhile, was ready to embark on step two of the awesome transition from a regional power to a major international brand.

HAIL, GRABOWSKIS!

Huskymania, which is loosely defined as unbridled enthusiasm on steroids, is widely believed to have been unleashed by Tate George's game-winning buzzer-beater against Clemson in the 1990 NCAA Sweet Sixteen.

That was, indeed, a seminal moment in UConn basketball history, but no less an august authority than the New England Historical Society traces the birth of Huskymania all the way back to March 13, 1964; to the moment that senior guard Dom Perno swiped the ball from Princeton's Golden Boy, Bill Bradley, dribbling away the game clock and sealing a Sweet Sixteen victory at Reynolds Coliseum at North Carolina State.

The Historical Society goes further in describing UConn versus Princeton as a classic "Grabowski versus Smith" contest—the Smiths being the uber-elite, Waspy, fair-haired Tigers and the Grabowskis a scruffy band of small-town kids with names like Perno, Slomcenski, DellaSalla, and Slimowicz.

UConn's jubilation after winning two NCAA tournament games for the first time in its history, unfortunately, was short-lived. The very next day, the Huskymaniacs got blown out 101–54 by Duke in the Elite Eight. It was, to put it mildly, anticlimactic.

Sixty years later, eighty-two-year-old Dom Perno remembers snatching the ball from Bradley—who first denied that it was a clean steal but later fessed up to the truth—like it happened yesterday. Hearing that he had been dubbed by an impeccable source as the father of Huskymania made the old point guard very proud, indeed.

As for the rookie UConn coach, Fred Shabel, he, too, was greatly pleased by the program's first extended run in the NCAAs. But being run off the court by Duke had to hurt at least a little, as Shabel had come to UConn after several years serving as an assistant at Duke under its legendary head coach, Vic Bubas. When informed that his assistant was leaving the vaunted Atlantic Coast Conference to coach in the lightly regarded Yankee Conference, Bubas did not offer very much in the way of support.

In any case, Shabel, in his four years in Storrs, brought to the program a new level of organizational discipline and coaching nuance.

Hugh Greer, an old-school coach very much of his time, mainly taught basic, fundamental basketball skills, whereas Shabel introduced a more tightly choreographed and sophisticated approach to daily practice, which included finesse drills that addressed specific skills sets, such as how to take a charge from the left. Shabel and his assistant coaches were also big on breaking down film and getting to know the strengths and deficiencies of each player so they could be placed in positions where their strengths would be maximized and their limitations minimized.

"Simply put, Fred was the guy who brought big-time basketball to UConn," says Tom Penders, who was UConn's floor general in the mid-1960s and went on to a forty-year D1 coaching career, with stops at Fordham, Houston, and the University of Texas.

Shabel, says Penders, recognized right away that his point guard's true value to the team lay less in his shooting, passing, and penetrating skills than in his highly outspoken leadership and chutzpah. Thus, throughout Penders's playing career, his coach remained confident in his ability to call plays on the floor and rally his teammates around a common pursuit.

But perhaps Shabel's biggest contribution to UConn basketball was in the area of recruiting, which, under Hugh Greer, was a rather haphazard, loosey-goosey enterprise. To wit, most of the recruiting was done by various and sundry alumni, who would go forth to watch a high-school kid in action and report back to the coach whether he was worthy of a scholarship. Even Billie Greer, the coach's loyal and accommodating spouse, would, on her husband's behalf, occasionally take on this recruiting function.

This was how Tom Penders got to UConn.

"I never met Coach Greer," he says. "Some alum saw me play and told him about me. Coach wrote me a letter notifying me [of a scholarship offer], and that was pretty much all there was to it. The main reason

I accepted the offer was that UConn was willing to allow the scholarship [to extend to] baseball *and* basketball."

Shabel was fortunate to have inherited Greer's all-time top recruit, Toby Kimball, a six-foot-eight center who was good enough to last ten years in the NBA. Shabel augmented his roster with other top-notch student-athletes, most notably Wes Bialosuknia, arguably the finest pure shooter in UConn history, who set an American Basketball Association (ABA) record of nine consecutive three-point field goals.

Bill Corley, a center/forward and one of Long Island's best high-school big men, was another major Shabel recruit.

Overall, the youthful, thirty-something coach posted an enviable 72–29 (71 percent winning percentage) record in his four years at UConn, which included a 23–2 regular-season mark in 1964–1965, three NCAA tournament berths, and four conference titles.

Nonetheless, coaching was not Shabel's dream job—he took losing very hard and was frustrated by not being able to have his teams practice year-round—and in 1967 he resigned to become athletic director at the University of Pennsylvania. In 1980, he left Penn to go into the sports business at Spectacor, a company that owns professional teams and arenas in the Philly area. He retired in 2020.

Shabel's old head coach, Vic Bubas, who didn't think much of his protégé's move to UConn, says his assistant ultimately got the last laugh, making more money in his lifetime than Bubas and all his other Duke cronies put together.

Today, there remain a lot of former players and UConn fans from the Shabel era who believe the late coach (he passed away in 2023) ought to be in the "Huskies of Honor" hall of fame. Shabel never spoke with UConn officials about his exclusion and indicated before his death that he never intended to do so.

"I'm not as concerned about it as I once was when I was younger," Shabel said in an interview, adding, "I never really understood [why]."

Jim Calhoun, a guy who ought to know about such things, offered up the view that Shabel was "one of the best that ever coached at our place" but noted that whether to induct a coach into the Hall of Fame was not his call.

Be that as it may, if we had that call to make, it would be a definitive yes.

DEE AND DOM AND THE BIG EAST

Next up on the coaching carousel was Burr Carlson, who presided over two dismaying seasons (a 16–32 combined record and not much to get Huskymaniacal about).

He was soon followed by a gentleman named Donald "Dee" Rowe, whose legacy and long-term impact on UConn and its basketball program would be measured far less in wins, losses, and coaching acumen than by his qualities as a human being.

Rowe was precisely the kind of guy who inspired the poet Maya Angelou to write that "people will forget what you said, people will forget what you did, but people will never forget how you made them feel." Just about everyone who played for, or knew, Dee Rowe can fully attest to that.

A native of Worcester, Massachusetts, Rowe took on the UConn job in 1969 after fourteen years as athletic director and head basketball coach at Worcester Academy, his alma mater. It took him little time to turn that program into a perennial New England powerhouse (nine New England prep championships and a 180–44 won-loss record).

His record at UConn was less impressive—eight mostly up and down seasons, a modest .577 win percentage, with a couple of NIT appearances and one (very sweet) Sweet Sixteen run in 1975–1976. As a coach, he was described as demanding at times but always fair, one who ran multiple sets and changed up his defensive looks while retaining an overall fondness for zones and an aversion to ordering up full-court pressure.

But, again, none of those minute details matter much in Rowe's case, as he was undoubtedly the right coach for the right time—a time of great tumult on college campuses across America, as the Vietnam War raged on endlessly, and civil rights came under fire. Rowe's warm and caring presence—"he was a second father to me" is a standard line among his former players—and his innate ability to personally connect with everybody in his orbit made him the perfect man to guide his teams through those harrowing years.

Rowe's impact on UConn continued well after his retirement from coaching. In 1978 he became a fund-raiser for UConn athletics, personally directing the raising of more than $7 million in private donations to build the Gampel Pavilion. He was part of the group who recruited Jim Calhoun in 1986; and after retiring from his fund-raising job in 1991, he remained close to the program for the rest of his life.

Still, it could be argued that Dee Rowe's most enduring contribution to the future of UConn basketball was his abiding friendship with Dave Gavitt, whom Rowe first hired as an assistant at Worcester Academy in the early '60s. The relationship (Rowe's kids called Gavitt "Uncle Dave") came into major play when Gavitt, then the head coach at Providence, was spearheading the effort to assemble the Big East conference in 1979. The friendship between Gavitt and Rowe certainly helped grease the wheels for UConn's entry into the Big East and all the glory that it has brought to the university over the past forty-five years.

Following Rowe's retirement as coach, Dom Perno, he of the immortal 1964 Princeton steal and the reputed inspiration for the birth of Huskymania, was named as his replacement. Perno had come back to UConn in 1972, taking over the assistant job previously held by none other than Jim Valvano. Valvano, who was leaving bucolic UConn for the head job at bucolic Bucknell, felt that Perno, who was shyer and less intense than Dee, shared his work ethic and would be a good complement to the staff.

By the way, isn't it strange how many interesting college basketball stories seem to feature Jim Valvano in one capacity or another?

Perno's coaching tenure witnessed a number of momentous developments, most notably the dawning of the Big East and the early stirrings of an eventual move into a state-of-the-art (well, maybe a quasi-state-of-the-art) athletic facility.

But Perno, looking back on it half a century later, is more inclined to recall less momentous events, such as when a starter's pistol went off in the middle of basketball practice (the track team held its practices at the same time) and scared his star forward, Mike McKay, half out of his wits. Perno also harks back to a camaraderie that existed among the entire athletic staff and the athletes themselves at that time, one that took its inspiration from small-town life and could never be truly duplicated in modern-day Storrs.

"We were a really tight group, all the coaches and their wives and kids . . . the picnics and the get-togethers in different coaches' homes. It was like nothing for us to be welcoming groups of players into our own home."

Andy Baylock, whose official title is director of football alumni/community affairs but whose unofficial role is UConn's resident sports griot (oral historian), has been at the university for sixty years. And, like Perno, Baylock derives pleasure from looking back fondly at those rustic idylls. But he is even gladder to have been around long enough to see the program grow with the times.

That was more than gratifying, he says. It was necessary.

"I'll tell you about the old field house," relates Baylock, referring to the Hugh Greer Field House, which opened in 1954. "It was a zoo. A multiple-use facility with a dirt floor and a leaky roof [the ceiling liners had been peeling for years]. Fans would sit on little bleacher seats under the basket, so close to the baseline that players would be tripping over their feet."

Baylock remembers a bomb scare at the 4,604-seat facility, which occurred during a 1971 game against Holy Cross. The place was evacuated, the facility was swept for explosives, and the game went on without fans in attendance. Although Baylock didn't say so directly, one gets the distinct impression that the UConn basketball community wouldn't have been too upset had a bomb actually detonated (with no injuries, of course).

As stated, the founding of the Big East was the catalyst for a sturdier, less zoo-like arena and a brave new era in UConn basketball. According to Dana O'Neil's book *The Big East*, Dave Gavitt and his team modeled the new league on the Atlantic Coast Conference, selecting schools that already had serious name recognition and were in or near East Coast media centers.

Initial calls went out to Georgetown and St. John's (DC and NYC), followed by Syracuse and Providence. Once he had those four locked in, Gavitt turned his sights on the Boston market and Holy Cross. But the

Cross turned him down, reportedly out of fears that big-time basketball might interfere with the school's academic mission. It also might have been more a matter of hubris, says another source.

"Holy Cross thought they could be another Notre Dame . . . the Big East was beneath them."

Gavitt turned instead to Boston College, which accepted the offer and became member number five.

Up next on the call list was UConn, which was a riskier play, as they competed in the lower-rent Yankee Conference and hadn't garnered much respect outside New England. According to O'Neil, the other five schools weren't particularly keen on sharing their table with a cow pasture college. Thus, Gavitt reached out to his longtime friend and mentor, Dee Rowe, who was then a chief fund-raiser, to use his influence to egg on the university to consider joining. Gavitt gave UConn athletic director John Toner and the school administration three days to make up their minds, after which he'd move along to the next candidate.

"Three days wasn't a lot of time," says Greg Ashford, an assistant to Dom Perno and one of several UConn staffers who were parties to those initial meetings.

Although the UConn folks could see the enormous benefits a Big East membership would bring, and were loath to get "left behind," there was some hesitancy on their part.

"We were a land-grant public school," says Ashford. "The private schools in the conference all had significantly greater resources. We had [a gym] with cracked windows and a high-school-level locker room, and we didn't recruit aggressively [even] in our own area. Would we be able to keep up with these other schools?"

But optimism ultimately prevailed in Storrs, and UConn signed on as the sixth member, to be followed by Seton Hall (which firmed up the New York metro market). Those seven composed the conference in its inaugural season. Villanova joined the next year, Pittsburgh in 1982–1983, and the fledgling conference was off to the races.

Dom Perno's nine years as UConn head coach were, like his predecessor's, up and down, but the heightened level of competition that

UConn faced during its first seven years in the Big East partly accounts for the lackluster results of the Perno regime.

In his first two seasons, while operating as an independent, the team posted a 36–24 record—21–8 in 1978–1979, when they reached the second round of the NCAAs. Three winning seasons and three trips to the NIT followed, with the team putting up fairly decent numbers in Big East conference play. But the next four years witnessed four disheartening losing campaigns, with UConn finishing no better than seventh or eighth in the conference and going without a postseason bid.

Again, those substandard in-conference results can be attributed to the fact that between 1981 and 1985, the Big East Conference had risen up and roared. Georgetown was a runner-up to North Carolina in the 1982 NCAA final and then came back to win the title over Houston in '84.

But 1985 saw the conference reach its zenith, as no fewer than three members—Villanova, Georgetown, and St. John's—made it all the way to the Final Four. Villanova ultimately took the crown from Georgetown, playing what has become known as the "perfect game" in the final. And that wasn't all. Boston College that year got to the Elite Eight and only narrowly missed making the Final Four an all–Big East affair.

These were, indeed, heady times. Unfortunately for UConn, they were not partying with the likes of Georgetown and Villanova. Dom Perno, to his dismay, was fired after the 1986 season and was succeeded by Jim Calhoun. Calhoun would eventually put UConn on its path to glory, but to be fair, even Calhoun did not experience much success against Big East competition right out of the box.

Although Perno's coaching record—a .549 win rate—is roughly on par with that of Dee Rowe, who is a member of the Huskies of Honor—Perno is not.

Still, he's in pretty good company with Fred Shabel. And like Shabel, he hasn't made a stink over it.

Should Dom Perno be considered for entry to the honor roll?

We might suggest consulting with the New England Historical Society. Or better, ask Bill Bradley.

OUR BRAND IS RELENTLESS

Brand: A distinguishing name or symbol embodying a set of beliefs, perceptions, experiences, and emotions that represent for your constituency an enduring promise of value.

In 1986, to paraphrase a well-known quote from the legendary college basketball guru Al McGuire, the fuse was already lit, and all that was needed was the right coach to ignite the flame. A smart, hyper-energetic, charismatic, no BS coach, who had a lot of experience in overcoming adversity and building basketball programs.

Jim Calhoun checked all those boxes, and then some. An Irish Catholic from Braintree, Massachusetts, he came up the hardscrabble way and knew all about taking on stiff challenges. The first big one came when he was just fifteen and lost his father, making him the man of the family when he was barely out of puberty.

Calhoun got a basketball scholarship to Lowell State but had to drop out after only three months to help support his mother and five siblings. For nearly two years, he ran the gamut of grunt jobs—grave digger, granite cutter, headstone engraver, scrap-yard worker. Eventually, he went back to college and graduated in 1968.

He coached high-school basketball for a few years (quite successfully) before moving up to college coaching at Northeastern University in Boston. He took that program from D2 to D1 in 1979 and to four subsequent NCAA tournaments. His record over his final three seasons at Northeastern was 72–19 (245–138 overall).

Says one former student who was there during those winning Calhoun years, "Everybody loved the guy. We hated like hell to see him go."

Calhoun says his fourteen years at Northeastern yielded indispensable lessons in how to coach young men, one of which came from the school's all-time greatest player, Reggie Lewis. Lewis went on to play with the Boston Celtics in the NBA and died suddenly and tragically at twenty-seven (while working out on his own in July 1993) at Brandeis University. His Celtics number 35 was posthumously retired by the team.

"I was going after Reggie really hard one day in practice, telling him to get the fuck off the floor if he didn't want to put out the effort," recalls Calhoun. "And after I'm done, Reggie comes up to me quietly and says,

'Coach, could you do me a big favor and don't yell at me in front of the fellas?'"

The critical lesson here, which Calhoun says he has carried with him ever since, was that "you can't lead people unless you know what's important to them."

The decision on UConn's part to hire Jim Calhoun was more or less a no-brainer. Not only did he possess all the above-mentioned attributes, but he knew the New England market and how to recruit it.

His decision to accept the UConn job, however, was not as much a slam dunk. According to the *New Haven Register*, Calhoun admitted to sports information director Phil Chardis thirty years later that he really had no idea what he was getting into.

But what swung the deal for Calhoun, or at least got him seriously thinking about it, was a game he played as a student at the old Greer Field House in the early 1960s.

"There were nearly five thousand people packed into the place, and the atmosphere was electric," recalls Calhoun. "Bobby Knight once told me never to go to a university that doesn't want success as much as you do. I knew from way back then this was a place that wanted it badly."

Of course, the challenge of coaching in the Big East and the promise of a swankier athletic facility weighed heavily in Calhoun's decision to come to Storrs.

The new coach didn't waste much time getting his house in order.

First, he began locking down the Connecticut talent pool, which had seen far too many enticing prospects get away. His first big in-state catch, Chris Smith, out of Bridgeport, became a Huskie in 1988. Smith went on to score a whopping 2,145 points in his four years at UConn, and four decades later he remains its all-time scoring leader. Smith logged three subsequent years with the NBA's Minnesota Timberwolves. Scott Burrell, a six-foot-seven forward from New Haven who went on to an eight-year NBA career, followed Smith to Storrs in 1989.

Wayne Norman, UConn's radio announcer for forty-plus years, says another significant move by Calhoun was putting in place a solid process that created a "safety net" for players in academic distress. This was an essential task, adds Norman, because every other serious program in the Big East already had such a process.

Calhoun's focus on process carried over into every seemingly minute aspect of the job.

"His attention to detail was unbelievable," says Steve Pikiell, currently head coach at Rutgers, who played four years for Calhoun at the beginning of his UConn tenure.

"You name it; from the start, he was on top of everything: how we traveled, how we ordered our uniforms, put a roster together, how to clean the locker room."

Calhoun's proprietary approach to the job took on more importance when applied to his players.

The coach recollects the day that the UConn athletic director called one of his unnamed players on the carpet for some unspecified infraction. When Calhoun entered his office, the AD gave him the lowdown on the kid's alleged misconduct.

"If he's a jerk," the coach admonished the AD, "then he's *my* jerk, and *I'll* handle it."

Calhoun says the player was listening to this conversation in the next room and thus gained a deeper understanding of where the buck stopped at UConn.

Once Calhoun had a handle on the Connecticut talent base, he faced a more difficult recruiting challenge—how to bring in great high-school athletes from out of state. Calhoun knew that it would be pointless and futile to venture into other big city/Big East domains and attempt to compete for top players.

"I wasn't going to get anywhere trying to recruit D.C. under John Thompson's nose," says Calhoun. Likewise, going head-to-head with Lou Carnesecca in New York, Rollie Massimino in Philly, Rick Pitino in Providence, or Jim O'Brien at Boston College. So, like Daniel Boone two hundred years earlier, Calhoun turned his attentions west.

"I had to begin recruiting nationally, and I'd go anywhere to get a great player," he says. His earliest out-of-area recruiting coups included Californian Kevin Ollie (later to succeed Calhoun as head coach) and Pennsylvanian Donyell Marshall.

But recruiting at this level posed yet another dilemma. Most of these out-of-town kids knew precious little about UConn basketball, and what they did know revolved largely around avoiding stepping in cow manure and gabbing with friendly clerks at the local feed store.

This is where Calhoun's recruiting gifts came to the fore; instead of trying fruitlessly to sell these kids on a pastoral UConn they didn't know, he sold them on the Big East.

And he sold them hard.

Call it counter-recruiting.

"I'd tell them, 'Come to UConn, and you'll be playing every week against Alonzo Mourning [Georgetown], Derrick Coleman and Pearl Washington [Syracuse], and Billy Donovan [Providence]."

Calhoun emphasized that going up against players of that caliber would not only make them much better at basketball, but it would get them recognized by the people in the NBA who pay a lot of money for those players capable of matching up successfully with the Alonzos and the Colemans.

Once again, Calhoun was applying the Reggie Lewis lesson: know your players' motivations if you want to lead them.

Anyway, Calhoun's unique recruiting strategy paid big dividends, although not instantaneously. A miserable 9–19 record in year one, which was good for ninth in a nine-team conference. And another ninth-place finish in year two. But the overall regular-season record of 15–14 was good enough to squeeze UConn into the NIT, and (surprise, surprise) the team got hot and won the title against the likes of West Virginia, Boston College, and Ohio State (in the tourney final).

According to Steve Pikiell, the team and the UConn faithful celebrated the NIT title as if it were an NCAA crown, which buttressed Calhoun's previously stated assertion that no coach should ever choose any college that does not crave success as much as he does.

The 1988–1989 regular season was likewise of the ho-hum variety, but there was a little something at which to rejoice. UConn finished seventh in the Big East and avoided the dreaded 8–9 play-in game, which they used to call the "UConn game."

"It may not sound like very much," says Pikiell, "but back then, moving up to 7, from 8 or 9, was a big deal."

Although Seton Hall bounced them out of the Big East tournament in their first game, UConn reached the NIT again and got through a couple of rounds.

Pikiell says that to compensate for a relative lack of talent, Calhoun was inclined in those first few years to mix and match various offensive and defensive schemes.

"We did a bit of everything during my time there," he notes. "We ran a number of offensive sets and on defense, we played 1-3-1, 2-1-2, 2–3 zones, man-to-man, whatever was working best."

As major league-level talent began filtering in and the win rate began its ascension, Calhoun's strategic thinking underwent changes. According to his players, he slowly gravitated to a more free-flowing, flexible NBA-style offense—basic ball screens and stagger screens (consecutive off-ball screens set by two offensive players) to free up the most skilled athletes to do what they do best, be it an open perimeter shot or a drive and a dish in the lane.

Who wouldn't love playing in a scheme like that?

On the defensive end, however, Calhoun never lost his penchant for preaching fundamentals and demanding maximum effort, especially under the defensive boards. His former players recall his defensive drills with groans and grimaces.

The very worst of these practice routines was positively diabolical.

"It was a brutal one-on-one, box-out drill," recalls Kevin Freeman, captain of Calhoun's first national championship team in 1999 and currently associate athletic director of the National "C" Club, which assists former and current UConn lettermen with mentoring, networking, and related services.

"Coach was looking to create an atmosphere of extreme toughness. The goal of the drill was to [pull in] three consecutive rebounds. If you missed on any, you went right back to square one; you stayed out there on the court until you'd completed the exercise."

Steve Pikiell, who as a six-foot-four guard was not particularly well-equipped to do battle with big, brawny forwards and centers, found this rebounding drill to be borderline tortuous.

"I couldn't get off the line," he says. "If I somehow managed to grab a couple of consecutive rebounds, I'd get matched up with Cliff Robinson [a strapping six-foot-ten center], and I'd have to start in all over again. . . . I could be out there forever.

"And the worst part," he continues, "is that the longer you're out there slogging away, the more exhausted you get, and the harder it is to compete."

Calhoun, although acknowledging that the drill could be a form of athletic purgatory, notes in his defense that he would give players in dire need of respite a bit of time to catch their breaths before putting them back out there.

Another typical Calhoun toughness drill was right out of the old-timey Coaches' School of Hard Knocks—roll a basketball out on the court and have a bunch of already depleted players dive on the hardwood floor to snatch it.

All this might make it seem like Calhoun was one of those hard-asses from a bygone era, who saw their mission as being similar, if not identical, to that taken by marine drill instructors (i.e., breaking down recruits emotionally before rebuilding them into lean, mean fighting machines).

And to some extent, that would describe Calhoun. But, according to Kevin Freeman, Calhoun had a way of breaking you down and building you up that differentiated him from the drill instructors at Parris Island.

"He was a master of psychology," says Freeman. "If, for example, you'd had a bad game over the weekend, on Tuesday and Wednesday at practice he'd be all over you, up in your face [about all the things you screwed up in the last game]. But come Thursday and Friday, he'd start building you back up. Now, he's your biggest booster, and by the next game, you've got all your confidence back, and you're ready to go out there and show the world."

Lots of big-name D1 coaches, adds Freeman, think they're doing just that.

"But the fact is, they don't and can't," concludes Freeman. "It's a tricky thing knowing the right levers to push. I don't believe there are any coaches out there who are as good at this as Coach Calhoun."

Moving on, it would be Calhoun's fourth season—the "dream season"—that would witness a new era in Storrs, heralding its true arrival on the national stage. It was the first team to play at Gampel arena (a critical factor), and it was led by Chris Smith, Scott Burrell, and Tate George.

Addressing the crowd at a halftime ceremony in 2020 honoring the thirtieth anniversary of that season, Calhoun called that group "the guys that got the whole thing started . . . the Big East championships, the national championships, the All-Americans; they started it all because they believed in each other and in our coaching staff."

The major highlight of that 1990 season, of course, was the miraculous buzzer-beater by Tate George against Clemson in the Sweet Sixteen, set up by a full-court pass from Burrell. Burrell later called it one of the top five moments of his life.

In the 1990 Elite Eight, however, UConn wound up on the other side of paradise, when Duke's Christian Laettner beat the Huskies with a last-second jump shot of his own. Laettner became well-known for dramatic buzzer-beaters and for his lack of gentlemanly play, but that's a story for another chapter.

The following twenty-three years of UConn were not all so good, just the large majority of them. The 1991 squad reached the Sweet Sixteen (ousted again by the Blue Devils on their way to the title) and were back in the NCAAs in 1992. In 1994, as the fourth-ranked team in the country—led by a cadre of future NBAers, including Ray Allen, Donyell Marshall, Donny Marshall (no relation), Travis Knight, and Kevin Ollie—they lost in overtime to Florida in the Sweet Sixteen.

The following season, that same sterling group, eighth in the nation, reached the Elite Eight. A year later they swept through the regular season and Big East tourney with a 32–2 record before faltering a bit in 1997. But that year saw the influx of a new crop of freshmen studs who two years later would lead UConn to the first of its six NCAA titles—Richard "Rip" Hamilton, Jake Voskuhl, and the aforementioned Kevin Freeman. And in 1998, freshman guard Khalid El-Amin joined the fun.

The 1999 team (34–2 overall), like so many UConn teams to come, seemed to find its mojo at just the right time, rolling over a fine St. John's squad in the Big East final and ending up in the NCAA final against—yes, its nemesis, Duke. UConn got revenge by the score of 77–74. In November 2023, ESPN named that team the best of the previous twenty-five years.

To its captain, Kevin Freeman, 1999 signaled the beginning of the UConn brand, predicated on toughness and a relentless desire to succeed. And nearly every recruit who has come through the program in the twenty-five years since, he insists, has "fallen in line with the feeling" of having been part of a special fraternity.

Whether the '99 team was the best of Calhoun's three championship squads is surely open to debate. One could make an excellent case for the 2004 group, which included Ben Gordon, Josh Boone, Emeka Okafor, Hilton Armstrong, Charlie Villanueva, and Marcus Williams, all future NBA draftees. They went 33–6 on the season; and on their otherwise smooth ride through the NCAA tourney, they knocked off Duke in a 79–78 semifinal thriller. UConn, down eight with less than three minutes left, outscored the Devils 12–3 down the stretch. Okafor scored all eighteen of his points in the second half.

Nevertheless, we would lean in the direction of the 2011 Huskies as the best story in UConn history. That team, tied for ninth place in the Big East at 9–9 and having closed out their regular season by losing four of five, somehow discovered their true selves in March and April.

Led by Kemba Walker's out-of-body performance, UConn beat five Big East teams on five consecutive days (four of them ranked teams) in the conference tourney and then ran off another six wins in the NCAAs. The eleven-game streak ended with a defensive effort that made all those tortuous practice drills worthwhile—holding Butler to 18.8 percent from the field and dominating on the glass.

Jeremy Lamb, Shabazz Napier, and Alex Oriakhi were other stars on that team, but junior Kemba Walker, who scored a record 130 points in the conference tournament and continued in that vein in the NCAAs, was the driving force on the floor. Walker won the Bob Cousy Award as the nation's top point guard; was named the Most Outstanding Player in the NCAA tournament; and at a pep rally following the team's return from Houston, became the first active player to join the Huskies of Honor.

Suffice it to say, he was among Jim Calhoun's favorite players—less for his great play and more for his leadership skills.

"The kids [on the team] didn't like Kemba; they loved Kemba," says Calhoun. "Shabazz and Jeremy [two freshmen], especially. Shabazz wanted to be Kemba, eat what he ate, and do what he did."

Calhoun says Napier was neither the right size nor did he possess the kind of game that would peg him as a surefire NBA talent. Nonetheless, he went on to have a serviceable six-year NBA career, a career based largely on his inner drive and a willingness to work his ass off.

"That was what he got from being around Kemba," says his former coach. "All in all, I've never seen a kid take on an entire team and lead them like Kemba did in 2011."

But a player didn't need to win a championship to make it to the upper echelon of Jim Calhoun's favorite players list. Caron Butler, a kid from the mean streets of Racine, Wisconsin, was dealing drugs at age twelve and getting busted fifteen times before his fifteenth birthday. His mom worked all night and wasn't around to set him straight.

"He got involved with some really bad guys," says Calhoun, who visited the Racine neighborhood where Caron had grown up. He talked to people who knew the youngster and got a true sense of what he had gone through on those streets. What Calhoun found was a kid with a good head and good heart, and a tremendous passion for basketball, not to mention the talent to match it. He decided Butler was well worth the risk and brought him to Storrs.

Butler ended up playing two years at UConn (2000 to 2002), averaging fifteen points as a freshman and twenty as a sophomore, where he led the Huskies to the Elite Eight. Butler, likewise a Huskie of Honor, left for the NBA after that season, spending the next fourteen years in pro ball.

Freshman Shabazz Napier gets ready to use a screen by Alex Oriakhi against Seton Hall in 2011. Led by Napier's mentor, Kemba Walker, UConn won the title several weeks later. Wikimedia Commons, Shabazz Napier

Since then, he's worked as an ESPN college basketball analyst, an NBA analyst at FS1, and an assistant coach with the Miami Heat. He and Calhoun touch base now and then.

"Last time I saw him, he said to me, 'Coach, I love you,'" recalls Calhoun. "That was nice to hear."

Now happily retired at eighty-two in his home in the Quiet Corner—and this is in no way meant as disparaging—Jim Calhoun maintains the chip on his shoulder as big as the Blarney Stone.

After all his successes detailed above, taking UConn to hoops heights that were unimaginable before he got there and impacting the lives of hundreds of young men, Calhoun somehow still feels the need to remind you that he won three championships and 625 games at UConn and is in the College Basketball Hall of Fame. And if you make any crack about the UConn men's basketball program, back then or even now, it had better not be a nasty crack or you'll get a disproportionate response.

The chip also comes into play vis-à-vis Calhoun's relationship—or lack thereof—with Geno Auriemma, his counterpart from the UConn women's side, whose personality can be just as prickly, and whose desire to be anointed King of UConn Hoops is just as strong.

UConn basketball observers have described the two men's feelings for one another in various ways. Some have termed it a mutual "loathing," which we believe to be on the extreme side. Most others refer to it as a marked dislike between two guys with lots of championship trophies and the egos to match.

Calhoun, for his part, once mocked the women's fan base as the world's largest nursing home, and Auriemma has stated that he and Calhoun don't get along and "don't have to."

There was talk over the years about the two finally declaring a *faire la paix* (kiss and make up). As far as we know, nobody has yet made any such conciliatory gesture.

Anyway, we were advised prior to beginning our research to refrain from asking Calhoun about Auriemma, and vice versa, and we felt it prudent to heed that advice.

Getting back to Calhoun's sizable shoulder chip, ask him where that comes from, and he'll tell you it stems from losing his dad at fifteen and having to learn how to be a tough guy. He'll talk about how the toughness is manifested in his ability to withstand several bouts of cancer dating to 2003, spinal surgery, and multiple major orthopedic issues.

But here's the thing: with a lot of accomplished men like Calhoun, that kind of tough-guy talk can easily come off as boastful, if not boorish. None of that comes through in an interview with Calhoun himself, which we found to be a delightful way to spend quality time on a lazy weekday afternoon.

Prior to the interview, we got some additional advice from Steve Pikiell:

"You're going to enjoy talking to this guy," Pikiell insisted, dismissing any notions about Coach Calhoun being narcissistic or conceited and noting that any coach worth his salt will stand up for his program against criticism from the outside.

What did Pikiell himself take away most from his four years with Calhoun?

"What it means to be a family guy," says Pikiell. "This is a job that by its very nature takes you away from them all the time, flying here and there, working crazy hours.

"But Coach Calhoun, who managed every game like it was life and death and won at the highest levels, still managed to be the most amazing dad and husband that I have ever known. That is, by far, the biggest lesson he ever taught me."

Calhoun's legendary career at UConn, unfortunately, was tarred toward the end with scandals, sanctions, and harsh criticism, especially from the media, which up to that point had been mostly in thrall to his coaching successes.

An NCAA investigation in 2009 involved irregularities in the recruitment of Nate Miles (who never played a game for UConn). Two years later, it was reported that a former team manager gave Miles impermissible benefits, and Calhoun ended up getting cited for failing to create an atmosphere of compliance with NCAA rules. Calhoun was suspended for the first three games of the 2011–2012 season. The school admitted to the violations, and Calhoun found himself under siege from several quarters, including the fourth estate.

On top of the recruiting excesses and the program's failure to meet the minimum scoring benchmark established under the Academic Progress Rate (APR), old complaints surfaced regarding Calhoun's failure to police the behavior of some of his players.

As much as the media admired the coach for assisting troubled youths such as Caron Butler, they dredged up several cases such as that of Ben Gordon, whom Calhoun played for nearly an entire game only a day after the player's arrest for assaulting a woman.

And then there was the notorious "Laptop-Gate" episode in 2005, in which two of his star players, A. J. Price and Marcus Williams, broke into a dorm and stole tens of thousands of dollars' worth of computers.

Calhoun drew media ire for not adequately holding them accountable for their actions.

Calhoun retired just prior to the start of the 2012–2013 season but insisted then, and still does, that his decision was not in any way related to all these unpleasant matters but, rather, to his strong feeling that "it was time." The underlying passion may still have been there, but the energy level was nowhere near meeting Calhoun's standards.

"To continue doing everything that I do in this job would require three naps a day," he quips. Staying on past his career expiration date would have entailed the strong possibility of "disappointing" Husky Nation, his players, and perhaps most distressing of all, himself.

Others are more inclined to suppose that all the extraneous goings-on had at least something to do with Calhoun's decision.

Either way, notes Steve Pikiell, "We don't always get to manage our exits."

Maybe not, but Jim Calhoun managed all the rest of it pretty well.

Still Relentless after All These Years

Kevin Ollie, one of Calhoun's prized early recruits, returned to the welcoming arms of his alma mater in 2010–2011, after a long and winding thirteen-year career in the NBA. As an assistant to his old mentor, Ollie proved his mettle, mostly as a bench coach. Ollie is widely credited with coaching Kemba Walker to achieve the magical feats he performed at the close of that championship season.

When Calhoun stepped away in September 2012, Ollie, despite his lack of head coaching experience, was the logical replacement, being a Calhoun mentee and a UConn fan favorite. His 2012–2013 team finished a respectable 20–10 but was barred from postseason play because of the APR issue that dated back years.

It was during Ollie's initial season at UConn that disaster struck.

In December 2012, the basketball-playing schools in the Big East—DePaul, St. John's, Seton Hall, Georgetown, Marquette, Providence, and Villanova, or the so-called Catholic 7—broke away from the football-playing members and formed a new conference (three months later, they announced that the new league would retain the Big East name).

All of that left the football-playing UConn holding the bag. Or to put it another way, landed them into a much less-esteemed American Athletic Conference, populated by football-playing former Big East schools.

"Kevin Ollie is a good coach who got screwed," says Kevin Freeman. "Because now [without the lure of the Big East] he starts losing all the local talent to Villanova."

Nevertheless, with a team composed of a few of his own recruits and some choice Calhoun leftovers such as Shabazz Napier, Ryan Boatright, and DeAndre Daniels, Ollie took the Huskies all the way to a fourth national title.

That team, seventh-seeded in its bracket, surprised the college basketball world by getting on another of UConn's patented March Madness thaumaturgic surges, knocking off Florida in the Final Four semi and Kentucky in the final.

A month later, Ollie signed a new five-year contract and, even in the tepid pools of the AAC, things were looking bright in Huskie Land.

But, being out of the bosom of the Big East, UConn fared less well over Ollie's next four years—two losing seasons, one trip to the NIT, and one to the NCAA round of thirty-two. Ollie was fired in March 2018 amid allegations of ineligible players, impermissible coaching from a video coordinator, improper benefits from a booster, and more.

Ollie filed a grievance seeking $10 million in back pay; and when UConn refused to continue with that contractual process, Ollie filed suit. Finally, in January 2022, an arbitrator ruled in Kevin Ollie's favor, and the school was ordered to pay him.

Not a perfect ending for Kevin Ollie, either, but in an interview following UConn's sixth title victory in 2024, Ollie left behind any lingering feelings of indignation and expressed his admiration for what his old program had achieved.

"That's a hell of a team," he said.

Danny Hurley, the coach chosen to replace Ollie, was perhaps a less likely choice, not being a Calhoun acolyte with a strong record of

Ryan Boatright, a stalwart on the 2014 UConn championship team, slams one down on Michigan State in 2012. Not bad for a 5'11" guard. U.S. Air Force photo

D1 success. In six years at Rhode Island, he had made only two trips to the Big Dance, both second-round ousters.

And he was a man who has experienced serious mental health challenges dating back to his teenage years—frequent panic attacks, suicidal ideations, and profound emotional peaks and valleys. One of his panic attacks occurred only nine days after he reached college basketball's summit, having just coached UConn to a fifth championship in 2023.

But, in other respects, Hurley was not only the right choice: he was the perfect choice. For Danny Hurley has a chip on his shoulder that sometimes makes Jim Calhoun's stone look like a pebble.

"He's a guy who can do [this job]," Calhoun says of the current UConn coach. "He could be 18–2 and lose a game and believe he's never going to win another . . . all coaches are like that, to some degree, but Danny really has that fire and the courage to stand up and defend his program [when it's disrespected]."

Moreover, like Calhoun, Hurley is a ferocious competitor, hard-driving and utterly relentless (there's that word, again) in his pursuit of excellence.

After two middling years coaching UConn in the lusterless AAC, things started looking up when the Big East invited the Huskies back into their midst in June 2019. Having the Huskies back has proven to be something of a mixed blessing for its conference mates, however, as Connecticut is dominating that conference right now in a way it never did in the old Big East.

Hurley's first two Big East teams finished third in conference play and were bum-rushed out of the NCAAs in the opening round. In 2022–2023, they went 31–8 but got knocked out of the Big East tourney in the second round by highly ranked Marquette. UConn went into the NCAAs as the fourth seed in the West; and once again, unexpectedly, the good times rolled. Six decisive double-digit wins.

The next season, UConn did precisely the same thing in the NCAA tourney—six consecutive survive-and-advance, double-digit wins, all of them blowouts or near blowouts. Only this title, UConn's sixth (matching North Carolina), was highly expected. UConn had been ranked first from mid-January to mid-February, slid to third for a week and second for another couple of weeks, before finishing the regular season where they always belonged: at number one with a bullet.

Danny Hurley, in a postgame display of Huskymania at its most grandiose, screamed out that UConn had been "running college basketball for the last thirty years."

That is undeniably hyperbole, if not out-and-out fiction, to non-Huskymaniacs, but it was reality to Danny.

Still, despite being at the very pinnacle of the college basketball universe, reloading rather than rebuilding his roster year to year, it may very well turn out that Danny Hurley's ultimate legacy will be less about championships than about opening the doors of perception toward a

A new dynasty is hatched: Huskies celebrate Championship #5 in 2023. Public domain, via Wikimedia Commons

greater understanding of—and empathy for—those souls struggling with mental health problems.

In a remarkable interview on the late-lamented HBO series *Real Sports with Bryant Gumbel*, broadcast prior to the 2024 championship, Coach Hurley peeled back the onion on his emotional life in a way that few, if any, sports figures have ever done.

He spoke exceedingly candidly about growing up in the shadows of his father, a demanding Hall of Fame high-school coach, and his brother Bobby, a star player on Duke's championship teams of the early '90s. Danny says he lived in subtle but constant fear of not living up to his father's standards of excellence.

As a student-athlete at Seton Hall, he totally "washed out" on the court as his interior life "cratered." On the road, fans would call out "Bobby's better," which didn't help his mood one bit.

Not being able to talk to anyone who could help him deal with the pain of feeling unworthy of being alive, Hurley quit school; and on the drive from the Seton Hall campus at South Orange, New Jersey, to his family home in Jersey City, he contemplated making a hard right turn into a tree and ending it all right there. Thankfully, he never followed through with an actual suicide attempt.

Shortly after brother Bobby was severely injured in a car accident, Danny confessed to a reporter that it should have been him in that car.

"I felt worthless," he told *Real Sports*.

What helped enormously in turning his life around, Hurley said, was the opportunity to coach at his dad's program at St. Anthony's High School after Bobby Sr. had to take a leave for a medical problem.

At St. Anthony's, Danny discovered a genuine facility for coaching; and after returning to Seton Hall and graduating, he embarked on a coaching career at the D1 college level. He became head coach at Wagner College, with his brother assisting him (a significant turnabout in the family dynamic), before moving to URI and UConn.

Today, Danny manages to effectively mix the emotional roller-coaster that comes with his ultra-intensive approach to coaching with family, meditation, and prayer, helping him to maintain a viable life balance.

As to his coaching acumen, apart from being a great motivator and a terrific Xs and Os guy, Hurley is making a name for himself as a master manipulator of the portal.

He grabbed two key 2022–2203 championship pieces, guards Tristen Newton (East Carolina) and Hassan Diarra (Texas A&M), out of the portal and followed the next year by spiriting away Rutgers graduate student Cam Spencer.

This, by the way, did not endear him at all to Steve Pikiell, who, despite his aforementioned affection for UConn basketball, hated to witness his best player sucked away through the dreaded portal.

Calhoun, who knows something about recruiting in the trenches, as well as fighting through the fearsome challenges of youth, is a regular and welcome visitor to Hurley's office in Storrs.

There, the old coach offers encouragement and advice to the younger man on how to get the most from his players and keep the pressures of coaching in the new NIL/portal era from turning an already volatile coach from Huskymaniac to just plain maniac.

Coach Hurley is clearly committed to UConn and to joining John Wooden as the only coaches in D1 history to take their teams to three straight NCAA titles. He expressed that commitment most unequivocally in June 2024 in turning down a six-year, $70-million offer to become the new coach of the Los Angeles Lakers.

As for Calhoun, asked if he would like to be younger and still be coaching championship-quality athletes at UConn or anywhere else, he was likewise unequivocal.

"Hell, no," he says.

Life is a lot sweeter these days, spending time with the family among the pickerel frogs and great blue herons of the Quiet Corner.

Duke University

Elite Winters

NCAA Titles (5)—1991, 1992, 2001, 2010, 2015
NCAA Runners-Up (6)—1964, 1978, 1986, 1990, 1994, 1999
Final Fours (17)—1963, 1964, 1966, 1978, 1986, 1988, 1989, 1990, 1991, 1992, 1994, 1999, 2001, 2004, 2010, 2015, 2022
Elite Eights (24)—1960, 1963, 1964, 1966, 1978, 1980, 1986, 1988, 1989, 1990, 1991, 1992, 1994, 1998, 1999, 2001, 2004, 2010, 2013, 2015, 2018, 2019, 2022, 2024
NCAA tournament appearances—46
Naismith College Players of the Year—8

TUCKED AWAY AMID THE LOBLOLLY PINES, ON A SPRAWLING CAMPUS IN the Central Piedmont of North Carolina exists a collection of resplendent gothic buildings, beautiful gardens, and in most every given winter across the past half century—fantastic basketball teams.

In the college hoops world, Duke University is as elite as it gets.

The championships, coach, venue, and national pedigree, but of course. Though perhaps to wholly synthesize the exclusivity, we should step back—similar to, say, the way Austin Rivers did with his Smith Center silencing buzzer-beating three-pointer in 2012—to fully celebrate, as Duke indeed did that night, the myriad ways in which the school is on something of a college basketball island.

Theoretically, Duke doesn't belong in this book. The school is an outlier for reasons seldom noted on national broadcasts. They ought to be a David, clearly, but they have earned their place as a Goliath.

Excellence on the court runs parallel to the privilege of the student body, more so than at any other institution detailed in this text. Duke University is the only private school featured in our book.

At barely sixty-seven hundred undergraduates, Duke's enrollment is less than a third of Carolina's, fewer than a quarter of the student body in Lexington, and roughly a ninth of the population walking about in Bloomington, Indiana.

So, kind of like David.

Yet Duke University's endowment—comfortably north of $13 billion at the conclusion of the 2023 fiscal year—is as large as the endowments of UNC, Indiana, Kansas, Kentucky, and Connecticut combined. This fluctuates with the markets, but you get the point.

More so, a Goliath.

Duke is one of the best research universities on the planet. It boasts more billionaire graduates, more Rhodes Scholars, and more Nobel laureates than any of their upper-echelon basketball counterparts. Duke also, er, boasts a president among its famed dignitaries: 1937 Law School graduate Richard Milhous Nixon.

Whereas the other six public, and in multiple instances flagship universities, with their massive alumni bases, represent a tool for upward mobility through higher education, Duke University's place among our basketball giants is far more selective.

Pull the curtain aside, and one finds a classism, superiority, an upper-crust veneer with halls inaccessible to nearly everyone. Consider that 95 percent of applicants to the prestigious private school in Durham, North Carolina, are met with rejection.

When it comes to basketball, instead of being a revered and a well thought of, if not appreciated, little guy (like, say, Villanova or Georgetown), Duke is widely viewed as elite, entitled, and eminently hateable. It's a dichotomy of sorts. And although it has become further calcified in recent decades, it is not new.

OBSCURE IRON

The coaching tree of Blue Devil basketball begins with eleven leaders across twenty-three years, eight of whom won more games than they lost. The first name of historic significance found among the school's hoop coaches is Eddie Cameron.

Cameron coached Duke for fourteen seasons—the second-longest tenure, and to be clear it was a distant second, in program history—during which time he went 226 up and 99 down (for a winning percentage just shy of 70 percent).

Cameron's teams claimed Southern Conference titles in 1938, 1941, and 1942. Then, in a sign of the times, he left basketball to coach the football team. Once transitioned, Cameron proceeded to post a 25–11–1 mark on the field from 1942 through 1945, a stretch during which the former basketball coach won three more conference titles and led the Blue Devils to a victory in the 1945 Sugar Bowl against mighty Alabama.

Cameron filled the void of Wallace Wade, created when the longtime Iron Dukes football coach entered the service. Wade spent an abridged sixteen years at the helm in Durham, and all but one of his teams managed winning records, as his undergrads racked up six SoCon league titles. Wade even led Duke to two Rose Bowls (not a typo), the most noteworthy of which was the 1942 contest.

The previous fall (in '41) Duke ran through everybody, smacking opponents by an average of thirty points, anchored by a stellar defense. After some invitational jockeying—Oregon State effectively got to pick its opponent—the '42 Rose Bowl was set to pit the Beavers against the Blue Devils.

At least that was the plan, until the Japanese attacked Pearl Harbor on December 7, 1941. After the Day of Infamy, unease understandably percolated. Among the major events sparking anxiety were the traditional New Year's Day festivities in Pasadena, California. First, the Parade of Roses (with an estimated one million spectators in the queue), before the Granddaddy of Them All (host to ninety thousand fans) got canceled.

The federal government banned any large gatherings on the West Coast for the remainder of the war, and it appeared for a brief while that the twenty-eighth edition of the Rose Bowl would have to wait.

But on December 16, Duke University invited Oregon State to come play the Rose Bowl—in Durham, North Carolina. University officials in Corvallis accepted, and the team spent nearly a week traversing the country on a train aptly called the Beaver Express. They arrived in Bull City (that's Durham) on Christmas Eve 1941.

Because the stadium didn't have enough capacity, bleachers were brought in from NC State and UNC. And on a chilly, wet, New Year's Day, the favored Blue Devils lost to the Pacific Coast Conference champs, 20–16, before an estimated crowd of fifty-six thousand. There was no parade of roses in North Carolina, if you're wondering.

What does all this have to do with Duke basketball?

Eddie Cameron—remember!

After the displaced Rose Bowl, head coach Wallace Wade, whose name now blankets the stadium where the '42 contest was played, joined the military, and Cameron left basketball for football.

Which leads us to the aftermath of the Cameron-led Duke basketball program. In the seventeen years following his departure, Duke posted decent records while dwelling in relative obscurity under the tutelage of Gerry Gerard and Harold Bradley.

From 1942 to 1959, Duke didn't have a single losing season. The problem was that during this stretch, they had but a single NCAA tournament appearance.

Enter Vic Bubas.

HOT-HEADED HEYMAN AND THE BIRTH OF A RIVALRY

As peculiar as it may seem now, for a time, the preeminent college basketball program in the Old North State reigned supreme in Raleigh. The NC State Wolfpack, under head coach Everett Case, helped build the Atlantic Coast Conference and constructed a program neighbors would seek to emulate.

UNC got so perturbed by Case, and losing to State, that it raided the St. John's athletic department, poaching Frank McGuire. Duke opted for a resolution closer to home. They went after Case's top assistant and recruiter, Victor Albert Bubas—Vic for short.

Bubas played at State, under Case, and graduated in 1951. He then served as the freshmen coach before being promoted to varsity assistant in 1955. Although State had seen a relative dip in the latter part of the decade, Duke administrators believed, accurately as it turned out, that Bubas was the man who could elevate the program over its recent position of above average but otherwise unnoteworthy.

The first big break of the Bubas era came in 1959 when a big-time recruit from New York City decided he didn't want to play in Chapel Hill.

Art Heyman initially had committed to play for McGuire and the Tar Heels, but during a recruiting visit a fight ensued between Heyman's stepfather and the UNC coach.

Inside the Carolina Inn—a place that still looks like Humphrey Bogart ought to be sitting at the bar sipping a scotch while holding a long, slender cigarette—Heyman's stepfather made a comment to which McGuire didn't take kindly.

"I had to step in between them," the younger Heyman told longtime Durham sportswriter Al Featherston years later.

"My stepfather called Carolina a basketball factory, and McGuire didn't like that. They were about to start swinging at each other."

The thing blew up, a verbal commitment was reneged upon, and Heyman ended up at Duke. The incident at the Carolina Inn served as an appropriate foreshadowing of Heyman's proclivity for finding himself in the middle of fights, which occurred regularly during his time at Duke.

Heyman was a brash New Yorker, unpopular with his own teammates and generally regarded as a hothead. His freshmen coach, Bucky Waters, understood that Heyman had a temper and suspected that taunting and anti-Semitism would be directed at the Jewish player from the Big Apple.

The Duke and Carolina freshmen teams met three times in 1960, with Heyman's squads winning each matchup. During one contest in Siler City—about an hour southwest of Durham—Waters even took extra precautionary measures.

"The team went on the bus, but I drove down with Art in a car," Waters remembers. "I said, 'I don't know what's coming, Art. But in any way they can they're going to try to pull you down.'"

Which they did.

First with "very anti-Semitic, awful" taunts before some elbowing and physicality. Waters took a time-out in the opening minutes. And he used two others to try to quell the looming disaster.

As Waters recounts this story, his jaw tightens, and he mimics a grunting Heyman in response to the coach's overtures.

"I knew what he wanted to do. He was a fighter," says Waters. "I kept telling him, you can't do that."

Waters's plan was to substitute Heyman out and have him glance up at the scoreboard (which favored Duke) as he walked by the Carolina bench. But it did not come off as planned. Carolina freshman Dieter Krause and Heyman got into it. Multiple accounts indicate that Krause threw the first shot, though the Tar Heel claimed self-defense.

"I remember a fist coming at me, and I instinctively ducked," Krause recounted to ESPN more than fifty years later.

"He missed in his effort to hit me with his right hand—and I instinctively counter-punched, and I connected with a punch to his face . . . and then total mayhem broke out."

Regardless of who started it, all these years later the matter still resonates. The two benches cleared; Blue Devil reserves surrounded Krause and delivered body blows with fists and feet as he resorted to the "embryonic position" to protect his head.

Waters, who boxed as a kid in New Jersey and later taught the sport at Duke, couldn't keep his cool either.

"Instead of going out there and trying to bring order to the chaos, I went right to the Carolina bench, grabbed the opposing freshmen coach by the collar, and threw him on the press table. His butt was hitting all the switches, and horns were going off."

Heyman, who averaged thirty points per game in that 1960 campaign, was melee-adjacent and bloodied, requiring five stiches. Krause, for his part, was ejected.

And if you can believe it, the Heyman-Krause fight was just the undercard.

The "Thrilla in Manila"—Muhammad Ali and Joe Frazier's third heavyweight title fight—might be the most celebrated fisticuffs in the history of mankind. But the biggest, baddest bout in the annals of Duke-UNC basketball had taken place fourteen years earlier.

A year after that car ride to Siler City, on February 4, 1961, the freshmen teams—now without Heyman or Krause—tipped off at Duke Indoor Stadium (later renamed for Eddie Cameron) as part of a double-header with the varsity teams.

Multiple fights broke out, and Carolina finished the game with only three players on the floor.

The freshmen were simply warming things up, as later that night, with Heyman once again on center stage, it got even messier.

Now briefly, for contextual buildup, it's worth noting that about a month earlier (on the final day of 1960) Duke and Carolina met in Raleigh at the Dixie Classic, a then-annual eight-team event that was the brainchild of Everett Case.

The Dixie Classic was, for years, a heated affair that pitted Carolina's Big Four—NC State, Duke, UNC, and Wake Forest—plus four other national notables, in a three-day tournament at Reynolds Coliseum in Raleigh.

A point-shaving scandal led to its demise, but not before the 1960 New Year's Eve game between the Blue Devils and Tar Heels. That's when UNC's Doug Moe pestered, annoyed, and eventually limited Heyman—who had eleven very quick points—to just sixteen by the end of the game.

Carolina won that game, 76–71. Legend has it that Heyman was furious, so much so that he tacked up a newspaper picture of Moe in his dorm room, psychologically readying himself for the next meeting.

By the time February rolled around, Heyman was ready. So, too, were his teammates, who had ticked off six straight wins and elevated themselves to fourth in the national polls, at the time Duke's highest-ever ranking.

UNC, meanwhile, hadn't been defeated since its Dixie Classic win against Duke, having posted twelve straight victories and garnering a number five ranking in the polls.

The 1961 clash was the very first in a long line of meetings that saw both rivals ranked in the top five nationally.

Heyman performed extraordinarily well, despite some—how shall we say this?—uncustomary defensive approaches from Moe.

"He spit on me," Heyman told the sportswriter Featherston. "Every time I took a shot, he spit on me. I told him I was not going to take that."

Heyman and Moe squared off in the first half. No punches were thrown as the tension kept mounting.

After the break, upon returning to the floor, Heyman got a tap on his bum from a Carolina cheerleader, and the volatile six-foot-five Blue Devil turned around and shoved that cheerleader to the floor. Assault charges followed days later, brought by a local attorney who happened to have graduated from UNC Law School.

Inside of a packed Durham courtroom, the case against Heyman—who had tossed the young cheerleader named Albert Roper, a man—was promptly dismissed.

Back to the game in progress, second-half tensions were now truly simmering.

Heyman hit two free throws with fifteen seconds to play, and Duke led by five. Larry Brown—the future coach—then collected the inbounds pass and drove to the hoop. Heyman fouled him, thinking that a whistle would allow for a substitution and a well-deserved ovation.

Brown had other thoughts, however. He took exception to the foul committed by his long-ago friend from Long Island and sharply threw the ball at Heyman. And then he swung at him.

The disaster in Durham was fully underway.

Heyman and Brown locked up, and the tussle escalated when Tar Heel reserve Donnie Walsh—yes, the future longtime NBA executive—attacked Heyman from behind. ACC Commissioner Bob Weaver would later describe Walsh's actions as "hit-and-run tactics."

Fans poured onto the floor seeking combat of their own, and the cops waded into the fray.

It required nearly a dozen officers to restore some level of order. Black-and-white footage of the brawl is pretty wild.

Inexplicably, Brown was not ejected and remained on the floor for the final seconds. Heyman, who scored a game-high thirty-six, was chucked.

Duke won 81–77, and the greatest rivalry in college basketball was born.

However, the season was about to unravel.

Weaver, the ACC commish, suspended Brown, Walsh, and Heyman for the remainder of regular-season conference play. For Duke, it derailed the rhythm of 1961. Wake Forest blew out the Blue Devils in the conference championship game, and the Demon Deacons snagged the ACC's lone spot in the NCAA tournament.

MR. AND MRS. ROBERTSON, I PRESUME

The early 1960s were a period of growth for the Blue Devils. Following the 1961 campaign that sputtered out, Heyman was joined in the backcourt by another New York guard (by way of Lexington, Kentucky) named Jeff Mullins.

"I was recruited by Kentucky," Mullins, who moved from the Big Apple to Lexington when he was in high school, recalls.

"But I had reservations about playing for Adolph Rupp. My reasons were that I was definitely a late bloomer. I had a great high-school coach, but my three years were really development years. And to be honest with you, I didn't think when I graduated that I was anywhere near a finished product."

Kentucky pushed, and Rupp enlisted the governor, Democrat Bert Combs, to help close the deal.

"I went to see the governor twice. And he very, very nicely stated that if I plan on staying in Kentucky, I definitely ought to go to the university. He was very nice about it."

Mullins opted for the dimmer lights of Durham, where he would team with the impulsive Heyman and play for the not-yet-established thirty-three-year-old Bubas.

"He was very competitive. He had tremendous character and integrity. He was a true gentleman, but he had a burning desire to win," says

Mullins. He also depicted Bubas as a tremendously organized coach who ran no-nonsense practices and rarely, if ever, raised his voice.

The Heyman-Mullins tandem each eclipsed an average of twenty points per contest as Duke finished second in the ACC. Many observers figured that the 1962 season would provide a conference tournament final rematch between Wake and Duke.

The basketball gods had other plans, however. Duke was upset in the conference tournament by an inferior Clemson team that it had twice defeated in the regular season, dashing any dreams of a March Dance.

Instead, the Demon Deacons rolled Clemson a day later, and then— piloted by Len Chappell and Billy Packer—marched to the only Final Four in school history.

Heyman and Mullins spent one more season together, and the 1963 campaign was their best. The Blue Devils won every one of their fourteen ACC games, defeating UNC twice, and exacted some long-overdue revenge against Wake in the league's title game, after which Heyman earned MVP honors.

Duke was back in the NCAAs following a two-year hiatus, and Bubas's team proceeded to defeat New York University and St. Joseph's to earn the first of many Final Four berths for Duke basketball.

At Freedom Hall in late March, the Blue Devils were blown out by a George Ireland–coached Loyola of Chicago team that would go on to defeat Cincinnati for the title the next night.

"College basketball was a little different then," Mullins notes. "We had never seen Chicago-Loyola play. They might have seen us. We were still on TV a little bit. But they were very good. We were probably not as prepared as we should have been. There were no videotapes."

It wasn't the culmination per se, but it was pretty darn close. Heyman was named the Associated Press National Player of the Year. In a misstep by the school, Heyman had to wait twenty-seven years (until 1990) for his jersey to be retired.

There are two little-known footnotes to that 1963 season, one that is just kind of wild and bespeaks, possibly, the Duke-UNC dynamic. The other offers up a real whopper of a what-if.

First, the zany.

Heyman was arrested that year in Myrtle Beach, South Carolina, charged with transporting an underage woman across state lines for immoral purposes. It's possible that Heyman tipped his hand when he attempted to check the two co-eds into a motel under the alias "Mr. and Mrs. Oscar Robertson."

Who made what calls to get the charges dropped remains unclear, at least publicly. For whatever it's worth, Terry Sanford, future Duke University president and U.S. senator, was North Carolina's governor at this time.

What is clearer was Heyman's position on the matter. Up until his death in 2012, the Blue Devils legend maintained his belief that private detectives were tracking him and exposed the tryst. Heyman said that after the brawl with Brown and Walsh two years earlier, private eyes tailed him on occasion; and he held that these private eyes had been hired by UNC supporters.

As for the what-if scenario, it goes like this:

Heyman and Mullins were stellar together, and they were supposed to be joined by another prized prospect. Two years earlier Bubas had received the commitment of a maniacal gym rat from Crystal City, Missouri.

But bad news arrived in August of '62 when, initially unbeknownst to the staff, the would-be freshman hadn't arrived for orientation. Assistant Bucky Waters recalls walking into the basketball office where he was told that "Mr. Bradley" had called. It sounded urgent.

"I called him back," Waters recounts, "and he said 'Coach, I'm sorry, but my son will not be coming to Duke. Any son of mine who can go to Princeton will be going to Princeton.'"

And so, the future 1965 NCAA Tournament Most Outstanding Player, 1970 and 1973 NBA champion, and three-term Democratic U.S. senator from New Jersey took his talents not to Duke but to Princeton.

What if Bill Bradley had been a member of the 1963 Blue Devils?

Even with Heyman gone to graduation, and Bill Bradley beginning his junior year at Princeton, the 1963–1964 Duke campaign didn't see any drop-off. The goal, just as a year earlier, was to advance to the Final Four.

"We had an electric record player in our locker room," remembers Mullins. "And from day one, the song that we would play, every day, was 'Going to Kansas City.' Back in those days, that was not something that went on in college basketball—this music in the locker room.

"He planted it in our minds on October 15. We knew we could be good, but I don't think many others did."

For months the Fats Domino classic echoed through the Blue Devil locker room, instilling a belief that helped boost Duke back to the Final Four in Kansas City.

Mullins improved his output to twenty-four points and nine rebounds per contest. Duke didn't run the table again in ACC play, though they were close. The lone league defeat came in Winston-Salem, a 72–71 loss at the hands of Wake Forest.

Bubas's Blue Devils won the league with a 13–1 mark, delivered the Demon Deacons some cold revenge in the ACC Tournament final (an 80–59 whuppin'), and moved on to the twenty-four-team tournament, where they quickly beat Villanova by fourteen (Mullins poured in forty-three points) and tormented UConn by forty-seven to earn a return trip to the Final Four.

The biggest win in program history at that point came in Kansas City. Senior center Jeff Buckley went for an out-of-character twenty-five points as Duke defeated Michigan, 91–80. The Blue Devils were on to the national championship for the first time in program history.

The fun ended there, as Gail Goodrich-guided UCLA dismantled Duke, 98–83. The future Laker outshone Mullins with twenty-seven points, and the Bruins won their first championship with a suffocating press and superior shooting.

John Wooden's teams proceeded to win nine of the next eleven.

Mullins departed for the NBA's St. Louis Hawks and went on to have a solid pro career, which included three All-Star nods and the championship that had eluded him at Duke, a 1975 triumph with the Golden State Warriors.

From Heyman to Mullins to the next machination, Bubas had a plan to keep the successes rolling. The 1965–1966 Devils reloaded with Jack Marin, Steve Vacendak, and Bob Verga, all three of whom would go on to play in the NBA. The trio helped the school to a third consecutive ACC regular season title before a defeat to NC State in the conference tournament.

"As Coach Bubas said, you have to be patient, organized, not get discouraged," Vacendak remembers. "He created the foundation during that time in a very methodical, planned, organized manner."

The 1966 season marked the senior campaigns of Marin and Vacendak and proved to be the last great unit under Bubas. He would later call the 1966 squad his best.

Duke lost only three games in the regular season by a combined seven points. They swept away UNC in their annual home-and-home meetings before a memorably slow triumph over their Tobacco Road neighbor in the ACC semifinals.

On March 4, 1966, Dean Smith called for the vaunted four-corners offense, a slow spread sure to lull the fans—and sometimes the opposing defense—into sheer boredom.

For his part, Bubas instructed the Blue Devils to sit in their zone and not chase the Tar Heels, which may have resulted in scoring opportunities for UNC. It was a stalemate that produced a 7–5 score at the break (Carolina ahead) and resulted in an awkward, pre-shot clock final tally of 21–20 in favor of Duke.

No, the fans didn't get a refund.

The Blue Devils handled NC State in the ACC Final, first danced through St. Joe's and next beat a Syracuse squad that included Dave Bing and a future coach named James Arthur Boeheim.

Duke had won the regular season and conference tournament and was back in the Final Four for the third time in four years. Kentucky awaited.

In his final collegiate game, Marin was exceptional, hitting eleven of eighteen shots for a game-high twenty-nine points. Vacendak, also suiting up for the final time with Duke, had seventeen. Verga, who was ill, managed just four points in truncated minutes.

Duke led by one at the half. It was tight throughout. And after a 71-all tie, Kentucky pulled away with a late 8–1 run, en route to an 83–79 victory inside Maryland's Cole Field House. Kentucky was closing in on its fifth national title; Duke was still seeking its first.

The next night Kentucky did not prevail. In one of the most important games in college hoops history, Don Haskins and his quintet of five black Texas Western starters, shocked Adolph Rupp and his whites-only Wildcats lineup, 72–65.

Bubas's six-year run—from 1961 through the '66 season—was unlike anything Duke basketball had experienced up to that point. Four regular-season ACC crowns, three league tournaments, a trio of Final Fours, a trip to the title game, a bevy of future NBA picks.

The foundation had been built, the program was ascending, and in a subtle foretelling of an historical trend that exists to this day:

During those six seasons, Duke lost precisely two games at home.

THE MECCA

Cameron Indoor Stadium is an unassuming place.

Seriously.

Or at least it is from the outside. As far as on-campus facilities go, the basketball cathedral in Durham doesn't stick out like a giant swollen thumb (see Syracuse) or necessitate a mile-long walk for entry (UNC). If you haven't been there before and were to take a summer stroll beyond the quad, it's entirely possible to mistake Cameron for a library or some other academic hall.

"It's Allen Fieldhouse at Kansas and Cameron Indoor Stadium that really are the Fenway Park and Wrigley Field of college basketball," contends Jay Bilas, the former Duke player and now TV basketball analyst.

"You know, there's just a unique, different feel to each one of those places, and the history and tradition are palpable inside both of those buildings.

"Cameron Indoor Stadium is to college basketball what Augusta is to golf and what Wimbledon is to tennis," adds Jeff Mullins, a 1964 graduate.

Like all those revered buildings, Cameron is in a historical class with Lambeau Field and Notre Dame Stadium. It is not a recommended reading assignment; attendance is a prerequisite for any true basketball fan. Even those from UNC.

Cameron is a chip shot away from Wallace Wade Stadium, where that World War II Rose Bowl played out. It is not adorned with advertisements or digital signage. It is natural in its beauty.

Then you go inside.

A game-day experience at Cameron is hot, loud, and inevitably filled with human contact. Luxury boxes? Try again. Air conditioning? Why? A courtside perimeter consisting of the uber-wealthy? What would be the point?

Cameron has remained in many ways untouched for the better part of a century since it opened in 1940. For its first thirty-two years known just as Duke Indoor Stadium, the Cameron—as in former basketball and football coach Eddie Cameron—was added in 1972. Like Fenway, Wrigley, and a few other sports landmarks, its mere existence is a gift to the game, an almost living, breathing museum with annual rotating exhibitions.

These days, Cameron lists a capacity of just over ninety-three hundred.

Mullins says the crowds used to be significantly bigger.

"You know in the '60s, there were no fire codes, and if there were, they weren't enforced. Now Cameron holds about nine thousand people. But back then we were getting closer to eleven thousand. Because every walkway was full of people; the sides of the court were packed. If you had to take the ball out on the side, referees had to clear out about twenty people so you could just step out of bounds."

Adding to the mystique on Tobacco Road was also the smoke. Smoking in arenas was permitted, and it was customary for a cloud of cigarette exhaust to form at the top of the arena.

Cameron has few, if any, bad vantage points. At the same time, it has few, if any, comfortable seats. As Mullins said, it's a sardine-like experience that wouldn't—couldn't—pass muster under current regulations.

The broadcast media must climb a ladder to a catwalk post, a location that generally results in everyone perched there having broken a sweat after two hours of action. The rest of the credentialed media sit courtside, opposite the benches, in what we contend is the best reporter viewpoint in college basketball, although certainly not the roomiest.

Journalists might have the width of a smartphone on each side of their laptop. Press row at Cameron is so tight that unless you're sitting adjacent to a break in the row, it's impossible to leave during the game. Should the ball bounce out of bounds in your general vicinity, a throng of hands will extend past your face, reaching toward the inbounding opponent, hands shaking and vocal cords reverberating.

"My freshman year I'm walking out on the court and I get hit in the head four times," says Dave Colescott, a former Tar Heel, describing his first trip to Cameron.

"[I got] pelted while we're waiting in the tunnel, with a Clearasil bottle."

The Duke fans had a special gift for two of Colescott's teammates, Mike O'Koren and Rich Yonakor, fellow freshmen who happened to have pimples.

"Yonakor and O'Koren had very bad acne. And they were white as a ghost because the fans also had pictures, and they called them the Clearasil poster boys."

In a subsequent trip up to Durham, Colescott remembers taking the ball out, with the fans chirping in his ear, using his mother's and sisters' names.

"It's the only place that you feel like they're a part of the game," Colescott continues. "I played a lot of tough places—but they get the award. The crazies—they're very smart. They did their homework, and they would try to get any psychological edge they could. They turned the heat up."

Remember, this is all long before the internet.

The unofficial, yet totally official, anthem of Cameron Indoor is "Everytime We Touch" by the German trio Cascada. It's an electronic track that starts slow, accelerates to 142 beats per minute, and invariably results in Cameron mayhem.

There are also certain aromas when sitting in front of the Cameron Crazies—that, of course, is the nickname for the student body fanatics who come painted, rehearsed, and laser-focused on every opponent. One smell is alcohol, because, well, this is college. And two is a little body odor. It's not hiking the Appalachian Trail for three months and in dire need of a shower, but it's bad. You catch a whiff, and you think, eh, someone has been working out or sleeping in a tent . . .

. . . and, indeed, they do live in tents!

Most, if not all, of them. The Cameron Crazies sleep out in a university-approved encampment, appropriately called "Krzyzewskiville." The home-court advantage that Vic Bubas helped to impregnate became the fiefdom of Mike Krzyzewski.

Krzyzewskiville began, organically, in 1986, with a small collection of students pitching tents outside of Cameron in advance of the regular season finale against Carolina.

Today, it's a school-sanctioned village, replete with tent monitors and an entry quiz.

Really.

These days anyone wanting the opportunity to live in a tent is first required to convene in Cameron to take a test. The top-performing seventy groups earn admission to Krzyzewskiville, where they get to sleep in the cold, imbibe with their classmates, and wait for the game of the season.

Depending on your perspective, this may be an opportune moment to remind you that the yearly total cost of attendance at Duke is now in excess of $83,000.

What do their parents think?

A SUPER SIGNAL

There is no question today about the strength of Duke's national brand. No need for any debate about the fact that it was crystallized through all the successes of Mike Krzyzewski-coached teams. Less appreciated is one of the roots from which the product was long ago built. Seeds that sprouted from a Charlotte radio station.

"The thing that I noticed that had the biggest impact back in the early '60s," Mullins begins, "Duke basketball was on WBT radio out of Charlotte. And WBT had a huge signal, north-south. My dad could listen to the games over in Lexington, Kentucky."

Charlotte to Lexington is a cool four hundred miles over the Appalachian Mountains.

"WBT was that super-powered radio station, a hundred thousand watts or whatever it was at night," notes Steve Vacendak. "The signal that was somewhat diagonal, parallel, I guess, to the run of the Blue Ridge Mountains. It ran up into Pennsylvania," where Vacendak's family could follow along.

Later, the WBT radio broadcasts helped propel a young color commentator to national fame.

"That actually helped my career," Bilas says. "I was doing Duke radio when I left as an assistant coach. I started working in Charlotte as a lawyer [and then] I started in broadcasting. I didn't know how radio worked, but at night, I was told the signal went up and down the East Coast, the WBT broadcast. And that's how I think I was heard by a couple of people at ESPN."

All the while, the nighttime fireside game calls of ACC action helped foment a regional audience.

Says Jeff Mullins, "I can't tell you the number of people from the Northeast who told me 'I became a huge Duke fan listening to Duke basketball on WBT radio on winter nights.'

"I remember one person who told me that. It was Bill Foster."

Foster Coach

Life after Vic Bubas in the confines of Duke basketball was far from remarkable. Bucky Waters, the former assistant, took over, returning from West Virginia where he had spent four seasons, and amassed a record of 70–41, along with a Southern Conference title and an NCAA tournament appearance. His four seasons in Durham went less swimmingly. Duke was barely above .500 in league play, didn't sniff a ticket to the ball, and finished no higher than third in the league standings during Waters's time.

Neil McGeachy was promoted from freshman coach, went on to compile a 10–16 overall mark (2–10 in league play) in an almost entirely forgettable one-year stint that, if nothing else, allowed him to lay claim to an obscure trivia question.

Q: Who was the coach the last time Duke had consecutive losing seasons?

A: Neil McGeachy.

Bill Foster spent eight years coaching at Rutgers from 1963 to 1971, a time during which he would, on occasion, catch broadcasts of Blue Devils basketball on his car radio. After six straight winning seasons and two trips to the NIT (played at Madison Square Garden), Foster headed west to the University of Utah.

By 1974, he was riding high, having taken his Utes all the way to the NIT title game, where they stalled out to Purdue. Duke AD Carl James—a largely forgotten figure from Duke history—made the call, later an offer, hoping that Foster could reinvigorate the Blue Devils to a place of national prominence, after those back-to-back seasons of futility.

It started slowly.

Foster's teams were a bleak 40–40 overall and a miserable 7–29 in ACC play across his first three years. Unrest was simmering.

But in the fall of 1977, it all began to click.

Upperclassmen Jim Spanarkel and Mike Gminski had breakout seasons, as Duke welcomed in talented freshmen Gene Banks and Kenny Dennard. All four would later play in the NBA.

Duke had integrated a few years earlier when C. B. Claiborne broke the Blue Devil color barrier. As Gminski notes, Banks was "really the first great black athlete" at Duke.

Banks was a Philadelphia native and coming out of high school was as coveted as Magic Johnson. He settled on Duke and settled in instantly, earning ACC Rookie of the Year honors in 1978. Three years later, as a senior, Banks led the ACC in scoring, outpacing future Springfield inductees Ralph Sampson and James Worthy.

Back to his freshman campaign, Banks played a supporting role to Gminski, the so-called G-Man, and Spanarkel, both of whom earned

Mike Gminski dunks against rival NC State in the late 1970s, as the Cameron Crazies watch. Courtesy of Mike Gminski

All-ACC honors. The Blue Devils went from last in the league to second and were ranked in the nation's top ten to end the regular season. They defeated Wake Forest in the conference tournament final, and the quartet barreled into the Dance with shoes full of steam.

After knocking off Rhode Island, Penn, and Villanova, Duke faced Notre Dame in the national semifinal. Gminski had an impressive twenty-nine-point outing, on thirteen-for-seventeen shooting, and Duke made its second trip to the title game, where top-seeded Kentucky—and Jack Givens—were looming.

"Anybody who says they go into a game like that, playing it like it's any other game, is lying," Gminski says. "I remember going out to run out on that floor, and the air was different. It weighed a thousand pounds."

Spanarkel had twenty-two points; Banks, twenty-one; and Gminski, twenty (along with twelve boards), but he went six-for-sixteen from the floor in what amounted to a relative off-night.

"If I make four more shots, we win," laments Gminski.

On the other side was Givens, in his last game for Big Blue. He logged a performance for the ages. A game-high forty-one points, as he drained eighteen of his twenty-seven attempts.

Without a shot clock, or a three-point line, the Wildcats edged the Blue Devils, 94–88, in what to this day is the highest-scoring title game in tournament history.

Duke was still without a natty.

The G-Man says, "I don't believe we understood the opportunity. We took for granted where we were. And I think that was the big difference in the game."

It was natural to think that the almost-champion Blue Devils would soon return to the marquee stage. After all, all five starters were back for the 1979 season. But another shot at winning it all would be eight long years away.

Duke was good the next season, and the season after, just not good enough. And the relationship between Foster and Athletic Director Tom Butters was eroding. Butters had replaced AD James, who had fallen out of favor with Duke donors for his money-losing athletic department.

Foster struggled with the pressure and grew to resent the giant shadow cast by the revered coach at Carolina. UNC beat Duke in the 1979 conference final, and the Blue Devils' campaign ended a few days later in the Dance at the hands of St. John's.

Nevertheless, in 1980, with Banks, Dennard, and Gminski still leading the team, Duke held the nation's number one ranking for four weeks. The season ended with another loss to Kentucky, this time in the Sweet

Sixteen, with the Wildcats enjoying now-prohibited home support—they played on their own floor inside Rupp Arena.

It was the end of Foster's sixth season, and he had righted Duke's ship, going an astoundingly excellent 73–24. Yet, Bill Foster would never coach another game for the Blue Devils.

"Coach Foster left for a couple of reasons," Gminski says.

"One, he was at odds with Tom Butters—they had issues. And second of all, he was very frustrated that even with all that success, in those three years, he never felt he would get his due, that he would always be way outshined by Coach Smith. And that really bothered him."

An opportunity emerged a couple hundred miles down the road when sixty-six-year-old Frank McGuire—the former St. John's-turned-UNC-turned South Carolina coach—announced his retirement after a sixteen-year stint with the Gamecocks.

"They backed up the truck, and Coach Foster made a life decision for his family," Gminski explains.

In South Carolina, Foster's run would be fine but unremarkable. Although he did pick up a memorable nickname in the Palmetto State, something of a finger-in-the-eye moniker. Strangely, rival Clemson had a basketball coach also named Bill Foster. The *New York Times* noted in Bill Foster's obituary (the Duke Bill Foster) that in 1980, fans needed a way to distinguish between the two Fosters. And thus, the new arrival from the ACC, the Foster who had departed amid the pressure and feelings of inadequacy, was labeled as "Chicken Foster."

What if Gminski had hit four more shots in the '78 Final? What if Givens hadn't gone off for forty-one? What if Foster had raised a banner before Dean? Would his relationship with Butters have improved? Would the Duke coach have received his desired respect?

Well, suffice it to say, if any of those things had happened, Mike Krzyzewski almost assuredly would not have arrived in Durham in March of 1980.

SPECIAL K
Mike Krzyzrewski is Bobby Knight 2.0.

The once-protégé is a reboot and enhanced software program, the rare sequel that outpaces the original box-office hit.

Krzyzewski won two more national championships and guided his home country to three Olympic gold medals, two more than his one-time mentor. Coach K went to twice as many Final Fours.

Whereas Bob Knight was a drill sergeant (if we're being honest), or maybe a "general" (if we're being kind), his understudy was far more complex in his approach to the job.

Krzyzewski was part tactician, part intimidator, part authoritarian, part (seemingly) gracious leader in defeat, and oftentimes ambassador of the game, all the while serving as CEO of the preeminent D1 program in the land.

Knight had two faces, as noted in our Indiana chapter. Krzyzewski, the most successful coach this side of Wooden, and arguably the GOAT, has many.

Coach K wielded a stick that would make Teddy Roosevelt proud and had a tongue during practice that would make George Carlin perk up.

He was Bobby Knight, improved.

Mike Krzyzewski didn't regularly act out in front of a television camera or ever toss a chair in front of a national audience.

No, that's child's play, or better, Knight's play. The pupil had a more evolved style, a keen sense of leadership, and an uncanny ability to code switch.

He was the second coming, the Foster replacement vehicle.

Still, the accolades didn't happen immediately.

With Foster's departure to Gamecock-land, Duke AD Butters needed a replacement—and preferably, soon.

Steve Vacendak, the 1966 ACC Player of the Year, was back at Duke as associate athletic director following a brief pro career, after which he was employed by the Converse Rubber Company. He had a recommendation for Butters, in the form of a fledgling young coach at West Point with a mediocre record and a mouthful of a name.

"My high school coach Jack Gallagher was a good friend of Bobby Knight," Vacendak says.

Gallagher did the scouting of East Coast teams that Indiana played and oversaw Knight's summer camp. Vacendak, a hoops head, was living in Annapolis, Maryland, when his former high-school coach invited him to attend an Army practice led by one of Knight's former players. The meetings would persist.

"I got to know the program very well," continues Vacendak.

"I was very impressed with the way Mike coached. You know the game between Army and Navy is not a game necessarily [of] natural talent. It's an X and O coach's game. The small things, the little things in basketball that count, [like] attacking, going over screenings or behind screens, just being in the right place at the right time."

Vacendak planted the seed with Butters who, in turn, captured the endorsement of Bobby Knight.

It was hardly an electrifying hire. Krzyzewski had posted a record of 73–59 at Army, and with due deference to the armed services, this is Army basketball, not some mid-major that carries any clout.

Imagine any blue-blood program today—only two years removed from playing for a national championship—opting for a coach from a service academy.

No way.

For the first three years under the now-iconic Coach K, Duke stunk up the joint. An overall mark of 38–47, with a 13–29 stretch in ACC play, his teams finished fifth, sixth, and—for good sequential measure—seventh in the league.

The Coach K Era in Durham was just about over, honestly.

"If Johnny's not there, K is a footnote," Mike Gminski says.

"I mean if Johnny Dawkins doesn't come to Duke, Mike is fired. And he's almost fired as it is. If Tom Butters doesn't stand his ground, Mike is gone in that third year. It's as simple as that."

There are many celebrated recruiting classes in D1 history—Michigan's Fab Five; UCLA (take your pick); the mid-2000s group that later hoisted a banner in Chapel Hill; and Duke's class of 1982–1983: Johnny Dawkins, Mark Alarie, Jay Bilas, and Dave Henderson.

Steve Vacendak holds the 1966 NCAA Regional Championship trophy after Duke defeated Syracuse, 91–81, in Reynolds Coliseum. The Blue Devils reached the Final Four for the third time in four seasons under Vic Bubas. Courtesy of Steve Vacendak; credit Angie O'Briant

Duke improved just barely with that class in the 1983 season, from ten to eleven wins. But there were glimmers of hope, most notably Dawkins averaging eighteen points per game.

Gminski continues, "Most of the Iron Dukes [boosters] wanted Mike's head on a platter, and Tom basically said screw you: this is my guy; I'm sticking with him. Eighty-four came along, and off we go."

Dawkins, Alarie, and Henderson all averaged double figures as Duke eked out a .500 record in ACC games and a 24–10 record overall. Then Tommy Amaker joined the team.

"You had to build over time," says Bilas, a member of that class. "And that's what Coach K did. It was pretty methodical and purposeful."

Duke lost to Washington in the opening round of the 1984 NCAAs.

In 1985, now a junior-laden team, the Devils spent a month as the second-ranked team in the country, finished fourth in the league, and bowed out of the Dance after collecting one win.

The methodical improvement became turbocharged in 1986 as experience mounted and future All-American Danny Ferry joined the roster. The Blue Devils went from twenty-three to thirty-seven victories, a win output that has since been matched—but never exceeded—in program history.

Duke won the regular season and conference tournament titles for the first time in Krzyzewski's reign. Dawkins was showered with awards and became the first of eight K-coached players to earn the Naismith College Player of the Year award.

Duke was sensational and advanced all the way to the championship stage—again—where they fell just short, 72–69, to Louisville and freshman phenom Pervis Ellison.

In their final season together, the high school class of '82 quieted those Iron Dukes and could have drawn up a lifetime contract extension for Krzyzewski and hand-delivered it to Butters themselves, even if they didn't realize it at the time.

"While we all thought he was the best coach, and certainly the best coach for us," Bilas adds, "I don't think anybody in their wildest dreams would have thought that he would become one of the greatest of all time in the next forty years. Who could wrap their head around that in the mid-1980s? It's been a remarkable, remarkable thing to watch."

PEAK DYNASTY

The title loss to Louisville marked the start of a sustained stretch on the ridge line with but one final peak to summit. Just as Chamberlain had to clear Russell; Jordan, the Pistons; and Dean, the field, most basketball legends must overcome a preexisting hierarchy or pecking order.

But not all legends get to the top. Lefty Driesell, Eddie Sutton, John Chaney, Bob Huggins, Mark Few. They've seen the top, but they haven't put their feet on that rarefied soil.

And this is precisely the position Krzyzewski found himself in, in the late 1980s. It's easy to forget now, but all those years ago this gargantuan query was looming: Would K, and Duke, ever win it all?

With the class that saved him now gone, and Ferry, a sophomore, leading the charge, Duke had not quite as good a 1987 campaign and lost to eventual national champion Indiana (and Bob Knight) in the Sweet Sixteen.

That fall would mark the beginning of an almost absurd streak—actually, it *was* an absurd streak—one that hasn't been eclipsed, or candidly, even sniffed in the more than thirty-five years since it happened. Duke embarked on a run of five straight Final Fours.

In 1988, back in Kansas City, just as Fats Domino had inspired the '64 squad, Duke ran into "Danny and the Miracles" and were ousted, 66–59, by the Jayhawks in the national semifinal. Adding insult to defeat, if not fuel for K's mountaintop dreams, was the sting left by losing to KU coach Larry Brown, a dreaded Tar Heel. Two nights later, KU handled rival Oklahoma for its first chip in thirty-six years.

In 1989, Ferry got a boost from bad boy Christian Laettner, and Duke spent the first half of the season ranked number one. At the Final Four in Seattle, the Blue Devils had a poor shooting night—missing nearly two-thirds of their field goal attempts and clanging ten free throws—and, despite thirty-four points from Danny Ferry, it was Seton Hall that prevailed, 95–78.

In 1990—and again, this five-year stretch was really an amazing run—the end only got worse. Ferry had graduated the previous spring, so senior Phil Henderson elevated to a leading role, and freshman point guard Bobby Hurley was handed the controls.

The Blue Devils, with a somewhat diminished roster and a freshman point guard, still managed to win five NCAA tourney games and get back to the title contest for the first time since '86 and the fourth time in program history.

But once there, things got ugly.

UNLV connected on better than 61 percent of its shots, including eight threes. The Runnin' Rebels had sixteen steals. Anderson Hunt poured in a game-high twenty-nine points, and Vegas, in a coronation of Coach Jerry Tarkanian, walloped Duke, 103–73.

It remains the most lopsided tournament final in history.

Afterward Krzyzewski told *Sports Illustrated*, "This wasn't a game of Xs and Os. It was one of complete . . . domination."

Coach K had lost in the Final Four three straight years, joining an elite but frustrated list that included Harold Olsen (Ohio State, 1944–1946), Guy Lewis (Houston, 1982–1984), and somewhat symbolically, Dean Smith (UNC, 1967–1969).

Although Dean had to wait another thirteen springs before his ultimate victory, Coach K would have to hold on for just twelve more months.

In 1991, it was—finally—Duke and Coach K's turn to ascend and sit atop the mountain. Not only was it the conclusion the school had been waiting for, but it also provided poetic justice, as well.

The Laettner-led Blue Devils won the ACC regular season, and after being relegated to a two-seed in the Midwest after falling to Carolina in the ACC final—rolled four hapless opponents, by twenty-nine, fifteen, fourteen, and seventeen, respectively.

Then, the rematch. A year earlier UNLV had throttled Duke in the most disparate of title games, and the Rebels hadn't lost since that culture clash.

Vegas entered the semis unbeaten, at 34–0, nine-and-a-half-point favorites, winners of forty-five straight games, against a roster nearly identical to the one they had dismantled the previous year.

Hunt again scored twenty-nine, but this time Duke took care of the ball, Laettner nearly matched Hunt's production with twenty-eight points of his own, and Duke prevailed in a back-and-forth game, 79–77. It is widely considered one of the greatest upsets—and games—in Dance history.

The other semifinal saw Kansas—led by Dean Smith understudy Roy Williams—beat the Heels, as the generally well-behaved Smith was ejected late for exiting the coach's box.

The Jayhawk upset prevented a Carolina-Duke Final Four meeting (it eventually came thirty-one years later, and, perhaps ironically, resulted in a KU title), and instead allowed K to deliver defeat to Kansas and a UNC man (Williams), along with any remaining doubters.

The 1991 final was Duke 72, Kansas 65.

The questionable hire from Army, who had nearly been run off eight years earlier, only to come up short in four different Final Fours, had at last stepped up the nine-foot ladder that eludes so many excellent coaches to the summit of the college basketball world.

Mike Krzyzewski was only getting started.

BECOMING THE HEEL

In 1992, Duke ran it back, decisively. The Blue Devils were nearly untouchable in their title defense. The preseason number one, Duke won every ACC contest, topped Carolina by twenty in the tournament finale, and save for a two-point loss in Chapel Hill and a four-point defeat at Wake Forest, were nearly undefeated rolling into March.

They smoked Campbell, Iowa, and Seton Hall in the tournament before an Elite Eight clash that fans are still talking about. It's a game now known as "The Shot."

Trailing Kentucky by a point in overtime, Grant Hill unfurled a nearly seventy-five-foot pass, which Christian Laettner caught, faked right, put it on the floor, turned left, and cashed a jumper just in advance of the horn.

Pandemonium in Durham.

In the semifinal, Duke overcame a halftime deficit and beat Indiana. Krzyzewski had exacted revenge against his mentor, Knight—for the '87 tournament defeat—in the process perpetually infuriated the headman from Bloomington. Duke completed the run of dominance with a twenty-point shellacking of Michigan's fabulous five freshmen in the title game.

Duke now had as many titles in two years as Carolina had claimed in the previous thirty-five. And K had eclipsed Dean for the time being.

It was also about this time, somewhere in the early 1990s, when America started to get sick of Mike Krzyzewski and Duke.

There were a host of contributing factors, some real, some silly, but to be clear, they all contributed to the mounting angst over Duke.

There was the upset of beloved and undefeated UNLV, Laettner's haircut, the overall preppy image, and the sheer domination.

In fairness to Duke, with the inexorable advance of cable TV, there was a need for a WWE-style heel to exist in the landscape.

Anyway, whatever you elect to attribute it to, the distaste for Duke was palpable.

Oh, and then there was, and is, the flopping.

From Hurley, to Shane Battier, to Greg Paulus, to Grayson Allen, and to the next great theatrical on-ball defender, Duke's flopping, K's whining, and the incessant working of the referees probably lopped off a few more undecided fans, if any remained.

After Carolina won the title in 1993, to restore some order to the hierarchy that had been, pesky Duke and the dogged Krzyzewski were back in the championship a year later, in Charlotte, North Carolina, no less.

Three titles in four years? Not possible.

Maybe the earnest fandom of William Jefferson Clinton (please remember, this is pre-Lewinsky) for his new-on-the-scene Arkansas Razorbacks with a wildly entertaining "forty minutes of hell" brand of ball also contributed to the growing dislike for Duke.

The Blue Devils lost the 1994 championship, on a memorable late three by Scotty Thurman, to Nolan Richardson and Company.

There seemed to be little sympathy for the Blue Devils.

"I'm sure some of it had to do with Coach K," Bilas reflects.

"I used to say, the more he spoke away from the games, whether it was at press conferences or people doing stories on him, I think the more people liked him. Once you get that—once you see him away from the game, he's an unbelievably good guy. And, you know, funny and engaging and wise, all these things.

"But if all you see is in that competitive environment, I guess I can understand how people would just see that and not care for it."

One of the odder twists underscoring just how much Duke is disliked is the extent to which they are reviled in what should be their own home territory. Maybe it isn't surprising with UNC just eleven miles south of the Durham campus.

A couple of anecdotes reflect this reality.

In 2007, the Joel Coliseum in Winston-Salem hosted first- and second-round NCAA tournament games. The Tar Heels were in the pod, along with Georgetown and Knight-led Texas Tech. Duke was a six seed in Buffalo. That didn't prevent the audience, when provided a chance, from celebrating their shortcomings.

In between games, the media room bustled, and a throng gathered around a flat-screen TV as Virginia Commonwealth, an eleven seed, sealed the deal, in Wing Town. The building's public address announcer, Jeffrey Griffin, a grand man with a booming, opera-trained voice, quickly pivoted to get back out of the tunnel and to his post but not before turning to a young reporter and telling him, "Come along, you're going to want to hear this."

A moment later, in this pre-smartphone era: "Some out-of-town scores now," Griffin bellowed. "A final in the West Region, Duke, 77 . . ."

Griffin paused for effect.

"Virginia Commonwealth," followed by another pregnant pause, "79."

The Joel Coliseum crowd erupted; it was the loudest roar of the night.

Five years later, the crowd turned again, only this time Duke was in the building, at the Greensboro Coliseum. Naturally, so, too, was Carolina, or at least some of their fans. The Tar Heels, a one seed in the Midwest Region, dispatched Vermont handily, 77–58, during the day session. The nightcap pitted Duke against Patriot League champion Lehigh.

This was the same Blue Devil team that had walked off as buzzer-beating winners in the Dean Dome a month earlier when Austin Rivers hit the step-back over 2012 ACC Player of the Year Tyler Zeller. Duke finished second in the conference, earned a two seed, and had realistic aspirations of a Final Four, as its roster boasted eight future NBA players.

The best player on the floor that night wasn't sporting blue. It was Mountain Hawk (that's Lehigh) C. J. McCollum, who led all scorers with 30. And late in the first half when the crowd, again with plenty of Tar Heel partisans, seized on what they deemed a tasty opportunity.

Across the next hour, Duke found itself in a virtual tournament road game, despite being less than sixty miles from Cameron. Find any pictures or highlights from that affair, and the leaning of the crowd is clear.

Fifteenth-seeded Lehigh stunned Duke, 75–70, and again, the place went nuts.

From 1980 until his retirement in 2022, Mike Krzyzewski charted new basketball waters. Rupp, Wooden, Knight, and Smith all built dynasties, though Knight and Smith inherited programs that had already won titles.

Krzyzewski took sustained success to new levels.

Coach K established a new record for victories. He went to more Final Fours than anyone (yes, that includes Wooden), won more titles than anyone other than Wooden, and presided over eight different Naismith Players of the Year—twice as many as Wooden, and amazingly, more than Knight, Smith, and Roy Williams combined.

He meticulously built up a program that remains one of the foremost in college basketball.

His departure after the 2022 season was both cruel and somehow fitting.

Duke lost to UNC in the final game K ever coached at Cameron, 94–81, with former lettermen lining the court left speechless. A visibly irate Krzyzewski apologized after the game, calling his team's performance "unacceptable."

Twenty-eight days later, Carolina sent him home forever with an 81–77 triumph in the national semifinals. UNC was so concerned with Duke, and with K, that this victory in the NCAAs was the climax.

"I thought it was kind of fascinating," says Bilas. "Where I live in Charlotte, there are North Carolina fans that gladly traded the idea of beating Duke and Coach K in his last home game and then beating them in the Final Four but not winning the national championship.

"I heard multiple times, who cares about the championship? We beat Duke!"

That was kind of an odd thing, concludes Bilas.

"Most people would rather win a championship than beat a rival, but I'm not sure how many Carolina fans would have."

It was a feat that only Mike Krzyzewski could have pulled off.

Indiana University

Will the Cradle Rock Again?

NCAA Titles (5)—1940, 1953, 1976, 1981, 1987
Final Fours (8)—1940, 1953, 1973, 1976, 1981, 1987, 1992, 2002
Elite Eights (11)—1940, 1953, 1973, 1975, 1976, 1981, 1984, 1987, 1992, 1993, 2002
NCAA tournament appearances—41
Conference regular season titles—22

THE GAME OF BASKETBALL WAS ENVISIONED IN CANADA; CREATED IN Springfield, Massachusetts; and brought by its creator to Lawrence, Kansas.

But when Dr. James Naismith arrived in Indiana in 1925 to witness a popular high-school tournament—some thirty-four years post-invention—he found basketball's spiritual homeland.

"While the game was invented in Massachusetts," wrote Naismith, "basketball really had its origin in Indiana, which remains the center of the sport."

Take that, Springfield and Lawrence.

Indeed, an extremely strong case can be made for Indiana as the seat of the game. A young reverend, Nicholas McCay, who hailed from a small, rural outpost called Crawfordsville, is said to have fallen head over heels in love with basketball while watching Naismith teach it to YMCA instructors in Springfield back in 1891. The Rev brought it back to his hometown and, within a year, young men and boys were playing it all across the state's gently rolling plains and river valleys.

Naismith, who had toured the nation for years proselytizing his new game, did not need to do any such promotion here. The truly legendary Indiana High School basketball tournament (check out *Hoosiers*, the movie) had started in 1911 and remains a perennial sellout.

There was—probably still is—a sign sticking out of a patch of soil in Crawfordsville that commemorates the town, and the state of Indiana, as the "Cradle of Basketball." The locals call this "Hoosier Hysteria," and it leads all the way from Reverend McCay, through John Wooden, Oscar Robertson, Bobby Knight, and Larry Bird; and finally, all the way to Gene Hackman, Hickory High, and the Hollywood dream factory.

All that is the hazy, magical, touchy-feely side of Indiana hoops history.

The hard reality is reflected in the following story, told by a former twenty-first-century assistant IU coach, who requested anonymity.

"I was recruiting a high-school point guard out of Detroit who was a hard-core Pistons fan," recalls the coach. "I said to him, 'Well, you know the greatest point guard in Pistons history played right here at Indiana.'

"So, the kid says, 'I didn't know Chauncey Billups played at IU.'" (For the record, Chauncey Billups played college ball at Colorado.) "No, I told the kid. I'm talking about one of the greatest guards in basketball history, Isiah Thomas!"

"The kid looks up at me and shakes his head."

"'Who's Isiah Thomas?' the kid says."

Suffice it to say, the kid from Motown wound up taking his talents elsewhere, as did the coach.

The sad fact is that Indiana University witnessed its last NCAA championship thirty-eight years ago and counting, and Isiah Thomas won his last title six years before that. For the youth of today, even remembering Chauncey Billups (who won a title with the Pistons in 2004) is an iffy proposition, let alone being familiar with a legendary point guard who's now old enough to be their grandfather.

Since the departure of Bobby Knight twenty-five years ago, IU has emerged as far as the Elite Eight just once, back in 2002, when they were runners-up to Maryland in the final. Otherwise, it's been a long, dry stretch for the IU Hysterics.

Yes, the passion is still there. Faithful fans still turn out to the 17,222-seat Assembly Hall in droves just to witness the Hoosiers practice, and age-old symbols and traditions, such as the candy-striped warm-up pants and "Martha, the Mop Lady" (an opera singer dressed as a cleaning lady who sings the IU fight song while sweeping the hall) remain in force. But those faithful fans and boosters are very restless these days.

James Naismith, who, as noted in the Kansas chapter, had no major interest in wins and losses, would probably still find his nirvana in Bloomington or Crawfordsville.

But he'd also find a lot of young people asking, "Who's James Naismith?"

THE FIRST SEVENTY YEARS

Indiana University began playing basketball in 1900, posting a 1–4 mark under its first coach, James Horne. Nineteen coaches followed over the next twenty-three seasons, nine of whom departed with winning records.

IU's first coach of any consequence or longevity was Everett Dean (1924–1938), who was an IU All-American ballplayer in 1921 and is the only coach to have been enshrined in both the Naismith Basketball Hall of Fame and the College Baseball Hall of Fame. He led the Hoosiers to three conference titles and 162 wins and set the stage for the first breakthrough era in IU basketball.

Branch McCracken (a great name for an old-timey hoops coach but an even better name for a tree surgeon) succeeded Dean in 1938. Like Dean, he was a young and eager former IU player, but the similarities seem to stop there. It was McCracken who brought the run-and-gun offense to Bloomington, sparking the nickname "Hurryin' Hoosiers."

McCracken was a hit right out of the box, finishing 17–3 in his first year as head coach and winning the NCAA title with his 1939–1940 team, which was led by All-American Marvin Huffman.

Three winning seasons later, McCracken joined the navy, serving as a lieutenant in World War II. He returned to IU for the 1946–1947 season where he and his teams continued putting up nice numbers.

In 1948, McCracken received a call from UCLA, which was looking to upgrade its less-than-estimable program to the big time. McCracken was a conservative-minded Midwesterner who had a good thing going at IU, so he turned UCLA on to his navy buddy, John Wooden, and thus did McCracken figure into the most extraordinary and magical period in college basketball history (see the UCLA chapter).

McCracken's IU team won its second NCAA title in 1953 and got to the Sweet Sixteen a year later, then again in '58.

But the good times were about to stop rolling. In the fall of 1960, the IU football team got nailed for a host of NCAA violations, which included players being offered free plane tickets, under-the-table stipends, and envelopes filled with cash.

The school was hit with a four-year probation, during which time *all* varsity sports, including basketball, were barred from postseason participation. The impact on current IU athletes, and on the university's ability to recruit new talent, was nothing short of devastating.

But for a pair of identical Indiana twin boys, Tom and Dick Van Arsdale, the problems confronting the IU basketball program didn't amount to a hill of beans. They had been living and breathing IU basketball practically since their infancy, and no scholarship offers from competing programs such as Kentucky or Purdue were going to deter them from realizing their dreams of playing for Indiana and Branch McCracken.

"He was like a father," says Tom. "A real country gentleman . . . more of a rah-rah motivator than a 'punisher.'"

In his book, *Journey Man*, Van Arsdale further describes his coach as a true servant-leader, a man who believed that his players were doing him a favor by coming into his program. He recalls a time when he and his brother were laid up sick at their fraternity house, and McCracken arrived with bags full of oranges, chicken noodle soup, and other groceries.

"Can you imagine John Calipari or Bobby Knight doing the same?" wrote Van Arsdale. "I love Coach Knight, but during his coaching days

The 1953 NCAA champion Hoosiers. Branch McCracken, the man in the middle in the light gray suit, was the last country gentleman to coach IU. Wikimedia Commons, photographer unknown

he'd be more inclined to accuse [you] of faking an illness to wiggle out of doing wind sprints."

During the Van Arsdale years (1962–1965), IU ran a lot of 2–2–1 zone presses and a free-wheeling, shoot-'em-up offense, eschewing any set plays. But to do this effectively, notes Tom, you need to have a big man who can scour the defensive glass, haul in a whole bunch of rebounds, and get the ball out quickly to the players running the fast break.

"Branch wanted to run an offense like Red Auerbach did with the Boston Celtics," explains Tom, "but Red Auerbach had Bill Russell on the defensive boards. We had one six-foot-seven guy and nobody else over six feet five."

John McGlocklin, a teammate and longtime friend of the Van Arsdales, likewise laments McCracken's failure to "get us a center" and half-jokingly alludes to the coach's tendency to play favorites.

"He'd yell at me all the time," says McGlocklin, who, like Tom and Dick, went on to a successful pro career. "But he never yelled at the brothers . . . he loved those guys."

For the Van Arsdales, the general lack of success in terms of wins and losses and the impossibility of ever playing in a postseason college tournament were mitigated by the opportunity to play in McCracken's pro-style offense. Tom says it wound up mirroring what they would face in the NBA and gave the brothers a decided edge on players from programs that ran less flexible and more rigidly enforced "systems."

Toward the end of his long tenure at IU, it was evident to his players that health issues were taking a toll on their coach's enthusiasm and what Tom Van Arsdale terms his "gravitational charisma." McCracken retired in 1965 and would pass away of a heart attack five years later, with 364 wins—450 if you include his time at Ball State—and grocery bags packed full of good wishes and fond memories.

It would be the last time Bloomington would witness a country gentleman in the coach's chair.

SUITABLE FOR A FINE INTELLIGENCE

There were basketball coaches who could jellify a player's knees with a glare, a bit of persiflage, or a "goodness gracious, sake's alive."

Then, there were coaches, generally soft-spoken, genial, phlegmatic individuals, who every now and then found it necessary to motivate their teams via some choice invective. Roy Williams is one who comes immediately to mind.

And then, there was this guy . . .

I'm tired of this shit. I'm sick and fucking tired of an eight and ten record. I'm fucking tired of losing to Purdue. I'm not here to fuck around this week. You may be, but I'm not. I'm gonna fucking guarantee you that if we don't play up there Monday night, then you're not going to believe the next four fucking days. Now I am not here to get my ass beat on Monday, and you better fucking understand that right now . . . this is absolute fucking bullshit. I'll fucking run your ass right into the ground. You'll think last night was a fucking picnic.

In case you can't identify the voice, which was as loud and raging as it was profane, this was Bobby Knight, addressing his team at practice. It occurred years before the internet and is in no way atypical of the coach's daily motivational approach. Only this specific burst of execration was surreptitiously taped and leaked to the media, going viral before viral was a thing.

It was the writer F. Scott Fitzgerald who suggested that the truest measure of a fine intelligence lies in the mind's ability to hold two opposing thoughts simultaneously without losing its capacity to function.

Taking F. Scott's suggestion to heart, then it would seem, at least to us, that the study of Robert Montgomery Knight is one that should best be left to only the finest minds.

Modesty and common sense forbid us from making any claims along that line, but we're going to forge ahead with this anyway.

We begin with the "A" side, the "Mr. Hyde" side, as it were. The side that Bobby Knight, coach of the Indiana University Hoosiers, chose to display to the world. Most who knew him well believe he needed, for whatever psychological reasons, to be seen as a tough guy. General Patton was one oft-cited role model. Or maybe John Wayne, only a little nastier.

For openers, Knight was a bully, a martinet, a misogynist, and, as is demonstrated above, a world-class vulgarian. He could be irascible, condescending, and imperious at different times, but occasionally as a package deal.

He carried a grudge like a priceless family heirloom; and he somehow managed, with considerable effort, to permanently alienate not only his perceived enemies (a list as long as Richard Nixon's) but many of those who loved and revered him the most.

He never seemed to grasp that foundational democratic principle that one man's freedom ends at another man's nose. Hence, the depositing of an obnoxious LSU fan into a trash receptacle; the shoving of a longtime assistant out of a chair and into a TV set; the choking of one of his players and any number of less violent aggressions against other players, including his own son. Not to mention his utter disdain for harmless pieces of furniture.

And, finally, although living one's life as if it were one long competition is not, in and of itself, a character flaw, Knight was prone to take the competition to extremes that bordered on—and frequently crossed over into—the preposterous.

Gary Cunningham, a former head coach at UCLA and longtime friend, says he and Knight, like fly fishermen everywhere, could talk fly fishing for hours on end without boring each other to tears.

"For years, Bobby would try to talk me into going with him on one of his fishing expeditions," says Cunningham. "But as much as I enjoyed his company, I've always thought of fishing as something that's relaxing and fun. There was no way I was going to go out with Knight and have it turned into a fly-fishing death match."

The Van Arsdale twins, Tom and Dick, did accompany Knight on fly-fishing excursions across the western United States and the former Soviet Union and recall those trips as being great fun for them but death matches for their competition-crazed companion.

"Four of us were trout fishing up in Montana, and we were competing in teams," relates Tom. "Dick was on Bobby's team; and as I remember it, Dick outfished him big-time. I think he caught fifteen more trout that day, and it made Bobby angry. After we're all back [in the lodge], Bobby takes out his rod and goes out there [in the dead of night] to catch another sixteen trout."

It isn't clear how Knight fared out there in the dark, for although early morning is widely deemed the best time to catch trout—low light conditions make the finicky fish more comfortable sitting out in the open—night fishing in the heat of summer in Montana can yield excellent results as well. In any case, Van Arsdale has a tough time imagining Bobby Knight giving up before nabbing those sixteen cold-blooded vertebrates.

All of this, suffice it to say, offers merely a snippet from Side One. The laundry list of Bobby Knight's transgressions against other human beings, and against the very notion of civility itself, is too lengthy to enumerate here.

We'll just leave it behind us, along with the observation that Bobby Knight was one f#$@%-ing piece of work.

But for every Side One, there is a flipside. In Knight's case, a "Dr. Jekyll" side. And trust us when we say that this opposing portrait of a very complex individual—the one Knight kept occluded from public view—was every bit as formidable, if not more so, as his execrable Mr. Hyde side.

To begin, Bobby Knight was a man of enormous generosity, especially with his time, but also with his money. He donated considerable sums to the libraries at IU and Texas Tech, where he coached for seven years after getting fired at IU; and endowed scholarships at Marian University. The sale of the chair he infamously tossed in anger onto a basketball court, and later autographed, raised $525 for two children in Iowa Park, Texas, who had lost their father.

According to at least two of his closest friends, Knight supported a homeless guy in Bloomington for years, eventually flying the man down to Texas to spend time with him in Waco.

Landon Turner, a former six-foot-ten standout player at IU before becoming paralyzed from the chest down in an automobile accident in July 1981 (four months after helping Knight win his second NCAA title), noted that before the crash, he couldn't wait to get out of Indiana, not being a big fan of Knight's over-the-top coaching style.

After the accident, Knight helped set up a fund to pay Turner's large medical expenses. Turner says his feelings changed when he got a good, honest look at Knight's Jekyll side. "I'd never seen it before. . . . I developed a love for him," Turner told a newspaper reporter.

"I had a lunch scheduled with Bobby one day, and I brought along another guy who wasn't very eager to join us at first because all he knew of Bob Knight was the jerk he'd seen kicking basketballs and throwing chairs on TV," says a longtime Knight buddy. "Part way through lunch, the discussion turned to Landon Turner, and Bobby began to tear up. Real, authentic tears. The guy asked me later why nobody ever sees that part of the man."

More than money, Knight's lasting contributions to humanity came in his expenditure of time, energy, and compassion.

For example, he was always up for meeting privately with the families of critically ill children and others in dire physical straits.

Steve Ahlfeld, Knight's second IU recruit and now an orthopedic surgeon affiliated with the university, recalls accompanying Knight, along with several other former players, to Riley Hospital for Children in Indianapolis. Knight had arranged meetings with the families of children housed in the pediatric oncology ward.

"When we get there, Bobby says to us, 'Okay, guys, I'm going up.' And we ask him if he'd like us to go with him for some support (given that there are few things in this life more distressing to behold than a ward full of cancer-ridden kids). Bobby turns to us and says, 'No, I'm going up there alone, and I don't want *anyone* to know about this!' Bobby was extremely adamant about that, and we weren't going to cross him. I can't tell you why he hated so much to show this human side of his personality. But, for him, this stuff was strictly for private consumption, between him and those families."

Knight was equally magnanimous when it came to sharing his basketball knowledge and coaching tips with others of his profession. He taught the motion offense—which he perfected but did not invent—to generations of Indiana high-school coaches and to college coaches all across the land. To those he liked, his beneficence knew few bounds.

Tom Penders, a former head coach at Houston and the University of Texas, notes that "nobody did as much [to further] my career as Bobby Knight." Penders recollects flying off to attend one of Knight's coaching clinics at IU.

"I got met at the airport by one of his assistants. We're in the car, and I tell the driver that this is not the way to my hotel. He pulls up in front of a house and says, 'You're not staying in a hotel. You're going to be staying with Bobby and his family during the time you're here.' This was Bobby Knight to me, warm and very kind."

Steve Ahlfeld suggests adding a charming demeanor and the faint hint of a waggish sense of humor to that list, two more attributes the coach camouflaged in vitriol.

"At the time Knight showed up for his recruitment visit, I was still talking to Michigan," recalls Ahlfeld. "Anyway, we're all sitting around, me, my parents, and my high-school coach, and Knight says, 'Well, I gotta tell you, you keep on talking to Michigan, and I might have to sic my guys on you.'"

Knight also served as a virtual one-man personnel bureau for dozens, if not hundreds, of out-of-work and out-of-luck basketball coaches. There weren't many basketball people in hiring positions back then who wouldn't take a phone call from Bobby Knight. On the minus side, if one didn't follow through with hiring Bobby's recommended candidate, that person would hear about it from Bobby. And oftentimes, in pungent Knight vernacular.

Moreover, if there is such a thing in major college basketball as a "clean program," then it was probably run by Bobby Knight. His players went to class and graduated, and there was no hanky-panky either before or after his recruits arrived on campus. Knight's words may not always have been nice ones, but he meant every one of them. He had no patience for liars, cheats, or scoundrels.

"Coach sat down with me and my family at his recruiting visit and promised us four things," says Steve Alford, a star of Knight's 1987 championship squad and one of his all-time favorite players.

"One, that I would obtain a degree. Two, that I'd have a chance to play for a championship. Three, that I would play with great teammates. And four, that I would have a friend for life in him."

Concludes Alford, "Say what you want about the guy, and as tough as he could be with me as a player, all I can tell you is that he checked off all four of those boxes."

Just as an aside, as a matter of synchronicity, our conversation with Alford occurred mere hours before Bobby Knight passed away at the age of eighty-three. He had suffered a stroke eight years earlier and was a diabetic. Those close to him said that he had been battling dementia as well. Stories were written at the time suggesting a strong link between his antisocial behavior and his cognitive decline.

Which brings us to the delicate matter of Bobby Knight's mental state during his coaching years. A common belief, shared by many journalists, is that the man was out of control a good deal of the time and that his ill temper and violent tantrums indicated a huge anger-management problem that he could not domesticate in any discernible way.

Dr. Jim Sherman, emeritus professor of psychology at IU, came to know, and ultimately befriend, Bobby Knight. Their relationship was hatched when a reporter called Sherman for input on a story that would examine whether the coach was truly off his nut or was just an angry son of a bitch. Sherman offered his take—that coach Knight, for all his faults, was aware of what he was doing at all times and showed no apparent signs of mental illness. According to Sherman, the reporter went on to write a piece that essentially depicted Knight as a near-lunatic and did not bother to temper that view with Sherman's observations to the contrary.

Anyway, Sherman reached out to Knight, and the two men initially bonded over their mutual distrust of the working press, a distrust that can be best summed up by the following vintage, pithy Knight quote:

"All of us learn to write in the second grade. Most of us go on to greater things."

Anyway, Knight and Sherman began hanging out together, and Sherman regularly attended Knight's practices, along with other faculty members. Just for the record, Sherman was in the room when Knight dumped the LSU heckler into the wastebasket.

Sherman recalls attending one practice where Knight was getting up in the faces of two of his best players, Alford and Daryl Thomas. Both were fully onboard the program and presented absolutely nothing in the way of disciplinary problems. Sherman was bothered by Knight's outburst, as it appeared to emanate from a dark, out-of-control place.

Suddenly, Knight halted practice and came up to talk to Sherman and the other onlookers.

"Let me tell you why I do that," explained the coach, in a calm, measured tone. "I do it because I know that those two young men can handle it, that they understand why I'm in their faces. I wouldn't act that way if I didn't know it would ultimately help make them better players.

"Now, with Uwe Blab [a center on that team who was in more urgent need of in-your-face coaching], I could *never* talk that way. He couldn't take it. It would destroy him."

Although Knight's words do tend to support the view that the man knew what he was doing, that doesn't mean that he always knew when to push his players hard and when to back off.

Take the cases of Alford and Thomas. Although Alford was wired from a young age to take in Knight's message and ignore the fury with which it was delivered, Daryl Thomas was a more sensitive lad who tended to take his raging criticism to heart. And as for Knight's relationship with Thomas, the anger didn't always yield the desired motivational result.

Nevertheless, in the end, Thomas, too, came to understand the affection that underlay the rage and over time grew more comfortable with the emotional oscillations that went hand in hand with playing basketball for Bobby Knight.

Sherman sticks by his assertion that even when his words and deeds far exceeded the boundaries of good judgment and taste, Bobby Knight maintained a semblance of stability. Even in his treatment of the LSU heckler ("he just kept chanting 'Tiger bait, Tiger bait'"), Knight showed restraint—albeit less than admirable restraint—in lifting up the man and putting him in the trash while bruising only his male ego in the process.

"Coach Knight was amazing to watch during practice or in games, the way his eyes would open wide when he was looking out on the court. He saw everything that was going on around him. I miss the way he'd come up behind me and slap me on the back, which was a friendship gesture, and, even more, I miss his advice, which was always sound. Once I got offered a post at Ohio State. I asked Bobby if he thought I should take it. He said, 'If you decide to go, just make sure you can come back.'

"The truth," concludes Professor Sherman, "is that this was a man who coached in a very different era. There were plenty of others in that time who crossed the line, and, yes, it was inexcusable even back then. But Knight never crossed it without having thought about it first."

So, that about wraps up the Dr. Jekyll side. And now, a la Scott Fitzgerald, how do we manifest our fine intelligence to put those two radically opposing views in perspective? How do we take the measure of a man whose mouth and heart seemed to be complete strangers to one another much of the time?

Perhaps we simply conclude that Bobby Knight was, indeed, a f@#$%&-ing piece of work.

But with a prominent asterisk attached.

IT'S NOT THE MEAT, IT'S THE MOTION

Now that we've completed our admittedly limited exploration into the multifaceted and much-debated personality of Bobby Knight, we turn our sights to a side of him that is not debatable: his brilliance as a basketball tactician, innovator, teacher, and motivator. The man of whom it was said by legions of Hoosier fans, "Bobby Knight *is* Indiana basketball."

Knight grew up in Massillon, Ohio, the son of a railroad worker and a schoolteacher. He was a star at Orrville High School and went on to Ohio State, where he was a reserve forward on the 1960 NCAA championship team featuring future NBA Hall of Famers John Havlicek and Jerry Lucas. Knight made two more (losing) trips to the NCAA final in '61 and '62.

After one year coaching high school, he joined the army and saw active duty for two years. During his time in the service, he became an assistant coach at West Point and was appointed head coach at the academy in 1965. He was only twenty-four years old but already carried the nickname "General." In truth, drill sergeant was more appropriate, but why quibble?

In his six years at Army, Knight began honing the reputation for outrageous behavior that would follow him throughout his coaching career and has already been detailed in this text.

Strategically speaking, Knight in his early coaching days was enamored of the "reverse action offense" run by the legendary Pete Newell at California in the late '50s. Without getting immersed in the exquisite intricacies of the Xs and Os, Newell's offense was based on players being able to recognize a defensive deployment and exploit it; and it required proper footwork, timing, and nonverbal communication. It came complete with a wide range of options that would counter any move by the defense and, when executed precisely, would lead to a low-post move and a high-percentage shot, or a layup off a back screen.

Knight ran this offense at Army and had excellent success with it, owing in large measure to the skills and savvy of his point guard—a kid named Mike Krzyzewski (see the Duke chapter).

When he got to IU in 1971, he took Newell's offense, as well as certain motion principles employed by Henry Iba at Oklahoma A&M and passed along to Iba's protégé, Don Haskins, at Texas Western, and went about creating a system that was all his own.

As it says in the name, the motion offense is about constant movement, with or without the ball. Speed and quickness can count for a lot, and when executed well—as Knight's teams generally did—the system will neutralize another team's size advantage. Indeed, Knight was quoted over the years as being more partial to speed than size.

Motion offenses differ from "continuity offenses" like John Wooden's vaunted "high post," which is based on a repeating pattern of passes, cuts, and screens. Motion offenses follow no fixed repeating pattern but are flexible and free flowing. Players are taught to pass, screen, and cut, depending upon how the defense is playing them, and then reacting accordingly. Only a few general rules are attached:

- Pass to one side of the court and move to screen for players on the opposite side, to create better spacing on the floor and driving lanes to the basket;
- Set back screens (behind a defender guarding another player) and "flare" screens, in which an offensive player cuts away from the ball to use a screen set by a teammate to receive a pass and either take an open jump shot or initiate some kind of action to create a better shot.

Former coach Fran Fraschilla, on one of his ESPN "Hoops 101" online tutorials, explained why the motion offense can be so effective. First, because no order of movement is predetermined, it's difficult for an opponent to prepare for and scout. Second, defenses can get confused by the constant movement, screening, and cutting, and the interchangeability of the system. Three, the system can be adapted to a team's personnel. It works just as well for a "power" team or a three-point shooting team. It can work with five guards on the floor or five big men. And finally, it promotes "team play," as every offensive player relies on his four teammates to create his scoring opportunities.

Bobby Knight's particular adaptation emphasized "a partnership of screening," given the coach's fondness for hard, legal screens. Moreover, this type of offense has a place for less-skilled athletes, as anyone who is fully ambulatory is capable of setting a screen to free up a teammate.

"There are so many [advantageous] aspects to Knight's approach," says Bob Starkey, a motion maven and assistant coach in the LSU women's program, which ran Knight's screen-oriented version for a decade. Starkey watched nearly two dozen Knight practices and attended several of his offensive clinics over the years and has never ceased to be impressed with the sheer beauty of the motion offense itself and Knight's canny ability to tweak it to his liking.

"First, there's the unpredictability. It can start with anyone, anywhere on the court making the first pass. Then it all comes down to thinking, reading, and reacting, and nobody could break it down [narrowing the focus to address specific actions within a play] and teach it better than Bobby Knight."

Steve Ahlfeld says his own education in the many virtues of the motion offense began at Willis Reed's summer basketball camp in New York, where Knight took a handful of players to introduce them to its basic concepts.

According to Ahlfeld, Knight rolled out the system gradually, as it was far too complex a mechanism to dump on his players at one time. Ahlfeld adds that most of the pieces were firmly in place by the conclusion of the 1973–1974 season.

It is certainly no accident that the teams that operated this offense with the most confidence, mutual trust, and nonverbal communication were the ones who won championships. Starkey says the great IU teams of 1975 and 1976 (a combined 63–1) were a case study in how to run a killer motion offense.

Those teams understood the system so completely and ran it more fluidly than any teams in NCAA history, he notes.

To accommodate the different set of skills that the 1987 championship squad possessed, Knight made some needed modifications in his system, making it possible for more players to be screening for Steve Alford, thus getting their best shooter better looks at the basket.

We could examine the ins-and-outs of the motion offense for another hundred pages, but there was another side to Knight's coaching philosophy about which he might have been even more passionate: IU's inimitable and indomitable half-court, man-to-man defense.

There's a classic story about Knight speaking at a clinic in Columbus, Ohio, fielding questions from a rapt audience of fellow coaches. One of them raised his hand and asked Knight which was his favorite type of zone defense. Knight responded with the fact that IU didn't play zone, making the man's question irrelevant.

Undaunted, the same coach raised his hand a few minutes later. Reluctantly, Knight called on him again.

"But coach," the guy went on, "what if you *did play zone*? Which style would you play?"

At this point, Knight was visibly agitated.

"I told you already," he answered brusquely. "We don't play zone!"

But just a few minutes later, the determined questioner was at it again, boldly raising his hand in the face of a glowering Bobby Knight.

Everybody in the audience knew what was coming: Bobby's stack was about to blow.

"OK, coach," the zone enthusiast inquired, "now let's just say the NCAA passed a *rule* that you could *only play zone defense*. What would you do then?"

Knight's patience, never all that great to begin with, had reached its limit.

"I'll tell you what I'd do!" he roared. "I'd quit this job! Now don't raise your fucking hand again!"

Bob Starkey says you have to admire any coach who exhibits that much passion about his defensive coaching philosophy.

AND SO IT BEGINS . . .

Bobby Knight arrived in Bloomington in March 1971 with some fanfare. The headline in the *Indianapolis Star* that day read, "Hoosiers Hire Disciplinarian."

The university was looking for just such a man, as things at IU had more or less unraveled under the previous coach, Lou Watson, the successor to Branch McCracken. Watson resigned with one game left in the 1970–1971 season amid what was described in the media as a player "mutiny" or "revolt."

Apparently, Watson hadn't done anything all that terrible to inspire his team to turn against him, except perhaps not being an especially conscientious or tenacious leader ("all he did was roll the ball out on the floor," noted one cynic) and overseeing an underachieving team of mostly underclassmen in his final year.

That team posted a pretty respectable 17–7 record (fourth in Big Ten play at 9–5), but the fanatical fan base had been expecting a great deal more. It probably didn't help Watson's cause that his teams had losing records in three of his last four seasons at the helm.

Anyway, Bobby Knight, the General, certainly seemed the right man to clean up Watson's mess. Knight, himself, was not about to bad-mouth his predecessor, noting that he had no interest in delving into the grim past, only with planning for the future.

Actually, Knight's original choice for a Big Ten job had been the University of Wisconsin. But after accepting that job in 1968, he backed out after his friend Bo Schembechler, the Michigan football coach, counseled Knight to stay put. Three years later, along came Indiana with an attractive offer, and Knight signed on.

Knight's approach represented a significant break from McCracken's Hurryin' Hoosiers run-and-gun offense, which, as previously mentioned, had resulted in two prior NCAA championships. But the old, reliable run-and-gun had run out of steam by the 1960s.

Still, a few members of Hoosier Nation questioned Knight's suitability for the job, given his lack of enthusiasm for traditional Indiana up-tempo basketball. "He'll never make it here," wrote one wag. And Jerry Oliver, a Watson assistant who coached the final game of the

'70–'71 season, expressed his displeasure about not even being considered for the top job.

Those negative vibes notwithstanding, it didn't take the thirty-year-old head coach very long to win over the skeptics. There was a 17–8 record (third in conference) and a seventeenth ranking in the final AP Poll in his first year; followed by 22–6 in his second (first in the Big Ten), with a season-ending ranking of sixth and a trip to the NCAA Final Four, where they lost to Bill Walton and UCLA.

But things were about to get a whole lot better in a hurry. Joining that excellent Final Four group of Quinn Buckner, Steve Green, John Laskowski, and Steve Ahlfeld were Kent Benson, Bobby Wilkerson, Scott May, and Tom Abernethy.

The IU '73–'74 squad went 23–5 and tied Michigan for the Big Ten title at 12–2 but lost to the Wolverines in a face-off game. And because NCAA rules at the time allowed only the conference champ to go to the Big Dance, IU was shut out and wound up in the "Collegiate Commissioners Association Tournament" (we had never heard of it, either).

Anyway, IU did win the CCAT title, for what that's worth.

The new no-Hurry Hoosiers hit their full stride in 1974–1975, rolling off thirty-one straight wins. Not a single, sentient college basketball observer anywhere in America saw anything but an NCAA championship in their immediate future.

But in one of those cruel twists of fate that can befall even the mightiest of warriors (see Sophocles, William Shakespeare, et al.), IU was a victim of extremely unfortunate circumstances in the Elite Eight versus Kentucky.

Though Indiana had walloped the Wildcats by twenty-four back in December, the Hoosiers came into this game with their leading scorer, Scott May, wrapped in a cast over his left forearm, having broken his wrist four weeks earlier. Moreover, the Kentucky team that they handled so handily way back in early December had morphed into a more cohesive and motivated bunch, with senior Kevin Grevey leading a cast of six future NBA (and one ABA) draftees.

May played only seven unproductive minutes and scored just four points, and even Kent Benson's tremendous

Scott May, now fully recovered from his wrist injury, cuts down the net after the 1976 title game. Public domain, via Wikimedia Commons

performance—thirty-three points, twenty-three rebounds—wasn't enough in a brutally disheartening 92–90 loss.

But the wound had healed by the following November, and neither wind, nor rain, nor busted wrist was going to stop Indiana from running the table in 1975–1976.

IU kicked off the season with a twenty-point pasting of reigning NCAA champion UCLA, followed by some sweet revenge against Kentucky in overtime. There were a fair number of other close shaves along the way, including another overtime win against Michigan at home and a couple of nail-biters against Purdue.

But when all was said and done, the '76 Hoosiers and their "fab five" starters—Buckner, Wilkerson, Abernethy, Benson, and May—stood alone at 32–0, with an (overdue) NCAA title and a whole host of accolades, most notably a nod from *USA Today* as the nation's all-time greatest college basketball team.

Forty-nine years gone by, the description still applies.

Mission accomplished.

The next few years saw more NBA-quality players flow through the system—Mike Woodson, Ray Tolbert, Butch Carter, Randy Wittman, the aforementioned Landon Turner—but only limited postseason success (second-round NCAA exits in '78 and '80, and an NIT title in '79).

But a cocky and profoundly gifted six-foot-one point guard from the harsh environs of Chicago's West Side—"we were poorer than poor," he once noted—was about to put IU back in the saddle again.

Isiah Thomas—although no longer a household name in Gen Z world—brought a different kind of energy to the program. Not the Quinn Buckner, coach-on-the-floor, total buy-in energy of 1976. Thomas was much less inclined to alter his personality to satisfy his demanding boss.

For two years, the two men engaged in a love-hate relationship, which had gotten off to a rocky start before Knight's home recruiting visit had ended.

As Isiah tells it, Knight made a glib remark when Isiah's mom expressed concerns about the Ku Klux Klan's major presence in Indiana. Isiah's brother took issue with Knight's cavalier attitude toward his brother's physical safety and challenged the coach to a fight. Knight, always ready to rock a good brawl, got up, took off his jacket, and rolled up his sleeves.

"Yeah, we can take it outside if you want," he said.

As usually happened in these situations, cooler heads intervened. Indeed, according to Isiah, his mom liked the coach's feisty attitude, and she approved her son's decision to attend IU.

As noted, Isiah's two years in the program did not progress entirely smoothly. Knight threw him out of practice in year one and made it a point to be especially tough on the kid to show the rest of the team that

Bobby Knight appears to be (almost) smiling beside Isiah Thomas during a 1981 NCAA tournament game. And why not? Knight was well on his way to the second of his three titles. Public domain, via Wikimedia Commons

no player, even one with Isiah's prodigious talent, was above the team philosophy.

In season two, 1980–1981, the pieces came together, and Thomas and Mike Woodson carried IU to another conference championship and IU's fourth NCAA title. This one concluded with a flourish—a decisive win over North Carolina and Knight's good buddy, Dean Smith.

More good results ensued—a trip to the Sweet Sixteen and the Elite Eight in '84. But things went far south the next year (a 7–11 conference mark, no NCAA bid, and lots of players being benched and excoriated). Knight took it all extremely hard, and his unfortunate habit of not letting go of disappointment caused friends to advise him to take a year off and chill the f—k out.

The fact that he didn't take the '85–'86 season off was a fortunate one for readers of sports literature, as it led to John Feinstein's masterly, best-selling *Season on the Brink*.

Feinstein, invited by Knight to be a fly on the wall at practices, team meetings, and midgame huddles, chronicled all the ups and downs of a season that took in all the many aspects of the Knight aura. That season, too, ended on a very sour note—a dismal loss to fourteenth-seeded Cleveland State in round one of the NCAAs.

Nevertheless, in their indomitable way, Knight and his Hoosiers got right back on the good foot the next year. That team, led by Steve Alford, Daryl Thomas, Keith Smart, Dean Garrett, and Rick Calloway, finished the season ranked number one with a 30–4 record and IU's fifth NCAA title. It would be the program's last, at least up to this writing.

The '87 campaign could not have ended more enjoyably or dramatically—a jumper by Keith Smart over Syracuse's Howard Triche with four seconds on the clock, sealing a 74–73 victory. Syracuse players insisted that they had called a time-out immediately after the made bucket, but the refs let three of those precious seconds tick away, leaving the Orangemen no option except a hopeless heave down the court.

Bobby Knight's record over his last thirteen years at IU would be a feather in any coach's cap (but certainly not in his): thirteen more NCAA appearances, a Final Four in '92, an Elite Eight in '93, and three trips to the Sweet Sixteen. But the last six of those seasons ended no later than round two.

Moreover, the last years of the Knight era witnessed arguably the most egregious, and unforgivable, of his violent outbursts—the choking of his player, Neil Reed, during a 1997 practice. A university investigation prompted the IU president to put Knight on a zero-tolerance policy, which he grossly violated in shocking fashion in September 2000, grabbing the arm of a student who had addressed him by his last name.

Knight was terminated immediately and finished his coaching career at Texas Tech.

But all his venial sins aside, Knight's basketball legacy by this point was solidly in place. It would infuse the IU basketball program for the next generation, and it would be an awfully difficult one for any coach to match.

AFTER THE KNIGHT AND THE MUSIC

Knight's sudden, painful departure on the eve of the upcoming 2000–2001 season elicited a bitter, angry reaction within the IU community. According to published reports, not only were the protesting students and alumni in an absolute uproar, but several players threatened to quit the team unless IU maintained some degree of program continuity by appointing a Knight assistant to the head job.

Mike Davis, with no HC experience and just three years spent in the Knight regime, and his fellow assistant John Treloar were offered the job as "co-coaches." This could be seen as a desperate effort on the part of the school administration to pacify the rage-filled IU community by at least giving them a Knight guy.

Regardless of the motive, Treloar declined the offer, and Davis was named sole interim coach.

Davis, for his part, dismisses the notion that his appointment was part of a pacification program. The problem, he says, was that it was simply too late, with the season scheduled to start in a few weeks, to go out and hire a (viable) outside replacement for one of college basketball's all-time hoop legends.

Davis, heartbroken by the nature of Knight's departure, admits he was a "little shaky" at first about taking on this awesome task. Nevertheless, he was well indoctrinated into the Knight way of doing things and knew something about establishing discipline, and organizing and running practices, in addition to recruiting and other duties he had assumed as an assistant.

"And besides," he says, "there was a system already in place for me to step into."

Davis, with a team featuring future NBA draftees Kirk Haston and Jared Jeffries, went 21–13 (third in conference) in his first season, which ended with a deflating first-round loss to thirteenth-seeded underdog Kent State in the NCAAs.

The next year would prove to be a very pleasant surprise. With much the same roster, IU got on a late-season roll all the way to the NCAA final, where they came up twelve points short against Maryland.

The future seemed bright enough to get everyone in Hoosier Land donning shades, and Mike Davis's contract was extended through 2007–2008.

But Davis, on some deeper emotional level, sensed that he was punching above his weight class, wondering if, down deep, he wasn't entirely prepared for the 24/7 maelstrom that's part and parcel of a job of this magnitude.

In December 2002, his desire to beat the "hated Kentucky" got the better of him and, angered by a foul call on the floor, bolted onto the court with 2.6 seconds left and his team down by one. Davis was hit with a technical foul and tossed out of the game, and the ensuing Kentucky free throws salted it away for the Wildcats.

A losing season in 2003–2004 and a marginal 15–14 record the next year sealed Davis's fate.

"You could see the frustration, and you knew the [losses] were wearing on him," says Adam Ahlfeld, son of former Hoosier Steve Ahlfeld and a walk-on at IU who played his first two years for Davis.

"But I certainly never got the sense that he had lost control."

Nevertheless, with the Knight aura having faded away, and the IU faithful calling for his ouster, Davis resigned in February 2006, with the resignation to take effect at season's end.

In 2018, Davis addressed his mind-set in stepping aside. I was never fully prepared for this, he said, but "I tried to walk out there like I was."

Davis says now that the whole experience was helpful in taking on the various professional challenges he has faced since then.

Such a challenge cropped up during his sixth and final season as head coach at Detroit Mercy in 2023–2024. Our conversation with Coach Davis happened to occur during the waning days of that lost season, with Detroit sporting an unenviable record of 1–26 on its way to a gruesome 1–31 finish and the unceremonious firing of its head coach.

In the midst of dealing with all the stresses that come with a one-win season, he took the time to assist a couple of complete strangers writing a basketball book. Which, to our minds, says something about the maturation and professionalism of Mike Davis.

Replacing Davis at IU was Kelvin Sampson, who carried a well-deserved reputation for high-quality coaching and turning troubled teams around quickly and equally well-deserved notoriety for his extreme laissez-faire attitude toward NCAA rules and regs.

In less than two seasons at IU, he demonstrated his aptitude for all of that.

"He was a great teacher who had us all buying in," says Adam Ahlfeld, who notes that Sampson was likewise very big on conditioning, which incorporated a particular 3-on-3 single bubble rebounding drill right out of the old GATA (get after their asses) coaching playbook.

Sampson's first year saw the Hoosiers finish 21–11 and, as a seven-seed, knock out the always dangerous Gonzaga before falling to UCLA. The following season got off to a blockbuster 17–1 start with a lineup that included freshman Eric Gordon, D. J. White, and Armon Bassett.

But the good vibes didn't last, beginning with the lingering resentment over the controversial recruitment of Eric Gordon, which occurred after the kid had already verbally committed to Illinois. Sampson was taken to task by the coaching fraternity for his legal but underhanded conduct in this matter.

There was also an investigation of improper recruiting calls (the kind that are legal now) and allegations by Eric Gordon that the 2007–2008 team was riven by disputes over drug use that the coach never adequately addressed.

"You couldn't tell what coach was going through in all this," says Ahlfeld, "but all the rumbling got to us."

After Sampson took a $750,000 buyout, assistant Dan Dakich took over on an interim basis with the team standing at 22–4. Six players skipped Dakich's first practice in an apparent show of defiance, and the team ran out of gas on the court, losing two of its last three regular-season games before getting ushered out in the first round of the Big Ten tourney and the first round of the NCAAs.

Left behind in Sampson's wake was a three-year, self-imposed probation, which the IU president termed a "one-time deviation from a half-century record of no major infractions."

The question now was who would step up and take on a job with major restrictions on recruiting calls, cuts in scholarships, and a greatly depleted roster. Eric Gordon took off for the NBA, D. J. White graduated, and a couple of players who were kicked off the team by Dakich were not allowed to return.

Why would anybody want the job under those restrictive conditions? This was especially so for the man who eventually accepted it.

Tom Crean was coming off a quality nine-year stint as head coach at Marquette, where he notched five trips to the NCAAs, including Marquette's first Final Four appearance since Al McGuire's team won the championship in 1977.

Crean's answer to this pressing question was a simple one: Indiana had a basketball tradition that no other college sports team anywhere could match, and he very much wanted to be a part of it, regardless of a bare roster and very little in the way of recruiting enticement.

Just his willingness to launch himself head-first into a thankless, no-win situation was enough to gain initial respect and admiration from his players. And when the direst predictions played out in terms of few wins and many losses, Crean's ironclad belief in the program's future would keep those players in his corner.

But it was still a very tough go in those first three years.

Kory Barnett, who was recruited by Sampson, had wanted to wear the candy stripes all his life. But when everything seemed to come apart in his freshman year, he called his dad back home to say that he felt himself to be in an untenable situation and didn't think he could deal with it. His father replied that staying put "will make you a better man."

And in the end, it did, says Barnett, who currently serves as an assistant to Steve Alford at the University of Nevada.

Barnett says Crean's approach to keeping his players' morale afloat, and their eyes on the eventual prize, entailed moving on every day, from practice to practice and drill to drill, just as if the Hoosiers were perennial title contenders.

"Coach taught us how to shake off all the losing [Indiana went 6–25 in the first year, 10–21 in the second, and 12–20 in year three] by maximizing what we did in practice four hours a day," says Barnett.

Crean also reemphasized the importance of IU's venerable traditions, earning the approval of the fan base by bringing back "Martha the Mop Lady," who had been on hiatus.

The wins did come at last, with the arrival of higher-skilled players, the most notable among them being five-star recruit and McDonald's All-American Cody Zeller, an Indiana native. Other major talent upgrades included Will Sheehey and Victor Oladipo.

Crean's 2011–2012 squad went 27–9 with a trip to the Sweet Sixteen, and 29–7 with another Sweet Sixteen finish the following season.

Collin Hartman, who came to IU as a freshman in 2014 (and currently runs its NIL program), recalls Coach Crean as a grand master of all the details that go with an all-encompassing job that in Indiana is not only higher paying but much more prestigious than the governor's. Everything from organizing practices and running a highly complex system loaded with difficult schematics and options, to shaking a million hands and kissing a million babies.

Crean's last four years at IU saw two more NCAA appearances, including another Sweet Sixteen run. But after a bitterly disappointing 18–16 in 2016–2017, he was fired.

Hartman played his senior year for Crean's successor, Archie Miller, whose four-year stay at IU was much drearier. No postseason berths and an overall 67–58 record. Miller's best season (20–12) came in 2019–2020, the year COVID shut down the whole shebang just prior to the onset of March Madness.

"There was a disconnectivity among the players and coaches the year I was there," says Hartman. "There was no buy-in at all . . . but I thought Miller was a good coach, too. One thing about him was that he was a young former player himself, and he'd get in there with us in our individual and group [workouts]. In my playing career, I'd never seen a coach shoot a basketball before."

Miller was fired in March 2021 and went on to coach at Rhode Island.

The following season, the IU Hysterics finally got their wish. Mike Woodson, a star of the 1981 championship team, came back to town as head coach. A real, dyed-in-the-candy stripes "Knight guy" was now in charge, and things in Bloomington would turn back to the old normal— lots of winning and more conference and national championships.

Three years into the Woodson regime, the jury's still out on that one. Two short-lived trips to the NCAA and a 2023–2024 campaign that yielded no postseason bid, not to mention a lot of discontent among the masses.

A clamor for Woodson's head grew steadily during the 2023–2024 season, until a late run, highlighted by an upset win over Wisconsin at home, calmed the restive IU faithful.

Jordan Hulls, born and bred in Indiana and similarly proud to have worn the candy stripes under Tom Crean, is likewise back in town after a professional playing career in Europe. Now IU's team and recruiting coordinator, he is convinced that his boss has the program back on track, regardless of the mediocre results to date.

Perhaps IU lacks the luxury of a recent history of enormous success, but the pride and the passion are still very much in evidence, notes Hulls, and the "player development" function—which expands the nature of coaching beyond offensive and defensive schemes to leadership skills, "coachability" skills, and locker-room management—can be a critical recruiting tool in its own right.

"The pitch is that if you come here, we'll make you a better all-around player, and that's an easy concept to sell," says Hulls. "Meanwhile, Indiana is still *the* basketball state. All we need is a season where we can stay healthy and generate some momentum."

That kind of optimism, awash in sentiment, is no doubt shared by the spirits of James Naismith, Mop Lady Martha, and the hayseeds who planted that sign in the fertile soil of Crawfordsville all those years ago, proclaiming their turf as hallowed ground.

Kansas University

Pride, Passion, and Prejudice

NCAA titles (4)—1952, 1988, 2008, 2022
Final Fours (16)—1940, 1952, 1953, 1957, 1971, 1974, 1986, 1988, 1991, 1993, 2002, 2003, 2008, 2012, 2018, 2022
Elite Eights (23)—1952, 1953, 1957, 1960, 1966, 1971, 1974, 1986, 1988, 1991, 1993, 1996, 2002, 2003, 2004, 2007, 2008, 2011, 2012, 2016, 2017, 2018, 2022
NCAA tournament appearances—52* (2018 vacated)
Conference regular season titles—58
Conference tournament championships—16

The past is never dead. It's not even past.

—WILLIAM FAULKNER

ON MARCH 3, 1932, MEMBERS OF THE KANSAS UNIVERSITY BASKETBALL team, coming off another conference championship season that ended with a flourish of big wins over archrivals Kansas State and Missouri, were cleaning out their lockers and looking forward to the spring planting.

Meanwhile, not far away, on a family farm in Blue Springs, Missouri, unbeknownst to the team and its legendary coach, Phog Allen, a very old man named Frank Smith was taking his last breaths.

His death may not have meant much to these players, but to a few aging longtime residents of Lawrence, Kansas, with memories still aflame, the passing of Frank Smith was a final, bittersweet rite of passage: from a nightmarish world of mass destruction to one where the young student-athletes of KU would be safe to conduct their battles on a basketball court.

Frank Smith, as it happens, was the last surviving member of Quantrill's Raiders, a gang of bushwhackers allied with the Confederacy who terrorized much of Kansas during the Civil War. On August 21, 1863, they turned all their vengeful fury on pro-abolition Lawrence. Smith rode into town alongside William Quantrill, where they and their comrades murdered nearly two hundred boys and men, looted the banks and stores, and burned every fourth building to the ground. Only two businesses in town were left standing in the aftermath of the infamous "Lawrence Massacre."

Just about everything in this town, and on its major campus, is drenched in historical Americana, nearly all of it horrific, sorrowful, or both (monuments honoring the victims of the massacre, and KU memorials to the dead of two World Wars, Korea, and Vietnam). So much of Kansas history is bound up in turmoil and pain, all the messy compromises and contradictions of a democratic republic at war with itself for 237 years.

The poet Langston Hughes, who spent several of his childhood years living with his grandmother in a two-bedroom house at 732 Alabama Street in Lawrence, learned all about racial prejudice on its mean streets.

There was the movie theater with the "No Coloreds Admitted" sign, the Bowerstock Opera House that let him and friends inside but relegated them to "N—ga Heaven" in the rear, and the school track team that barred the future championship high-school relay runner from participation.

"Lawrence was where I discovered books [in which] people suffered in beautiful languages, not in monosyllables, as we did in Kansas," wrote Hughes in 1949.

But books were not his only salve.

Young Langston Hughes rooted for KU.

Millions of future hoops fans would follow his lead.

"So much of what goes on in Kansas is bad," noted the late writer Steve Singular, who was raised in Emporia, where his dad grew up playing with Dean Smith.

"The politics are bad, the landscape is boring . . . the older I get, the more Kansas basketball functions as the source of my pride in my home state."

Such feelings are hardly limited to the left end of the political spectrum. Rock-ribbed conservatives, who comprise the majority of Kansans, are similarly inclined to consider the sovereign state of Kansas and KU basketball to be one and the same.

Which brings us to the one campus monument that reflects that pride and joy, rather than cruel fate and melancholia. That would be the seventy-year-old Allen Fieldhouse, storehouse of 127 years of fond memories, and (according to *Guinness World Records*) the planet's loudest indoor sports venue and, by extension, the biggest home-court advantage.

Larry Brown, for one, ought to know, having coached basketball in just about every American nook and cranny. He lives the game in his bones.

"It's the best building ever. . . . I don't think anything compares to it," he said at Allen's sixtieth anniversary celebration in 2014. Brown's KU teams went 71–5 there over his five seasons.

Ted Owens, who coached at KU for nineteen years before Brown arrived, reflected on the building's early days, when it housed a dirt track that had to be swept and watered down for dust several times a day.

All good, according to Owens. "This is a special place."

But, aside from the cacophony, the cherished memories, and the won-lost record, what makes Allen Fieldhouse and KU basketball so special?

Ask former players, coaches, boosters, and fans, and they'll tell you essentially the same thing: it's "continuity" that distinguishes Kansas basketball from every other major D1 basketball program. Only eight men (including an interim coach) have helmed a Kansas team, and despite significant differences in their personal styles and coaching philosophies, they have shared one common characteristic: they knew what they were doing.

"That's what is most remarkable about the program," says Tad Boyle, the current head coach at the University of Colorado who played four years under Ted Owens and Larry Brown. "In 127 years, the university has *never* had a bad hire."

That is no doubt a product of the program's lineage, which traces all the way back to coach James Naismith, the inventor of basketball, who passed the job on to his number one protégé, Phog Allen. Allen proceeded to pass his teachings along to his former player and assistant, Dean Smith, a Kansas native who elected to leave Lawrence for Chapel Hill, North Carolina. So, another Allen assistant, Dick Harp, took the Kansas coaching reins from Phog and eight years later gave way to one of his assistants, Ted Owens. Owens, ninety-four years young as of this writing, is an Oklahoman but with a spirit that's at least half Jayhawk.

Owens was followed by Larry Brown, a basketball savant from Long Island who was mentored by none other than Dean Smith at Carolina. Brown, after a typically short sojourn in Lawrence, stepped aside to make way for Roy Williams, yet another Carolinian and acolyte of Dean Smith. After Roy went back to Carolina in 2003 to assume his ultimate dream job, Bill Self, who came up as an assistant under Larry Brown in the 1980s, was named head coach. Self's autobiography is titled *At Home in the Phog*, which pretty well sums it up.

Indeed, it's a title that any Kansas coach, past, present, or future (aside from Naismith and Phog himself), could slap on his autobiography.

As stated so succinctly by Tad Boyle, among the relative handful of men who have carried the standard of KU basketball across six generations, there is nary a bum in the bunch.

One other salient point in the evolution of the KU basketball program is how it is interlaced through the years with the history of its Carolina counterpart. A T-shirt that Kansas rooters wore years ago pointed to this powerful connection:

The front of the shirt read "KANSAS." The back read "BIRTH-PLACE OF CAROLINA BASKETBALL."

To us, it seems more like they birthed each other.

Whither the Soul of Basketball?

One of the seeming oddities of KU basketball is the fact that the program's first coach, the man who invented the game and brought it to Lawrence—and presumably understood all its fine points and idiosyncrasies better than any other living human being—was also the only coach in KU history to sport a losing record. James Naismith's teams went 55–60 in his nine years as coach.

And it wasn't as though they faced big-time competition during that period. Naismith's boys played mostly against nearby YMCA teams, a tribal land-grant college, and other small schools. The only major Big Eight school on the schedule during the Naismith years was Kansas State, and KU played them only once.

But, upon even cursory examination, nothing at all is odd about the tally of wins and losses, because Naismith did not consider winning to be an essential goal of the game. Although he didn't have anything against it, per se, the won-loss thing was extremely far down on his priority list. Likewise, Naismith had no regard whatsoever for the act of coaching itself. He believed that all that was needed to play a rigorous, healthy game of basketball were ten willing and able young men and a referee.

When his ultimate successor, Phog Allen, advised Naismith in 1904 that he was leaving to coach at Baker University, his mentor corrected him.

"You can't coach basketball, you just play it," he said.

A coach who doesn't believe in coaching is not likely to leave behind a legacy that fits on a championship banner or trophy.

Naismith, from the start, had a different type of legacy in mind. Back at the YMCA in Springfield, Massachusetts, in the late 1800s, the goal was encouraging young "ruffians" to embrace Protestant values—cooperation, nonviolence, concentration, creativity.

The popular sports back then—bare-knuckle boxing, football, hockey—did nothing to inculcate these values in the boys at the Y. Thus, Naismith came up with a new game—one based very loosely on a childhood pursuit from back in Canada called "duck on a rock."

This boldly innovative new game eliminated running and tackling, replacing them with passing the ball. Agility, speed, and accuracy were elevated over remorseless bodily contact. It was a monumental change in the American sports landscape, away from individual exploits on the field toward cooperative, interdependent action, based on building trust among teammates. This groundbreaking new game also did away with the violence and roughhousing that made those other sports "tools of the devil." At the same time, basketball promoted physical fitness, which made it a perfect representation of a relatively new philosophy known as "muscular Christianity."

Novelist and die-hard KU basketball fan Andrew Milward, in his memoir, *Jayhawker*, notes that Protestant leaders in the mid-nineteenth century were concerned that their religion was becoming feminized. Muscular Christianity put testosterone-charged oomph back in the faith, combining those fundamental religious values with the image of the body as a temple.

Anyway, this is how the inventor viewed his invention: as an enjoyable, salubrious, character-building endeavor that rightfully belonged to the players themselves. Naismith was put off by watching coaches "mechanize" their players through repeated drilling to run specific plays. Players should be allowed "to think for themselves," he said, and determine the outcome of their own games.

Nevertheless, Naismith's top pupil, Forrest "Phog" Allen, to whom he would turn over the coaching reins in 1907, did not share his views. And the hearts-and-minds battle that the two men engaged in over the spirit and purpose of the game would determine its path over the coming decades.

To whom does the game truly belong?

Phog Allen believed it belonged to the coach, in his role as a "benevolent dictator," setting the terms of what constitutes success on the court. That would, of course, be measured mainly in wins and losses. Allen, from the very beginning, preached the gospel of "playing to win." Naismith thought of winning as an idea that might inspire a young man to play the game more meaningfully but never as a primary goal, or worse, as an end in itself.

According to Andrew Milward, the two men maintained a respectful working relationship when Naismith ran KU's physical education department, and Allen ran the basketball program, but they were never friends. That would have been quite difficult, says Milward, given their "Obi-Wan versus Darth Vader" duel for the soul of basketball.

It is not necessary here to proclaim the victor, as that would be obvious to anyone who has watched a high-school, college, or pro basketball game in the past sixty years. But even if Allen's view had not prevailed at KU, some other enthusiastic young coach would certainly have come along in his wake, picked up his light saber, and marched the game forward into the commercial world of TV networks, social media, NILs, and portals.

With all due respect to the esteemed founder of basketball, from the very outset he was fighting a historical inevitability.

And that's a fight no one can win.

INTO THE PHOG

There must be many stories about Phog Allen (whose nickname derives from the foghorn sound of his voice): stories about his coaching exploits, his amazing osteopathic skills, and his good deeds. Funny stories about his little quirks and whimsical utterances (i.e., his grandkids called him "Phoggy," and when he learned that Wilt Chamberlain was coming to KU, his immediate reaction was "that's great. I hope he comes out for basketball").

Nevertheless, the stories we heard, from old coaches and players, were not about Phog himself but the awe-inspiring, communal experience of encountering Phog, attending his funeral in 1974, or meeting people who had met Phog. And these stories, which generally feature a nonsectarian form of genuflection, tell more about Phog himself than any actual Phog story.

They tell you that this was an almost mythical figure on the KU campus, who was more than respected, more than admired, more, even, than idolized. Lots of coaches fit those descriptions, quite a few of them spotlighted in this book.

Phog Allen, by contrast, was and is a *beloved* figure.

Which puts this benevolent despot (accent on benevolent) in very, very exclusive company within the upper echelon of the college coaching

Phog Allen throws up a rather awkward shot to herald the opening of Allen Field-house in 1955. But give the man a break; he was seventy years old and a bit out of practice. Courtesy of Kenneth Spencer Research Library, University of Kansas

fraternity. It puts him in a select group with Dean Smith, and . . . well, to be quite honest, only Dean Smith.

One doesn't get to that exalted status by simply winning 590 games and three national titles (two prior to the advent of the NCAA tournament), although all of that certainly helps. One gets there by being the first basketball coach to actually "coach" the game and to have positively role-modeled the profession for every coach who came later. In other words, every coach in college basketball history.

Forrest "Phog" Allen was, by no means, larger than the game itself. But he sure embodied the hell out of it.

Phog's early life was no barrel of laughs. The fourth of six sons of William Allen, a produce wholesaler, he grew up traveling town to town in Missouri, as his dad found it hard to support the family. According to his grandchildren, Phog was able to contribute to the finances, earning a few bucks in the prizefighting ring and working for a time as an "axman" on the Kansas City Southern Railroad, pounding stakes on the tracks. He also played ball for the Kansas City Athletic Club, captaining that team. This is where Naismith took note of the young man, encouraging him to come to KU and become a part of basketball history in the making. Allen entered college in 1905 without having graduated high school, which was likely easier back then than it would be today.

After two years of playing ball under Naismith, Phog assumed the head coaching job at KU in 1907. He held the job for a couple of years before taking up Naismith's suggestion that he attend medical school. After getting his degree in osteopathic medicine (again, without graduating high school), Allen picked up his coaching career at several small Midwestern schools.

In 1919, he came back to KU, where he would spend the next thirty-seven years of his working life. His teams won "Helms Athletic Foundation" championships in 1922 and 1923 and the NCAA tournament title in 1952, led by a future NBA star, Clyde Lovellette. Making a much lesser contribution to that team's ultimate success was a bench-warming math major named Dean Smith (as in the beloved Dean Smith). Allen also coached Kansas's Final Four teams in 1940 and 1953.

The already legendary coach anticipated that his career would be capped off by yet another championship or two once Wilt Chamberlain had come onboard in the fall of 1955. Phog had actively recruited the big man, beating out an estimated two hundred schools that were offering Wilt the moon and the stars.

Coach Allen took a different tack, first turning his considerable charms on Wilt's mom and then bringing in heavy artillery to sell Mrs. Chamberlain and her son on Kansas being a place where he could get an education as well as a championship trophy. Allen's key reinforcements most notably included KU chemistry professor Calvin Vanderwerf, who called on mom when he was passing through Philly. Olivia Chamberlain noted at the time that lots of other colleges had spoken to her about "Wilton" but added that Vanderwerf was the first "professor" she had encountered.

"I'm so happy," she gushed, "to have someone talk about the academic side."

Nevertheless, there might have been a bit more to it than that, as Wilt later claimed that KU alumni had slipped him about $15,000 or $20,000 in cash. Still, that was reportedly a good deal less than what other schools were offering.

Anyway, once Wilton was enrolled at KU, Phog began working with him regularly on his basketball skills. According to an article in *Time* magazine, that training extended to having the freshman read Helen Keller's autobiography to give him a greater awareness of the importance of touch and feel: the goal there was to improve Chamberlain's classic finger roll and his ability to use it to spin the ball from all angles when he found himself in heavy traffic under the offensive basket.

The coach celebrated his seventieth birthday that November, gleefully watching Wilt's freshmen team obliterate the varsity and imagining more such obliterations to come.

"We could win the national championship with Wilt, two sorority girls, and two Phi Beta Kappas," Allen famously quipped.

But Coach Allen's final, glorious hoop dream did not materialize. The KU powers that be, for whatever reasons, refused Allen's request to waive the rule mandating retirement for state employees at seventy. Allen would never get to coach Wilt Chamberlain or anyone else.

Sources have suggested a couple of possible reasons for their decision: fear that sports were becoming more important at KU than academics (can you imagine that happening now at any major D1 program?) and maybe just a tinge of envy, as not even the beloved Phog Allen was beloved by everyone.

In any case, the Allen era came to an abrupt end, and a seven-foot-one, 275-pound wunderkind was heralded as the irresistible force who would bring KU into the next one, replete with championships and Big Eight conference bragging rights.

But not so fast.

An immovable object was still in the way. One that is nearly as old as time itself and as virulent as those repulsive Kansas bushwhackers of a century ago.

Big Man on Campus

Why, man, he doth bestride the narrow world like a Colossus.

—William Shakespeare, *Julius Caesar*

Another seeming oddity in the history of Kansas basketball is that the place that served as a beacon of antislavery sentiment in the mid-nineteenth century was, a full hundred years later, about as segregated as Philadelphia, Mississippi.

Carmaletta Williams, executive director of the Black Archives of Mid-America, explained how that can happen in a 2020 essay titled "Free Did Not Mean Welcome for My Family."

All those big ideas of freedom, wrote Williams, mean next to nothing when the same people preaching the promise of freedom don't hold that notion in their hearts. The people of Lawrence might have been repelled by the horror of human slavery one hundred years ago, suggested Williams, but in 1956 they sure didn't want black people shopping in their stores or eating in their diners.

Wilt Chamberlain, although he hailed from a different Philadelphia—the one in Pennsylvania—must have had some familiarity with racial bias, having grown up in the late 1940s and witnessed the ugly treatment of the rookie Jackie Robinson in the City of Brotherly Love (not being able to stay with his team at a whites-only hotel and having to endure silently the vile epithets slung at him from the opposing dugout by the odious Phillies manager, Ben Chapman).

Nevertheless, Wilt surely did not expect to find this level of segregation in Lawrence. He may have gotten a little heads-up from Maurice King, the second African American basketball player in KU history and its first black starter. King had arrived in Lawrence a couple of years before Wilt and was already well-versed in the downside of PWB—playing college basketball while black.

King reported receiving repeated taunts and threats both at home and on the road, although the antebellum road version was worse. In Dallas, where KU went to play Southern Methodist University, the rules in place at the time prohibited the young man from being housed with the rest of his team at the Hilton. King had to stay in a student dorm with the SMU players. At plenty of places in and around Lawrence—movie theaters, in particular—King got the same hostile treatment accorded Langston Hughes a generation earlier.

Wilt Chamberlain's impact on Kansas went well beyond the court. Here he co-hosts a Christmas party for thirty orphans at the Leavenworth Guardian Angel Home with KU football halfback John Traylor. Courtesy of Kenneth Spencer Research Library, University of Kansas

In this regard, King was perhaps less fortunate than Wilt in that he was not a nationally celebrated phenomenon, just another N-word, so when the fans unfurled a sign reading "N—gers Go Home," they were likely referring more directly to him.

King handled all this in a quiet, "dignified" manner, noted Max Falkenstein, the Jayhawks' radio broadcaster.

Wilt, on the other hand, was more vocal in confronting the racial animus he found in Lawrence.

According to Carmaletta Williams, one of his first stops upon his arrival in town was at the KU chancellor's office, where he demanded that the school do something about the situation. And the chancellor reportedly responded affirmatively, getting the word out to the business community that Wilt Chamberlain was a very important addition to the team and the town, basketball-wise and business-wise, and that all the townspeople would be wise to treat him in a manner befitting the BMOC.

Phog Allen, although not an outspoken opponent of segregation up to that point, did step up in support of the big man and urged the Lawrence community to lighten up on the overt racism.

Wilt, for his part, took a multipronged strategy to the desegregation of Lawrence. He tried some of that Quaker-like friendly persuasion, which worked in the case of the Dine-O-Mite diner, an establishment that drew the color line. Chamberlain befriended its owners and reportedly got them to be more inclusive in their choice of customers.

In other instances, Wilt took a more aggressive posture, sauntering into a segregated diner, planting himself at the lunch counter, stretching out his massive seven-foot-one frame, and daring anyone to escort him off the premises.

This approach was generally deemed to be an even more effective deterrent to segregation.

Nevertheless, Wilt was also widely known for his propensity toward exaggeration, so it should come as no surprise that he claimed to have desegregated Lawrence "single-handedly."

This was, by no means, among Wilt's more flamboyantly improbable boasts. We refer specifically to his later claim to having bedded approximately twenty thousand different women in various configurations over the course of his life.

This statement was decried by legions of feminists and was eyed skeptically by others capable of doing the math (so exactly when did the man find the time to eat three meals a day and play professional basketball?).

Wilt did ultimately apologize to females, noting that the twenty thousand was just a figure of speech meant to connote the importance of sex in his life.

When it came to basketball, at least in his younger years, Wilt was more inclined to temper the bravado. And when it did go untempered,

Wilt didn't need to walk back the rhetoric, as he had the game to back it up.

Chamberlain was deeply disappointed in not being able to play for Phog Allen. Although he liked the coach who had taken his place, Dick Harp, describing him in his autobiography as a "decent, moral man," he had limited respect for Harp's coaching prowess.

"I sure as hell don't think he was much of a basketball coach," wrote Wilt.

Jerry Waugh, Harp's assistant, insisted that Harp was a pretty good basketball coach and a "technically" sound one but lacking in communication skills.

"At times he was a little uptight with the kids. He put a lot of pressure on himself," Waugh noted.

As for Wilt's teammates, they reportedly got along well with their new star player and accepted him without jealously, understanding that he was their meal ticket, and everything on the court would, and should, be funneled through the big guy.

Dick Harp had even bigger things than basketball on his mind.

He told a reporter that his true aim was to foster closer relations between the white players and their two black teammates, Wilt and Maurice King. He wanted to instill in his white players a desire "to walk that extra mile" in support of their black counterparts, and he hoped that sports would become a powerful force for integration in the United States.

Sadly, according to Harp, only Maurice King bought into his plan. Wilt, on the other hand, was described by his coach as a sensitive "loner" who chose to do his socializing off campus and away from the team.

Based on his experience coaching at KU, Harp concluded that the whole concept of sports as an engine of integration was "a myth," perpetrated by those who should know better.

And from an integration standpoint, he added candidly, "Wilt was my most conspicuous failure."

That was off the basketball court. On the court, Wilt was a conspicuously smashing success.

In his first-ever varsity game, Wilt scored fifty-two points and hauled in thirty-one rebounds against Northwestern. Both stats remain school records.

He continued in that vein throughout the 1956–1957 season, which featured only two losses—a buzzer-beater by Iowa State and another two-point loss to Oklahoma State.

Jerry Waugh says opposing teams tried just about every manner of constant physical and verbal harassment to foul Wilt out of games or get into his head. But Wilt was having none of it. He kept his cool and his temper firmly in check throughout the season.

In the 1957 NCAA's, KU breezed by Oklahoma City and San Francisco to get to the Finals showdown with North Carolina.

Prior to tipoff, UNC coach Frank McGuire spelled it out for his team in the simplest of terms. This was a game of 5-on-1. If you don't let Wilt beat you, you'll beat KU.

That simple.

And McGuire's strategy worked. Although Wilt, as noted in the introduction, played great that night, his teammates couldn't find the basket, let alone put the ball in it.

Tommy Kearns, UNC's talented point guard out of the Bronx, New York, said Harp also made a crucial mistake on defense in not being more aggressive in guarding UNC's outside sharpshooters.

The triple-overtime, 54–53 loss to Carolina was Wilt's most heartbreaking defeat, and worse, according to the big man, it started the whole "Wilt's a loser" narrative, which was not only false but demeaning to a kind, thoughtful man who deserved considerably more respect.

Kansas finished seventh in the nation the following season but only second in the Big Eight. Wilt departed KU after his junior year, and after a year-long fling with the Harlem Globetrotters, he entered the NBA, rewrote the record book, and remade the league. His list of astounding NBA personal achievements includes a hundred-point game and an entire season averaging more than fifty points and twenty-five rebounds per game.

And, while he was at it, notwithstanding the braggadocio, the man had a lot of wild sex on the side.

Dick Harp, meanwhile, coached at KU for another six years—only two of them winning seasons—before quitting in 1964. Several observers say that Harp's commitment to integration played more of a role in his decision than did his mediocre won-lost record.

His 1960–1961 team, for example, featured seven black players, of whom four were starters. This was years before Texas Western started five blacks in the 1966 championship game, helping to integrate college basketball in the South.

Harp reportedly took a lot of heat from boosters and fans who thought he was blatantly overdoing the integration thing. *Sports Illustrated* reported years later that Harp was especially incensed by all the alumni who confronted him directly about playing so many "[n—gers]." He also didn't like the earful he got from the KU cheering section at home games.

"All the insults from the fans and digs from alumni wore him down," wrote Jack Olsen of SI. "He could feel the pressure for a quota system and didn't want to be a part of it."

This is a coaching legacy of which anyone can be proud.

A FINE HANG-UP

Before we discuss the KU career of Ted Owens, who replaced Dick Harp as head coach in 1964, a couple of quick items by way of introduction:

- During our conversation with Coach Owens—ninety-four years of age and possessed of the memory and the golf swing of a sixty-year-old—he suggested that a team that had once gotten the better of his guys had the distinct advantage of less than rigorous adherence to academic standards. About a half hour after the interview had concluded, Owens called us back to request that we not use that team's name, as his offhand comment was unsporting and ungracious. We acceded to the request, as Ted Owens is someone to whom one likes to say yes.

- Coach Owens, some sixty-one long years after beginning his career at KU and forty-two years after coaching his final game there, conducts annual Zoom reunions with his former players.

These virtual get-togethers draw eighty or more Owens loyalists from across the country and overseas, and that doesn't include the many others who don't log in online but keep in regular telephone contact with their favorite coach. "If you've met the man, you know why," says Dale Greenlee, a member of the 1974 Final Four team, arguably Owens's best.

Well, then, ladies and gentlemen, let's meet Ted Owens.

Growing up on a cotton farm in southwest Oklahoma during the Great Depression, Owens began formulating a sound strategy for coaching and living, which was based on something known as the daily "hang-up."

"At the end of the day," Owens explains, "we would figure the total weight of the cotton we had pulled. We called it the hang-up."

One day, in a competition with his dad to see who could pull the most cotton, Owens was well in the lead and probably razzing his father about it when his old man laid a life lesson on him.

"It's not what you have now," his father said. "It's what you have at the hang-up."

Owens says he got similar advice from Phog Allen when he asked the former coach to name his greatest players.

"Coach Allen says to me, 'I don't know. Let's wait twenty-five years and see what they all did with their lives.'"

In other words, wait for the hang-up.

Owens, like Dick Harp, is one of those Kansas coaches who tend to be overlooked among all the legends.

Owens is more than OK with that, taking a measure of pride in being the college game's Forrest Gump, coaching against and meeting a panoply of all-time greats—Adolph Rupp, Henry Iba, Nat Holman, Dean Smith, Bobby Knight, and Joe Lapchick, to name a few. It seems they each passed along to Owens some nugget of coaching wisdom or encouragement that Owens has carried with him to this day.

"During my rookie year, Joe Lapchick comes over in the final seconds of a game and sits next to me on the bench. We had just upset St. John's at Alumni Hall," recalls Owens, as if this event occurred yesterday.

"'Congratulations, you did a good job,' he says to me. Such a classy thing for an old coach to [give a thumbs-up] to a young coach after he's just beaten him."

Jeff Guiot, who played for both Ted Owens and Larry Brown, says that to Coach Owens, there was no such thing as a stranger.

"He was always smiling [he was known as 'Smiling Ted'], and the way he had in connecting with other people made him an excellent recruiter."

Tad Boyle says he remains forever loyal to Owens but feels a bit guilty about one aspect of his recruitment.

"I was a big guard, and Ted liked big guards. As I recall, we were playing a lot of 2–3 zone, very physical, very patient. There was no shot clock, no three-point shot, in his last two years at KU."

Boyle notes that in his emphasis on size over speed and quickness, Owens was a bit behind the times, and it showed up in a losing record over those two seasons, which led to the coach becoming the first and only coach in KU history to be fired.

"I always felt bad about that," notes Boyle, "because I think he got fired for recruiting players like me."

"Coach Owens taught us basketball plays," sums up Jeff Guiot. "Larry Brown taught us how to play basketball."

Coach Owens, for his part, fully concurs with Guiot's assessment.

"Basketball has changed so much since I was coaching," he says. "Looking back, from a coaching perspective, if I'd had it to do over, I'd have tried to do things differently, focus less on plays than on running plays out of plays."

Overall, Owens's teams over those nineteen years put up some pretty fair numbers—348 wins, a .657 winning percentage, Final Four appearances in 1971 and 1974, seven trips to the NCAAs, and a half dozen Big Eight regular season titles. Owens was a four-time winner of Big Eight Coach of the Year honors and *Basketball Weekly*'s 1978 National Coach of the Year award.

Not too shabby for a guy with a two-handed set shot.

Dale Greenlee recalls his coach as the epitome of calmness and rationality on the bench, which was especially needed in light of the "dogfights" that characterized every conference game.

"Allen was rocking all the time because you needed to win every game to win the conference championship," explains Greenlee.

For example, after KU clinched the '74 championship with a win over Kansas State, students stormed the court and carried away the players. Later, seven thousand crazed fans celebrated on the Hill at midnight, where newly minted KU graduates take their first steps toward the future.

"Nobody wanted to sleep," says Greenlee, who credits Owens and his staff for fostering a "tight, family feeling" among the players, inviting them into their homes and encouraging all that critical male bonding.

But Owens's nineteen-year run was anything but smooth. There were too many ups and downs, a few too many 11–15, 8–18, and 13–13 seasons mixed in with the 20-plus win years. The coach never had the kind of support from his bosses that his predecessors had been given.

"One Jayhawker has observed that Owens may be the only coach in America who has never had next year to count on," noted sportswriter Jim Lassiter.

"Every December through March you can hear rumblings from the Sunflower State that Owens is history. His teams have either not won enough games or not been exciting enough."

In 1983, Monte Johnson came aboard as the new AD and, according to press reports, he was not an especially big fan of Ted Owens. The last two losing seasons (13–14 and 13–16, respectively) were the proverbial straws on the camel.

Owens acknowledged taking the firing very hard in his 2013 autobiography, *At the Hang-Up*.

"I was absolutely devastated. I had hoped [the chancellor] would block the move, but he had been at the university only the last two years, when our teams weren't as strong as previous years."

Nevertheless, Owens's initial bitterness passed with time, and the age-old smile returned, as did his devotion to KU and its basketball program.

"I did something some say a coach should never do," confesses Owens. "They'll say a coach shouldn't fall in love with the fans and players. But I did."

At ninety-four and living quietly back in Oklahoma, Ted Owens is not quite ready for his own personal hang-up. And that is enough to generate a whole lot of smiles in Kansas.

ONE FLEW OVER THE FIELDHOUSE

All my life I've been like this
You can love me at your own risk
When the dust hits my shoes
I got the urge to move
'Cause I'm a road runner, baby . . .

—JUNIOR WALKER, "ROADRUNNER"

After the many hundreds of thousands, if not millions, of words expended in spelunking through the cavities of Larry Brown's psyche, two aspects of his personality can be stated as incontrovertible facts:

For one, Larry Brown was a true basketball savant whose profound understanding of, and passion for, the game of basketball was baked into his DNA. Like Mozart, if players were musical notes. Those who know Brown say it has always been awfully hard to get him to talk about anything other than basketball, especially when he gets going.

"The guy is amazing," says Tad Boyle. "He could watch a scrimmage with ten guys running three times up and down the court; and after the whistle blew, he could tell you everything each of those players had done on each trip."

There are all kinds of stories of Brown leaving a practice, coming back two hours later and telling every player where he was positioned on the court when he left the building.

However, his otherworldly memory was only half of it. Brown had the innate ability to make those memories pay off. Another commonly told Brown story features the coach on the sideline diagramming a play that he once saw being run on some high-school playground in a faraway place twenty-five or thirty years ago.

And those ancient but never-forgotten plays tended to work.

This was yet another inborn talent that made Larry Brown one of the game's finest teachers.

"His life revolved around basketball; he was consumed by it in a way that nobody else [could match], and he was super-organized all the time," raves Jeff Guiot.

His profound understanding of the game and his fondness for young people made him an especially effective college coach. Indeed, Brown was oft quoted as saying that it was so much more fun teaching college kids than spoiled NBA professionals.

"I learned how to play the game from him," adds Guiot. "For example, he taught you how to react to what a defense was doing. You had some freedom [to freelance out of the play] as long as you were operating within certain principles of the game."

The problem was getting Brown to stick around long enough to apply those lessons to more than a relative handful of young men. They didn't call him "out-of-town Brown" for nothing.

Which brings us to the second irrefutable fact in the basketball odyssey of Larry Brown, which can perhaps best be illustrated in the lexicon of the early-twentieth-century Wild West fiction writer:

Larry Brown was "fiddle-footed."

He made his gun-slinging reputation by riding into town and cleaning up a mess (often leaving another mess behind). And he never stayed in one place very long, which meant that if you loved Larry Brown—as did many people on his basketball voyage—you were doing so very much at your own risk.

Kansas University was the sixth stop on Brown's career-long thrill ride through the vast landscape of modern American basketball. It would eventually take him to some sixteen coaching jobs, fifteen in the United States and one in Italy. His longest stay was six years with the

Philadelphia 76ers and Allen Iverson, which in itself generated a career's worth of good stories.

Brown, by all accounts, felt at home, and at peace, in Lawrence, and among the populace and some sportswriters, a feeling was that this might just be the place where the fiddle-footed coach would finally settle down contentedly.

As it happens, he lasted only five years in Kansas, which, for him, was a fairly long sojourn but not long enough for the Kansas basketball community to embrace him as they wished.

Students at KU sensed early on that this guy was a radical departure from the five head coaches who preceded him.

"You'd see Larry occasionally in student bars on the Hill, like the Hawk and The Wheel, just kicking back with the kids," says a KU alum. "It was weird. The notion of a Dick Harp or a Ted Owens hanging out at The Wheel was inconceivable. This was a very different kind of guy."

Another thing that made Brown stand out in Kansas was the awesome cadre of coaches he mentored during those five years. Brown's Kansas coaching tree included John Calipari, Mark Turgeon, R. C. Buford, Alvin Gentry, Bill Self, Gregg Popovich (a volunteer assistant), Bill Bayno, and Bob Hill, among others. A truly extraordinary array of coaching talent, and a very tight group.

His assistants reportedly had a ball following in the path of their Pied Piper. Brown and his merry band of coaches enjoyed running together, staff meetings over drinks (ten-cent beer nights) at The Wheel, breaking down plays, and talking nonstop basketball.

Scooter Barry, one of Brown's players, told the *New York Times* that all these assistants eventually learned to "adapt and adjust" to wanting to be just like Larry, going on to forge their own identities and substantial basketball careers.

Larry Brown is said to have taken a particular liking to Mark Turgeon.

"I believe at that time, coach had only daughters, so Mark was like the son he never had," says Jeff Guiot. "And the two were very close. Larry wore number 11 at NC, so Mark wore 11 at KU. I remember them sitting together on [the team bus], talking or playing cards. It was a special relationship."

If Brown had one weakness, it was recruiting, an activity that he detested. But he managed to find his way around that problem, landing his greatest player, Danny Manning, by simply hiring his dad, Ed, as an assistant.

A pretty slick recruiting move.

As usual, Brown got Kansas back on the winning track virtually overnight. They went 22–10 in his first year with a trip to the NCAA second round; and 26–8 in year two, with a final national ranking of seven and another second-round exit in the NCAA.

The 1985–1986 team led by Manning, Greg Dreiling, Cedric Hunter, Ron Kellogg, and Calvin Thompson went 35–4 (number two ranking) and got all the way to the Final Four, losing to number one Duke in the semi.

After a Sweet Sixteen finish in year four, KU put it all together after a disappointing eleven-loss season and a ho-hum third place in the conference. "Danny and the Miracles," as that team is known, won the title on the wings of Manning's thirty-one-point, eighteen-rebound performance against Oklahoma in the final.

That would be Larry Brown's swan song—a perfect ending to a short but noteworthy coaching gig.

Nevertheless, this happy time came with an unhappy coda, as Brown was accused of violating NCAA regulations by giving a player an airline ticket to visit the gravely ill grandmother who had raised him.

It seems absurd now to punish a coach and his team for that kind of basic humanitarian gesture. Brown has said that he would not hesitate again to give a player money to visit a dying family member.

Anyway, Larry and his staff left en masse for the NBA's San Antonio Spurs, and the Jayhawks got slapped with a three-year probation and a one-year ban on postseason play.

As to why Larry Brown left Kansas—given his fondness for the place and his coaching success there—there are multiple hypotheses.

Perhaps he felt that he had already accomplished his mission. Or maybe it was the looming probation, or his deep-seated insecurities

This image of Brown celebrating the sheer joy of coaching, ran in the newspaper alongside the announcement of his resignation from UCLA. *The Cincinnati Enquirer*, Public domain, via Wikimedia Commons

causing him to fear getting fired. Or it could just have been his fiddle-footed feet going to sleep again.

All of these are reasonable guesses.

And then, there was this bit of conjecture from a KU alum.

"Well, you know," he says, "Larry being Jewish and all, it might have been the money."

We feel obliged here to point out that one need not be Jewish to be lured away by a job offering a ninefold increase in salary.

As of this writing, Larry Brown is finally retired, reportedly for health reasons. Going forward, it wouldn't be at all shocking to hear that this mercurial coach had come back to the sport to which he has given his life and soul.

As for the rest of us roundball fans, his return to the sidelines would always be welcome as something is amiss in a basketball universe that doesn't have Larry Brown in it.

DAGGUM ROY

To replace the iconoclastic New Yorker, Kansas went back to the basics, hiring a down-home North Carolinian right out of the Phog Allen-Dean Smith coaching tree.

Today, after Roy Williams has retired as a Hall of Fame coach with three national titles, it seems strange to say that Kansas was taking a significant risk in hiring him.

But it was.

"You're talking about hiring a second-assistant coach from North Carolina without any head coaching experience," explains Greg Gurley, who played under Williams from 1991 to 1995, going to a Final Four and a pair of Sweet Sixteens.

"Kansas had a number of [heavy hitters] under consideration for the job, like Gary Williams [who later won a title at Maryland] and Charlie Spoonhour [who had made a name for himself at Southwest Missouri State]. This was a very big choice for Kansas, and it was by no means an easy one."

Indeed, if that decision were to be made today, it is highly unlikely that Roy would have gotten the job. Blue-blood programs these days shy away from hiring assistant coaches in a traditional hiring cycle.

Nobody knows this better than Roy himself.

"I thought it was a tremendous gamble [for Kansas]," Roy told ESPN on the eve of his induction into the Naismith Hall of Fame in 2007.

"I jokingly said I was choice number ninety-three. I know I wasn't one, two, three, four, five, six, or seven . . . thinking about it, nobody would do anything like that."

Williams believes that Kansas AD Bob Frederick was prepared to go out on a limb based on his respect for Dean Smith, for whom Williams served as an assistant for ten years; and for Dick Harp, the Kansas head coach of yore who was then also an assistant under Smith at UNC.

Frederick gave some other reasons, which included being impressed by Williams's organizational skills and his respect for Kansas basketball traditions, as well as the training he got from Dean Smith on how to fill the role of head coach. Frederick saw in Williams the kind of guy who would stick around for more than a few years, which was important to the program after its experience with the peripatetic Larry Brown.

And, finally, noted Frederick, Roy Williams had another key attribute that would not be expected to emerge in a job interview, that being the man's inner drive to be successful.

In Williams's early days at Kansas, that drive manifested itself most dramatically on the recruiting front. In his first few years, he hauled in a big crop of major talents, including Adonis Jordan (in year one), Rex Walters, Greg Ostertag, Jacque Vaughan, and Scot Pollard.

According to Greg Gurley, Williams had no problem traversing the country in search of quality athletes and had success recruiting out of California and Washington State.

To the court, notes Gurley, Williams brought his mentor's "system," which incorporated Dean Smith's renowned "secondary break" (how a team moves into a half-court offense after its fast break has been stymied); the employment of multiple screens against zone defenses; and plenty of analytics (Smith had pioneered the concept of "possession-based analytics," a natural application of his undergraduate mathematics studies).

Williams also organized his practices in the highly structured manner that Dean Smith had taught him—the idea being that with maximum efficiency one can bring to bear more drills, more sprints, and more scrimmaging in two hours than a less organized coach can manage in four.

Williams's fifteen years at KU witnessed an extraordinarily consistent record of success—fourteen consecutive NCAA appearances (KU was barred from the tourney in his first year); four Final Fours, two of them as NCAA runners-up; and one Elite Eight finish. Williams's winning percentage was a remarkable .805.

However, the record is missing one very significant accomplishment, and we all know what that is: zero national titles.

Heaven knows, the man came close. Oh, so achingly close.

We refer to Roy's final game as KU head coach: the 2003 championship game against Syracuse, which was coached by another future Hall of Famer, Jim Boeheim. The Orange coach at the time was under similar pressure from an even more frustrated fan base, having yet to cop his first title.

The game came down to a final shot by Kansas's Mike Lee, left alone on the wing for an open three-pointer with but a couple of seconds on the clock and KU down 81–78. Hakim Warrick, doing his very best impersonation of a condor in full flight, arose from out of nowhere to bat away the shot and forever cement his name in Syracuse basketball history.

In Syracuse, they still call this game "The Block."

In Lawrence, we imagine they have less congenial names for it.

In any case, after that season, the job that Roy Williams had always longed for—head coach of the North Carolina Tar Heels—opened up, and Roy moved on (more on this in the UNC chapter).

Loyalty was a prized virtue to Williams, as it is to so many coaches. Indeed, he did have a previous opportunity to return to Chapel Hill in 2000, after Bill Guthridge retired. But Williams elected to stay on after a large-scale outpouring of love from the KU community—emails begging him not to go, signs, flowers, and so forth. That decision dismayed the Carolina folks as much as it delighted the Jayhawkers.

But by 2003, the ties that bound Roy Williams to KU had weakened considerably with the departure of Bob Frederick and the coming of a new AD with whom Williams had no history or sentimental attachment, making this decision to leave a relatively easy one.

As for the KU fan base, most understood the pull of the Carolina job. Others viewed it as treachery, which may have been dumb, but it was still their feeling.

"Traitor!," a KU fan shouted at Williams at a banquet after his announcement.

More than two decades later, there's still a lingering feeling of ill will among those fans not yet willing to completely forgive Roy's supposed act of duplicity.

Responds a longtime KU watcher, referring to those relative handful, "Having a great fan base doesn't mean having an idiot-free fan base."

WILLIAM THE EIGHTH

Bill Self's career at KU did not begin with his hiring on as head coach in 2003, making him the eighth coach in its storied history. It began at age twenty-one, working at Larry Brown's summer camp forty-one years ago.

Self injured his knee one day, and his boss, perhaps out of sympathy, asked Self if he could do anything to lend the lad a helping hand.

"Hire me as a graduate assistant next year," replied Self.

"You're hired," responded Brown, who had a penchant for assisting young men who shared his passion for coaching.

Self spent the 1985–1986 season as a member of Brown's lively band of assistants, where every day was a different clinic, and on any loose paper towel or table napkin you might find a new play that had just been drawn up—a play you might use down the line to win you a game.

Jerrance Howard, a member of Self's staff at KU from 2012 to 2020, says his ex-boss's connection with Larry Brown has been a deep, lasting one.

You might well ask, aside from the aforementioned love of coaching, what would bring together a native New Yorker with Woody Allen-level anxiety issues and a country boy from Okmulgee, Oklahoma? One who held sixteen coaching jobs over fifty-seven years, the other six jobs over forty years (two at KU, including a current gig that's lasted twenty-two years). Larry's KU gig, by comparison, lasted just five.

Howard would tell you that the connection begins with their basketball DNA. Just as much as Larry Brown's basketball sense is inbred, so, too, is Self's, argues Howard.

"Bill, like Larry, is a kind of basketball 'Rain Man,'" he says. "The way the [film character] could count a thousand toothpicks on the ground, Bill and Larry share the ability to watch ten guys on the floor at once and see and remember everything each of those guys do. It just floored me."

Self, however, isn't anywhere near as complimentary of his innate coaching ability.

"As a player, I thought I knew what to do," he wrote in his autobiography. "But I'd never been behind the scenes of coaching before. I was so enamored of Coach Brown [because] I suddenly realized I knew nothing."

This alleged intrinsic connection notwithstanding, the two men do share a fierce underlying ambition. For example, an entry on KU's Law Blog addresses the importance of persistence in job hunting, using none other than Bill Self as a case study in tenacity.

First, there's the way he got to KU, beginning in that summer of '84. Then there were the constant letters he wrote to Brown after he was back at Oklahoma State, finishing up his bachelor's degree. Not having heard back from Brown, he piled all his belongings into his car and took off for Lawrence, walking into Brown's office uninvited and announcing his arrival.

"What do you need me to do?" he asked.

"Sit over there at that desk and start working," said Brown.

Self did much the same to wangle an assistant job under Leonard Hamilton at Oklahoma State, selling him on the fact that Hamilton was in desperate need of a point guard, and Self knew just the right kid to fill that need.

"But he won't play [for you] unless you hire me as a coach," Self advised Hamilton.

Hamilton agreed to hire Self if he could deliver on that promise. Self left the office and called an Oklahoma State senior and close friend named Jay Davis, who had played the position in high school.

"Man, you've got to play basketball for Oklahoma State this year," implored Self.

Davis was quite happy at school and had no interest at all in playing organized ball, but Self kept right on prodding his friend.

"You don't understand," he told Davis. "You have to play! I won't get the job unless you play, so you're playing."

Perry Ellis, a six-foot-eight forward who logged 144 games for Bill Self from 2012–2016, plays defense with a certain stylishness. Public domain, via Wikimedia Commons

And that was it. Davis played the 1986–1987 season for the Cowboys, leading the team in assists and steals. Self got the assistant job and remained in that post for five years.

And that's Bill Self, rather subdued on the outside but on the inside a boldly determined—near-fixated—coach whose ambition got him to the pinnacle of college sports. That ambition has not yet abated, at least as it relates to the success of his program.

At the same time, notes Jerrance Howard, Self, again like Coach Brown, is a sensitive and attentive teacher who adheres to the philosophy of "teaching it better than you learned it."

"There was no ego with him," concludes Howard, "no pride that got in the way of his relationships with his players and staff. He'd let his assistants run the drills in practice and [take on] other responsibilities. He was great to work for."

The one major difference between Brown and Self is that the former abhorred recruiting while the latter is quite good at it. This skill shows up on the KU program's balance sheet in the form of four trips to the Final Four (including titles in 2008 and 2022), six to the Elite Eight, and twenty NCAA tournament berths. Add to that, 565 wins as of this writing and a win percentage of .806, exceeding Roy's by one thousandth of a point.

Not bad for a kid from Okmulgee.

Still, it hasn't all been rosy for Bill Self and his program.

A sweeping but ultimately less than fruitful 2017 FBI investigation of corruption in college basketball started a process that led to sanctions and charges—specifically, that Self had failed to maintain compliance with NCAA bylaws. The violations involved payments from an Adidas bagman to people associated with former Jayhawk players.

All of it ultimately resulted in sanctions against the program but didn't prohibit participation in postseason play. Nor did it significantly stain the coach's reputation as a worthy successor to the legendary coaches who came before.

Perhaps Self's most glorious moment came in the immediate aftermath of "Mario's Miracle," the 2008 championship game that featured a miraculous three-pointer by Mario Chalmers that tied the game in the closing seconds and sent it to overtime, in which KU prevailed over Memphis.

Back at the hotel in San Antonio, a relatively quiet celebration was going on in Self's hotel room. He was the new King of College Basketball, as he wrote in his book. This was everything good that he had ever imagined about being a big-time collegiate coach.

Nonetheless, there was no hint of hero worship in the room, no shouting or cheers for the newly crowned king. Just Self and a crowd of well-wishers.

There was but one significant detail that made this night different from all other nights when winning coaches are crowned:

Bill Self knew the name of every celebrant in the room. And not just their names, but the names of most of their spouses and kids. He had that ability to remember names, faces, and places, and those things about people that matter more than their names.

Which is a *Rain Man*-like gift that far surpasses the memorization of all the player positions on a basketball court.

University of Kentucky

Big Blue Nation

NCAA Titles (8)—1948, 1949, 1951, 1958, 1978, 1996, 1998, 2012
NCAA Runners-Up (4)—1966, 1975, 1997, 2014
Final Fours (17)—1942, 1948, 1949, 1951, 1958, 1966, 1975, 1978, 1984, 1993, 1996, 1997, 1998, 2011, 2012, 2014, 2015
Elite Eights (34)—1951, 1952, 1956, 1957, 1958, 1961, 1962, 1966, 1968, 1970, 1972, 1975, 1977, 1978, 1983, 1984, 1986, 1992, 1993, 1995, 1996, 1997, 1998, 1999, 2003, 2005, 2010, 2011, 2012, 2014, 2015, 2017, 2019
NCAA tournament appearances—62
Naismith College Players of the Year—3

ON SUNDAY, MARCH 12, 1933, FRANKLIN DELANO ROOSEVELT DELIVERED his first Fireside Chat. Two weeks earlier, the Wildcat basketball team defeated Mississippi State for the SEC Championship. In the Commonwealth of Kentucky, listeners intently tuned in to both events.

Across the next eleven years, FDR gave thirty Fireside Chats, the most listened to on December 9, 1941, two days after the Japanese attacked Pearl Harbor. An estimated sixty-one million Americans— about half the country's population at the time—tuned in.

The basketball broadcasts, of which there were hundreds during the same period, were far less internationally relevant than the messages beamed out of the White House, although in some facets just as culturally important.

Before the days of television, the Fireside Chats were supposed to calm calamity, succinctly communicate a vision for America, build trust, and patriotism, if not provide the president with a successful political strategy.

Meanwhile, on crackling radios across the state, hoops fans were treated to the trusted sounds of squeaking sneakers on a hardwood floor, orange leather ripping through a polyester net, and the indiscernible, raspy barking—both fierce and exhausted—of a legendary coach.

FDR was seeking to build unity through audio.

Kentucky basketball was building a sort of union using a similar method.

To be clear, we're not saying Kentucky basketball is as important as World War II, just maybe for some Kentuckians.

Radio is far more romantic than other mediums. Reading a newspaper results in ink-covered fingers and that general noisy chore of folding the B section just right to finish your article. Watching television is overstimulating, particularly these days, with scrolling updates, flashing graphics, double boxes, and overcaffeinated anchors with a proclivity for yelling.

Same for smartphones.

Radio lets the mind wander, fill in some of the illustrative blanks, finish the partially completed canvas. It has a certain mystique. Which is why it has long been such a natural fit to disseminate the fables of the 'Cats.

"When I think of Kentucky basketball, the first thing I think of is a young kid getting ready to listen to the radio at night," says Oscar Combs, a resident of Lexington and a resident historian on UK hoops.

"It was a very special night if you got to stay up and listen to Kentucky. Most of the big conference games throughout my lifetime were Saturday–Monday contests. In fact, they would play two-game road trips. And, of course, this was before TV."

By the time World War II concluded, a smattering of stations already carried the games of the most elite, consistent program in the South, if not the country.

In the 1950s, Cawood Ledford took the microphone and served as the voice of Big Blue nation for thirty-nine years, the soundtrack of the 'Cats. He helped to voice history and encapsulate a way of life. Ralph Hacker was with Ledford for much of the journey.

"I can't tell you how many people have told me, 'You know, I'm a UK fan because my grandfather grew up listening to the Kentucky games on the radio,'" shares Dan Issel, two-time All-American and 1970 Kentucky graduate.

"They wouldn't know Coach Rupp if he walked into their living room, but they knew everything there was to know about him and Kentucky basketball, and that has just gone from generation to generation."

Throughout the generations of college basketball, fans have had little reason to change course. Kentucky has won more, won more frequently, landed as often in the NCAA tournament field, and produced more NBA draft picks (128, if you're wondering) than any other school. Seven former Wildcats have busts in Springfield, Massachusetts. So, too, do five of their past coaches. Only UCLA has more championship banners.

In the past ninety years. Kentucky's longest drought without a conference championship was a whopping five years. It only happened once.

And in case this list of accomplishments isn't wowing you, try this one: Kentucky last had consecutive losing seasons during the pandemic. Not the recent pandemic. You must go back to the Spanish (or Great) Flu of 1918 to come up with two straight instances in which the Kentucky basketball team lost more than it won.

The Kentucky Wildcats are also, importantly, the only show in town. Of course, we know that a three-time national champion is posted up just eighty miles down the road. Please don't mention the four-letter word that starts with Louis and ends with Ville to any member of Big Blue Nation. Outsiders may view it as a rivalry; fanatics in Lexington do not. And acknowledging the trio of titles—two under Denny Crum and the latest under former Kentucky leader Pitino (blasphemy!)—the head-to-head *competition* is, well, scarce.

Consider, Kentucky has an all-time series "edge" of 39–17. And despite the big banners hanging in Freedom Hall, you-know-who has also spent some extended stretches in the dumpster of college basketball. As Eddie Sutton once said, the Cardinals are like a little brother.

Anyway, it's not a true rivalry. To truly understand the history of Big Blue, it's also imperative to turn it back about a century, when a twenty-eight-year-old high-school coach arrived in Lexington and changed the place forever.

RUPP'S DOMAIN

Adolph Frederick Rupp was born on September 2, 1901, in Halstead, Kansas, a speck of a place not quite forty miles outside of Wichita. He was among six siblings born to German immigrant parents and grew up on a 163-acre farm. When he was nine, his dad died. In the aftermath, to help his family, he served as a young custodian at the one-room schoolhouse he attended.

Rupp was a high-school basketball standout who demonstrated a knack for leading his team on the floor. Upon graduation, Rupp went to Kansas, where he played for head coach Phog Allen and assistant James Naismith, the creator of basketball.

Kansas had some very good teams during Rupp's run in Lawrence. The 1922 and 1923 Jayhawks were retroactively honored with the Helms National Championship. Rupp was a reserve. Upon graduating in 1923, Rupp attended Columbia (New York) Teachers College, where he earned a master's degree and then headed back to high school.

In the Midwest, Rupp spent the latter part of the 1920s coaching basketball (as well as a season of wrestling) and teaching economics for high-school students. At Freeport High School, a couple hours west of Chicago, Rupp developed a reputation as a winning coach. After just five seasons, he was ready for a major step up.

When the University of Kentucky hired Rupp in 1930, the program had been just fine. Across the first twenty-seven years of the Wildcat program, fifteen coaches totaled 183 wins.

There wouldn't be any more coaching searches for a while.

Former players recall a disciplinarian, a perfectionist allergic to losing, who would, once in a great while, drop the veneer of stoicism and share a personal moment of connection.

"He was always a strict fundamentalist," two-time All-American center Alex Groza told ESPN. "I recall in practices we'd run a play and sometimes even when we would score a basket, he would blow his whistle and say, 'Now boys, you didn't run it my way.'"

His way would come to include turning up the tempo with fierce man-to-man defenses leading to crisp fast breaks.

Rupp's childhood farming roots continued into adulthood. He had a five-hundred-acre farm outside of Lexington, where he bred cattle and grew tobacco. He served as president of the Kentucky Hereford Association for seventeen years.

He became the king of Kentucky. A figure of basketball royalty who didn't just have nicknames; he had nicknames that rang out like they should be the titles of blockbuster movies: "Baron of the Bluegrass" and the "Man in the Brown Suit."

Ah, yes, the brown suit: it turns out the blue one was no good. While coaching at Freeport in the late '20s, Rupp bought a spiffy new, *blue* suit. He wore it to a game; his team got blown out. Not only did Rupp toss the brand-new, blue suit in the garbage, but he also went back to brown suits forever.

"He was amazingly superstitious," remembers Dan Issel. "He thought it was good luck if he found a bobby pin on the ground on the way into the arena, to the point that our trainer would get ahead of him at the visitor's arena and sprinkle a few bobby pins outside for Coach Rupp to find."

Issel says Rupp also had a lucky urinal—seriously. And you better not have been using it when coach came in to take a pregame leak.

"I'll give you another one," Issel says, his voice rising. "When we went to Knoxville, we stayed in an old hotel. It was called the Noel Hotel—in downtown—and it was a dump. It still had that metal accordion thing on the elevator. I think it was more a house of ill-repute than it was a hotel.

"My sophomore year they had built a brand-new hotel out close to campus. So, we stayed at that hotel, and we got killed."

Final score: Tennessee 87, Kentucky 59.

"I think it was the worst margin of defeat, at least one of the worst defeats coach Rupp ever had," Issel says.

"My junior year, we were back at the Noel Hotel."

Some years before the memorably unlucky Knoxville hotel, the Rupp regime began, appropriately, with a decisive win. His first game as coach of the Wildcats was a 67–19 win against Georgetown (Kentucky, not D.C.), one of fifteen victories that inaugural season. Fans in the Bluegrass State would grow accustomed to these types of wins until Rupp's retirement in the early 1970s.

Rupp's next five campaigns included a final SoCon title, before Kentucky's impressive transition to the Southeastern Conference, where he followed with four straight championships, in case anyone in the league was unsure about them.

Winning was sustained throughout the Depression, and when the NCAA tournament began in 1939, Rupp and his Wildcats would soon earn a larger, national audience.

The first of Rupp's six Final Fours came in 1942. That season ended with a loss to Osborne Cowles's Dartmouth squad, winners of the now-defunct Eastern Intercollegiate Basketball League.

Then, things started to get quite fabulous.

THE ORIGINAL FAB FIVE
Long before the baggy shorts, black socks, and bald heads of Michigan's culturally influential "Fab Five" sits a lesser-known, dust-covered chapter of hoops history. You've heard of the Fab Five from Ann Arbor, a group that lost in back-to-back title games as it ushered in a new era.

What about Ralph Beard, Alex Groza, Wallace "Wah Wah" Jones, Cliff Barker, and Kenny Rollins?

Meet Kentucky's *Fabulous Five*. It's an alternate quintet of the times from five decades earlier that, in fact, was even more successful than the Wolverine group: a great collection of players who won consecutive championships while barnstorming their way to an Olympic Gold Medal.

"Stop me if I get too long-winded here," Oscar Combs warns, "but very few people know the story, and it's an incredible part of the game's history."

It was a wartime group, some of whom fought for their country, all of whom represented America. Groza, Beard, Jones, and Barker were all juniors in 1948. Rollins was the lone senior.

He was a six-foot guard who had his college career halted for three years of service in the U.S. Navy, after which time he was an All-SEC performer. He was also closing in on his twenty-fifth birthday when his eligibility expired.

In 1948, the fabulous Wildcat roster included six players who would later play in the newly formed NBA. They ran the table in the SEC, and dispatched Columbia, Bob Cousy-led Holy Cross, and Baylor to win the national title in Madison Square Garden.

Rupp had brought Kentucky its first championship.

"Perhaps the best way to describe Kentucky's 34th and certainly most important triumph of the campaign," wrote Louis Effrat in the *New York Times*, "is to report that form held up. Nearly every pre-game prediction pointed to the size, speed, and depth of the Wildcats from Lexington and figured that these would determine the outcome."

Effrat went on to note that Rupp did not substitute any of the Fabulous Five until the 6:30 mark of the second half.

That summer, the Olympics were to take place, and the United States had to select a men's basketball roster. The process was a little different than it is today. The national champion Wildcats took on the Phillips Oilers of the Amateur Athletic Union (AAU) in three separate exhibition contests. The games were designed to raise money for the Olympic team.

"One of the games was played at the football stadium in Lexington," Combs notes. "They put up a floor right there, the long way, and played in front of a packed stadium."

It was a precursor to how football stadiums are used today: to maximize the in-person Final Four audiences and minimize the number of seats with a good basketball view.

The Fabulous Five, plus five members from the Oilers, comprised the bulk of the 1948 roster that went to London in July. The United States was perfect on the international stage, defeating all eight of its opponents, including an overwhelmed French National Team, 65–21, in the

Gold Medal game. Groza, a soon-to-be senior, led the team in scoring, and Rupp was an assistant coach.

Of the original Fab Five, only Rollins rolled off the roster for the 1949 season. Joining the now senior quartet of Barker, Beard, Groza, and Jones was junior Dale Barnstable.

Kentucky was again perfect in SEC play, 13–0. The Wildcats proceeded to tear through the smaller NCAA tournament field. After wins against Loyola (Illinois), Villanova, and Illinois at MSG, they headed west to Seattle. There, Groza, a six-foot-seven senior center, scored twenty-five points, and Kentucky did away with a Hank Iba-coached Oklahoma State squad, 46–36, making it back-to-back for Big Blue.

Although this achievement is remarkable in and of itself, the individual narratives within this Fab Five group only add to the compelling story. Wallace "Wah Wah" Jones was an all-state football, basketball, and baseball selection from Harlan (Kentucky) High School. He dropped baseball when he arrived in Lexington and became a merely two-sport star.

On the hardwood, he was a three-time All-American and four-time All-SEC selection. As he told the University of Kentucky Oral History Project in 2009, "In four years we won 130 out of 140. That was pretty good."

In addition to the two NCAA titles, Kentucky also earned an NIT championship in 1946, Jones's freshman season.

But that wasn't all. Wah Wah was also a two-time All-SEC football player, where he played for the iconic Paul "Bear" Bryant. It's reasonable to forget that one of college football's most legendary leaders had thirteen seasons and three stops *before* getting to Tuscaloosa. Bear Bryant was the headman in Kentucky from 1946 to 1953.

Jones had the rare distinction of playing for Rupp *and* Bryant, two coaches who are on the hypothetical Mount Rushmore of their respective sports.

"They both stressed the responsibilities of what you had to do and the way they were telling you to do it. If you didn't do it, you were on the bench," Jones recalled.

And the sideline is where Jones ended up at one point, albeit briefly.

"I was playing up at Cincinnati and sacked the quarterback. They put in a substitution, and he hit me in the mouth with an elbow. Back then we didn't have face masks, and we had leather headgear.

"So, I was bleeding, and one of my cheeks got moved. I come out, and I'm standing on the sideline, and Coach Bryant has his arm around me and says he's going to send me back in. And I said something about my teeth. Coach Bryant said, 'Well, you don't run on your teeth.'"

A fellow fabulous senior on the 36–3 title team in 1949 was six-foot-one point guard Cliff Barker. He had five points in the finale against OK State and an undetermined number of assists, as they were not part of the official record. Regardless, Barker had developed a status as a splendid distributor.

"He was a phenomenal passer," Combs says, adding that he had clear similarities to Cousy, his Final Four opponent a year earlier.

"Naturally the press was interested in his passing style, and they asked him how he became such a good passer."

Combs describes Barker's answer: "He said, 'Well, when you're a prisoner of war, your only recreation is passing a ball from one prisoner to another. And we had a lot of time.'"

Sixteen months, to be exact.

Barker grew up in Yorktown (Indiana), a small community of about nine hundred people. After high school he entered the air force and was a gunner on B-17 bombers. According to the American Air Museum, on January 30, 1944, Barker's plane—named Fancy Nancy III—was shot down during a bombing mission over Brunswick, Germany.

Captured, Barker became a POW for the next sixteen months and subsequently filled much of his idle time bouncing and passing a volleyball. The repetition resulted in magnificent ball-handling skills.

"He had exceptional hands," former teammate Rollins told the museum. "His hands were very sensitive to the ball. And he was able to visualize things on the floor that other people couldn't see."

By the time Barker completed his service, survived POW status, and graduated following a bifurcated time at Kentucky, he was twenty-eight years old.

After the back-to-back titles and gold medal, the jerseys of Barker, Beard, Groza, Jones, and Rollins were retired and continue to dangle from the rafters of Rupp Arena.

THE SCANDAL

Alex Groza was selected by the Indianapolis Olympians in the first round of the 1949 NBA draft. He was honored as an All-NBA First-Team pick. The NBA didn't officially name a rookie of the year back then, but voting members of the media bestowed that honor on him, as well, after he averaged better than twenty-three points per game.

Beard, a three-time All-American at Kentucky, was taken in the second round by the Chicago Stags and traded, before ever playing a game, down the road to Indianapolis, where he linked up with his former teammate. Beard blossomed in his second season, averaging nearly seventeen points and five assists.

In 1951, Beard and Groza were both NBA All-Stars and All-NBA First-Team honorees before their careers came to a catastrophic halt. A massive point-shaving scandal was uncovered, and it had connections to organized crime.

Born out of the 1950 CCNY (City College of New York) men's basketball team, thirty-two players from seven different schools were implicated in the improprieties, including Kentucky.

Beard, Groza, and another former teammate, Dale Barnstable, were charged with taking bribes from gamblers to affect the outcome of Wildcat games. The following April, all three pleaded guilty to conspiring to shave points and were subsequently issued suspended sentences. NBA President Maurice Podoloff banned them from the league for life.

"If taking $700 was wrong, then I was guilty," Groza told the *New York Times* in 1995. "But I was totally innocent of influencing games. I never had two dimes to rub together. My mother cleaned six apartments so we could have one to live in. I took the money, and that was it. I always gave 101 percent on the court."

Two highly promising professional careers ceased abruptly.

Meanwhile, there were other consequences in Lexington.

"Rupp didn't take a team back to New York City, following the scandal, for the rest of his career," Combs explains. "That was another twenty-one years."

Rupp, notes Combs, "loved to take his teams to New York and Chicago, because that's where all the media was. I mean, at one point you had something like forty-seven newspapers in New York City. And he would take them up there, and then the scandal happened, and that was it for Kentucky in New York for a long time."

THIRD AND FOURTH

In the same year that the point-shaving scandal ended careers and shook the foundation of college basketball, Kentucky was up to its usual early spring shenanigans. Led by Bill Spivey, Shelby Linville, and future pros Cliff Hagan, Frank Ramsey, and Bobby Watson, Kentucky ran through the largely inferior SEC and lingered in the top five of the national polls all season.

The team had two minor setbacks in 1951. The first came at the hands of St. Louis, a 43–42 overtime defeat. The other was an upset versus Vanderbilt in the SEC tournament final. It was a moderate stunner that kept Kentucky from claiming its *eighth* consecutive tourney win.

Rupp's Cats rebounded and defeated Louisville, St. John's, Illinois, and finally Kansas State, 68–58, as the big man Spivey totaled a game-high twenty-two to win Rupp his third national title.

Then, the scandal unfolded. After the arrests, trials, and sentences, the inevitable NCAA investigation commenced. That inquiry ultimately found that Kentucky had violated several rules, chief among them allowing ineligible athletes to compete and providing players with illegal spending money.

In the wake of the NCAA investigation, the conference then acted on its own, with member institutions voting to ban Kentucky from playing for a year.

It was an unofficial death penalty. Kentucky did not play basketball in the 1952–1953 season.

Naturally, the next year saw Rupp post his only undefeated season, as Kentucky concluded the regular season atop the polls. The 25–0 team blew out just about every opponent as well. Only Xavier kept the final tally within single digits.

Things got messy again when the NCAA ruled three players ineligible prior to the start of the postseason. The punishment stemmed from the fact that the trio had graduated the previous spring but missed their senior season. Without any career-extending COVID provisions, the NCAA came down hard, barring Hagan and Ramsey from the tournaments. Rupp pulled his team from the 1954 Dance.

Despite the external uproar, Kentucky practices under Rupp were not never-ending, grueling affairs. They were silent.

"We couldn't talk in practice," remembers Dan Issel, the Wildcats' all-time leading scorer. "The only time you could talk was if a coach was asking you a question."

The systematic practice sessions began with a half hour of shooting.

"It was bouncing of the balls and the squeaking of the tennis shoes and coach Rupp's whistle and voice, and that was about it. We weren't allowed to, you know, be goofing around or chatting with our buddy," says Issel.

"And believe me, I'm not being critical of coach Rupp. Everything I have in life was because of my life and experience with Coach Rupp. I love him. I grew up on a farm, had a good work ethic, and that was the kind of player he wanted.

"There are two ways to motivate—one is to pat 'em on the back, one is to kick 'em in the tail . . . and if you weren't tough enough to take it, he wouldn't let you on his team in the first place."

Issel laughs as he remembers the message from Coach Rupp: "It was conveyed—you didn't speak in practice unless silence can be improved upon."

"You didn't speak in practice unless silence can be improved upon," Combs reiterates, "and Rupp told me, 'Nobody can improve upon silence, if anybody is talking other than me.' If you walked into the top of the gym, and he could hear chatting to a friend up there, you were thrown out of that gymnasium."

Adolph Rupp's fourth and final national championship team was the least consistent of his championship groups.

Dan Issel, an Illinois native, created a legacy at Kentucky where he became a two-time All-American and had frequent battles against "Pistol" Pete Maravich.

In 1958, Kentucky started Vernon Hatton, Johnny Cox, John Crigler, Don Mills, and Ed Beck. It was common for Rupp to have a short bench.

In the slower-tempo, pre-shot clock era, he generally went with as few guys as he thought were necessary.

The starters in '58 earned the coach's moniker the "Fiddlin' Five" after Rupp declared that they "fiddled around enough to drive me crazy." Hatton led the offense with seventeen points per game, as inconsistencies persisted. The team struggled to win close games and, at one point, dropped three of four.

Still, they managed to peak, as opponents shot poorly at opportune moments. In the national semi, Kentucky won at Freedom Hall, 61–60, over Temple, when the Owls bricked ten of their twenty free throws.

It was the second tight victory against Temple that season. Months earlier, Hatton had sunk a half-court shot with one second remaining in overtime, forcing another extra session. The forty-seven-foot heave is a legendary shot in the Kentucky annals. The 'Cats won 85–83 in triple overtime.

In the NCAA final, Rupp's team didn't fiddle around.

Instead, they focused on Seattle All-American forward Elgin Baylor. The Wildcats' defense forced Baylor into a lousy night shooting (nine-for-thirty-two), and he logged limited, foul-troubled minutes. Hatton, a Lexington native, led everyone on the floor that night with thirty, and Kentucky won, 84–72.

RUPP'S RUNTS

> *Was Coach Rupp a racist? Probably by today's standards, but you have to remember that was a different time.*

> —DAN ISSEL

The time was the 1960s, the civil rights movement was in full swing, and Kentucky basketball remained an all-white ensemble. Rupp infamously passed on New York City legend Connie Hawkins in 1960, reportedly calling a newspaper to ask if the young phenom who was being pursued by so many colleges was white or colored.

Informed that Hawkins was not of the Caucasian persuasion, the story goes that Rupp lost interest and passed.

We will not defend any bigotry. We will only note that at this time, Rupp, despite his baron status, existed as part of a larger ecosystem in the still deeply segregated South.

Kentucky administrators were a contributing factor and resisted athletic integration at the time. Another obstacle was the Southeastern Conference, which had no black athletes until 1966. That's when Vanderbilt added Perry Wallace and Godfrey Dillard to its basketball team, and Kentucky's *football* team integrated with Nate Northington and Greg Page.

The year 1966 was an incredibly important one for Kentucky, indeed, due to the courage Northington and Page exuded, in addition to the lessons learned from Don Haskins's Texas Western basketball team.

The 1966 edition of Wildcat ball was a smaller unit. Only one player stood above the six-foot-five threshold (sophomore forward Cliff Berger, six-feet-eight). The so-called runts were led by a superb starting backcourt of Louie Dampier and Pat Riley, both juniors. Coming off a mediocre 15–10 1965 campaign, Rupp's Runts were unranked to begin the next season. By the time they had rattled off twenty-three wins to start the season, they sat at number one.

In the tournament, Kentucky polished off Dayton, an already integrated Michigan team, in the Elite Eight, and then a talented Duke squad in the semifinals, 83–79. The national title game pitted Rupp's Runts—all of whom were white—opposite the five black starters on the Texas Western Miners.

"To us, race was not involved at all," Dampier told the University of Kentucky Oral History Project in 2016. "We just looked at it as the championship game. Even after the game, you didn't hear anything about the white guys got beat by the black players. Through the years, it has been built up as a racial game."

Dampier was introduced to Texas Western's starting point guard, Bobby Joe Hill, early on.

"There was one point in the game where Bobby Joe Hill stole the ball from Tommy Kron, and then next time up the floor, he took it from me.

He got two steals in a row, right at midcourt. It was embarrassing. People say that could have been the turning point of the game."

Dampier and backcourt mate Riley each had nineteen points; Bobby Joe Hill led everyone with twenty. In front of a capacity audience at Cole Field House in College Park, Maryland, Texas Western (today UTEP) defeated the favored Wildcats, 72–65.

"It was the first time I had ever seen Coach Rupp be upset, really sad about it," Dampier remembered. "Usually, he would come in as his strong self and holler at us. But he was meekly quiet."

Texas Western's victory has led to books, movies, and a long-view cultural appreciation that may have been cloudier in the moment. The 1966 NCAA final is now considered among many as the most socially consequential game in college basketball history.

In any case, Rupp was denied a fifth title. He never again reached the Final Four, and it would take three more years before Tom Payne arrived at UK, breaking the basketball team's monochromatic history.

RUPP'S BEST HORSE

By the time Dan Issel concluded his illustrious offensive career at Kentucky, he had set twenty-three different school records, which is to say, he came a long way.

Issel, a six-foot-nine scoring machine nicknamed Horse, tallied 2,138 points in his Kentucky career, a standard that still holds more than half a century later.

Impressively, Issel did this in only three seasons, as freshmen remained ineligible until 1972.

Despite his eventual success in the Bluegrass State, Issel grew up largely oblivious to Kentucky's prowess; he didn't know who the heck Adolph Rupp was.

"I wasn't that aware of Kentucky," admits Issel, who grew up in Batavia, forty miles west of Chicago. "I took a recruiting trip to Kentucky. It was the first time I was ever on an airplane.

"While I was there, I picked up a copy of the school newspaper, the *Kentucky Colonel*, and there was an article about recruiting in there. It mentioned about fifteen different people, and my name wasn't on the list.

I went back home, and I signed a Big Ten letter—they had conference letters and national letters [of intent] back then—with Wisconsin."

Issel later learned that Kentucky was going all-in on George Janky from nearby Chicago. But when Janky chose Dayton instead, the Wildcats had another scholarship, and Issel got some advice from his dad.

"At that time, Kentucky had had more All-Americans and more professional players than any other school. And I can still remember my father coming into my room and saying, 'If you're really serious about this basketball stuff, Kentucky might be a pretty good place to go.' So that's why I took a second recruiting trip with my father. And I wound up going to Kentucky."

As a sophomore, Issel averaged sixteen points—second on the team. He helped UK to another SEC title before getting upset in the Elite Eight, at home, by Ohio State, 82–81.

Later that year he was also on the court for basketball history. On December 30, 1967, Kentucky defeated Notre Dame, 81–73. It marked Rupp's 772nd career win, surpassing his former coach, Phog Allen. Rupp amassed another 104 victories, and his career mark of 876 wins stood for a generation until Dean Smith eclipsed it in 1997.

As a junior, Issel improved his scoring average to a team-leading twenty-six points per contest, led Big Blue to a second straight conference crown and, *again*, lost in the Elite Eight by a point. This time Miami (Ohio) prevailed, 72–71, on what was once supposed to be Issel's home floor: Wisconsin Field House.

As a senior, Issel amped up his output again, to thirty-three points per game, still the school's best single-season mark. Kentucky ripped through the conference with a 17–1 mark—making Issel's career SEC record a silly 48–6.

His college career concluded when he met a third and final loss in the regional final. On this occasion, it was the Dolphins of Jacksonville ousting Kentucky, behind future pros Artis Gilmore and Rex Morgan. The pre-shot clock, pre-three-point era score was 106–100.

Issel was a first-team All-American in 1970. He was not the SEC Player of the Year. And respectfully, he shouldn't have been. The honor went to the guy who averaged eleven points *more* than Issel, Pete Maravich.

"Pete was unstoppable because he was so clever with the basketball," says Issel, whose collegiate career spanned the same years as "Pistol Pete," who starred for Louisiana State.

"A lot of other teams would run two or three guys at him, but Pete would still get a shot. And Coach Rupp's philosophy was exactly the opposite. He said, 'We're going to let Pete get what he gets, but we're not going to let anybody else on that team beat us.'"

Issel and Maravich met six times. The Horse says the Pistol *averaged* fifty-two in those contests. Kentucky went 6–0 against LSU. The closest game was a twelve-point margin.

Their final SEC meeting, in Baton Rouge on February 21, 1970, saw Maravich pour in sixty-three. Issel had a relatively pedestrian fifty-one. The Wildcats tamed the Tigers, 121–105.

"I tell people as far as passing and ball handling, nobody's come close—not Magic, John Stockton, nobody has come close to what Pete could do with a basketball. He was flashy, and people loved him. And, you know, as long as we won the game, it was pretty fun to watch Pete play."

After the "Glory Road" defeat in 1966, Adolph Rupp coached six more seasons at Kentucky. As he began his fifth decade leading the program, it became clear that retirement would soon arrive. Not necessarily because Rupp wanted it but, rather, because it is what Kentucky law required. Rupp was facing a mandatory retirement in the months after his seventieth birthday. (He got to conclude the season following his September cake.)

Now, why Governor John Y. Brown didn't offer some sort of executive order, that is a bit unclear. Though candidly, it seemed to be time. The seventy-year-old Rupp—who had long lived on the heavier side—was dealing with complications from diabetes. And then there was his complicated past when it came to race relations.

Rupp had exactly one black player on his forty-two teams.

Hatton, the star of the 1958 team, once remarked that "it takes six or eight years to get over playing for Coach Rupp. Once you get over it, you get to like him."

However, in his final decades, away from the game, Rupp became more likable to many.

Combs, the de facto Wildcat historian who spent considerable time with Rupp in the later stages of his life, says, "He was your typical seventy-seven-year-old, gray-headed grandfather . . . you would just sit and listen to story after story after story.

"He told a lot of great ones, and I learned so much. And I also learned earlier in life that sometimes you see it the way you want to see it as the time goes by, and if you repeat a story enough times, you'll get to believe in the things that you sort of embellish."

One thing that *sounds* like an embellishment is Kentucky's home winning streak between 1943 and 1955. Across twelve years, Rupp's teams ripped off 129 consecutive wins at Memorial Coliseum. The NCAA record, which, of course, hasn't been surpassed, ended with a one-point loss to Georgia Tech.

Again, after 129 straight victories.

Issel reflects that along with the four national titles, 27 SEC regular season championships, a gaggle of All-Americans, and five national Coach of the Year honors, there was the importance of elevating Kentucky in the pride department.

"You know, there aren't any professional teams in Kentucky. And Kentucky has always been toward the bottom of any list, as far as states are concerned, in just about any category. Except they were number one in basketball, and people were so proud of the university and of the basketball program and what Coach Rupp was doing."

Adolph Rupp, in his forty-two years as the head coach at Kentucky, never had a losing season.

Joe B.
Five different coaches have taken Big Blue to the top. Rupp, Rick Pitino, Tubby Smith, John Calipari and . . .

Joe Beasman Hall.

If you're south of fifty, you might not remember Coach Hall. If he were around today, the younger generations would likely refer to him as "a real one."

Hall had spent eight years as Rupp's top assistant by the time that pesky state statute forced Rupp to the barn (literally; remember, he had a huge estate and lots of horses).

Rupp's imposing demeanor did not linger directly with the next coach of Kentucky. Joe B. Hall was genuinely liked by his players, staff, and fans. He was primed to sustain the culture of excellence in Lexington. However, things were going to look—and feel—quite different, even if Rupp did keep his old office, and his presence continued to loom.

"Here's one of my favorite stories about Coach Hall," says Issel, who was recruited by Joe B.

"He called and said, 'I'm in town. Can I stop by the house?' And I said, 'Yeah, but I have a date tonight at seven.' So, he arrives around five o'clock or so, and I thought that'll give me plenty of time. We sat at the kitchen table—my mom and dad and coach Hall and myself—and come seven o'clock, I got up and went on my date. I came home at eleven, and Joe Hall was still sitting at the kitchen table with my mother."

At his introductory press conference, Hall indicated that he would recruit black players. This was a noteworthy pledge in 1972, especially when you consider that Tom Payne had been the one and only black ballplayer in Lexington under the previous regime.

Hall's arrival also coincided with freshmen becoming eligible. These changes would coincide in big ways for Kentucky basketball, most notably with the addition of Jack Givens in 1974.

Givens—nicknamed Goose—was a local kid, a product of Bryan Station High School in Lexington. The six-foot-five guard arrived on campus along with the six-foot-eight big man, Rick Robey, and the 'Cats were in business. Senior Kevin Grevey led the way as Hall's team handed him the first of several SEC titles. UK went 15–3 in the league and 26–5 across the 1974–1975 season.

Their postseason saw a big upset of top-seeded Indiana in the Elite Eight, 92–90 (after which the Hoosiers went on a winning streak that didn't conclude until December of 1976, a year and a half later).

Then, UK upended Roy Danforth-coached Syracuse in the national semis. Finally, in the Final Four, they succumbed to UCLA, 92–85. Grevey had thirty-four points, more than anyone on the floor. Still, it wasn't enough to spoil John Wooden's final game.

Givens had eight off the bench in that title game, and he averaged nine per game that freshman season. He made a sophomore jump that saw averages accelerate to twenty points, seven boards, and three assists per contest. More importantly, Kentucky had its first-ever black standout.

It was long after it should have, or could have, happened, but despite the late arrival, Givens brought Kentucky into a more contemporary mold.

"I was not recruited by coach Rupp. I never interacted with him," Givens notes. A decade before his Wildcat career, he had watched the 1966 Final against Texas Western and is candid in his assessment:

"I was cheering for the other team to win. Just because of the situation. I wasn't a Kentucky fan at that time. Most of the people in my neighborhood, my community, housing project, felt the same way. It was a huge moment."

Ten years later, Givens was, as much as any other individual, the change. His second season saw statistical improvements, as things sputtered out without a postseason berth. In 1977, his junior year, Kentucky breezed through the league again before being ousted by another heavyweight, deep in the tournament.

This time it was UNC, led by Walter Davis's twenty-one points, who ended any Final Four hopes with a 79–72 defeat of Kentucky in the Elite Eight.

Givens, Robey, and the bulk of the team had one more year to put it all together. The 1978 installment of Big Blue began with a preseason number two ranking. Hall's team won its first fourteen games and was without a blemish until a trip to Alabama in late January.

They lost just once more: a 95–94 overtime decision in Baton Rouge. Otherwise, the 1978 team was on a mission to finish what had twice eluded them.

Kentucky went 16–2 in SEC play and 30–2 overall. In the Dance, Kentucky beat Florida State, then Miami (Ohio). In the Elite Eight,

Kentucky trailed Michigan State at the break, 27–22, before UK defenders tormented freshman Magic Johnson. Magic, a year away from his own tournament triumph, had six turnovers on the day, as the 'Cats came back to win the regional final, 52–49.

Looming in the penultimate game was Arkansas, not yet a conference foe, still then a member school in the Southwest Conference. Givens paced all scorers in that semifinal with twenty-three (on ten-for-sixteen shooting) and hauled in nine boards. The Arkansas team—which included longtime future pro Sidney Moncrief—was coached by Eddie Sutton, who would oversee seven more seasons in Fayetteville before heading north to Lexington.

Kentucky was through the national semifinals, 64–59.

This time, Duke served as the final obstacle between Kentucky and its first parade in twenty years.

"Kentucky had to win that game," explains Mike Gminski, the Blue Devils' starting center. "If they didn't win that game, they were not going to be let back into the state of Kentucky. They were playing with an unbelievable sense of urgency."

Givens offers a counterweight.

"I didn't feel any different going into that game than going into any other. We were very fortunate. We had some really good players on that team. If you look at our march through the tournament, every game someone else kind of stepped up and was kind of 'the man,' if you will."

Givens was *the man* on March 27, 1978. Duke implemented a 2–3 zone, stretching the floor, and left the middle wide open.

"Hank Iba once told me, if you move your front line up, you have to bring your back line up," Coach Hall told the Kentucky Oral History Project years later. This is a well-understood tenet of the 2–3 zone, from Iba to Boeheim. But for whatever reason, Duke didn't adhere to it in '78.

"There was a huge gap in the middle, and we just kept going to it," Hall explained.

Running a Rupp offense, the final option of the set was a weak side forward, flashing to a doughnut hole of the zone. Kentucky kept feeding the middle. Givens scored Kentucky's final sixteen of the opening half and had twenty-three in the first frame. In an offensive exhibition, both teams scored at will in the second twenty minutes.

The Blue Devils never found a way to slow Goose, and Givens finished eighteen-for twenty-seven from the floor. His forty-one points remain the second most in title game history.

Kentucky outlasted Duke, 94–88, for its first title since 1958.

After the horn, Hall sought out his son.

"I was thinking back to the UCLA loss, and I remembered going into the dressing room after that game, and my son—who was a young kid at that time—was sitting up on the taping table. And I went over to him and said, 'Don't worry; we'll get one, one of these days.' After that win, I went over and told Steve, 'See, I told you we'd get one.'"

The win took an immense amount of pressure off Hall as Kentucky readied to celebrate. But the party in Lexington was delayed, temporarily.

"We went to the airport and couldn't find the plane," recalled Hall. The delay departing St. Louis was not due to a mechanical issue or a missing crew member. No, the national champions literally couldn't find their plane.

"No one was there to direct us, and I got out on the tarmac and walked the whole length of the terminal and found our plane at the other end. We were late getting back into Lexington, and by that time, the crowd was shoulder to shoulder," Hall said.

"Just a great reception."

The year after the title was an unmemorable one for Hall and the Wildcat fanatics, as the team finished sixth in the SEC, its worst league finish since 1940.

After that, Hall ushered in a five-year run, bookended by twenty-nine-win seasons, with three more SEC league titles, and, in 1984, his third and final run to the national semifinals. This stretch was also bookended by Sam Bowie.

"Sam Bowie, in my mind, would have been one of the greatest pros and college players of all time," Hall said. Bowie is, unfortunately, one of the game's all-time what-could-have-been narratives.

"He had so much ability for a big man," Hall said of the seven-foot-one product from Lebanon, Pennsylvania. He was, when healthy, a complete player on both ends of the floor.

Following a freshman year that produced an average of seven points, just shy of ten rebounds, and two blocks per game, Bowie made what Hall described as "astonishing" improvement. As a sophomore, Bowie averaged seventeen points, nine rebounds, and three blocks. He was honored as a third-team All-American. In one game, he swatted away nine shots, a school record that remains.

It all changed in a lopsided home win against Vanderbilt when Bowie landed awkwardly on his leg. It was later diagnosed as a stress fracture, which marked the beginning of a painful series of injuries that derailed his career.

Bowie missed the 1982 and 1983 seasons. He was in a cast for ten months. Once finally removed, Hall said Bowie was only a portion of his former self. Still, the 1984 'Cats saw a strong campaign with the additions of Kenny Walker and Melvin Turpin. Kentucky went 26–4 overall and won the SEC regular and tournament titles.

They topped BYU, the school from Louisville (aka Louisville) and Illinois to set up a meeting with Georgetown in the Final Four. Sam Bowie logged a double-double, All-American Patrick Ewing struggled (eight points), and Kentucky led by seven at the break.

Then, the Hoyas held UK to eleven second-half points and moved on with a 53–40 win.

Sam Bowie's unfulfilling Kentucky career ended.

Joe B. Hall's days were numbered.

SUTTON DEPARTS—WITH A PULSE

As bad as were the Billy Gillespie years in Lexington—and to be clear, they stunk—Eddie Sutton's tenure was far more awful.

Under Gillespie (2007–2009), the 'Cats missed the Dance for the first time in eighteen years, put up a crooked eight-loss conference effort in 2009, and found themselves in a toxic coach-team relationship. What should not have continued past a first date (or interview) developed into a cohabitation where neither party was happy. It was a match made in purgatory.

Gillespie never signed a contract with Kentucky. He initially worked under a "Memorandum of Understanding," and that arrangement continued throughout his brief stint in Lexington after the coach and the school failed to formalize a contract.

Gillespie lost his second game, at home, to unranked Gardner-Webb by sixteen. This, in the same program where *The Guy* rattled off 129 consecutive home wins across a dozen years, was an ominous start.

Gillespie didn't win an NCAA tournament game. He posted a pedestrian mark of 20–12 in league play and a decidedly un-Kentuckian 40–27 overall. Athletic Director Mitch Barnhardt fired Gillespie after only two seasons, citing incompatibility among other failures.

Gillespie sued the school.

Kentucky countersued the coach.

In the end, Billy received a settlement of about $3 million.

Truly, it was a mess.

Despite all this, somehow, Eddie Sutton's time in the land of bluegrass is a bigger stain on the program.

Sutton was forty-nine years old when he was hired to replace Joe B. Hall. The outgoing keeper of the Wildcat flame said he didn't want to be an "old coach," which is kind of an odd explanation when you consider that Hall was just fifty-six and a year removed from the Final Four when his departure arrived.

In thirteen seasons, Hall won three of every four games, along with eight regular-season SEC titles, the NIT in 1976, and the big championship in 1978.

It wasn't good enough. As the great Jack McCallum wrote in *Sports Illustrated*, plenty of people saw Hall as—wait for it—a *failure*.

In other words, Eddie Sutton never really had a chance.

He arrived from Arkansas with strong credentials: eleven seasons, an aggregate record of 260–77, victorious in 80 percent of league games, three outright league titles, two other shares of the top spot, and the aforementioned 1978 Final Four, where he lost to Kentucky.

Although it was a good stretch with the Hogs, it was also only natural to wonder: Was Sutton an *improvement* over what had been? Could he meet the demands of Big Blue Nation? Somehow improve upon Hall's success?

At his opening press conference, Sutton offered this:

"All I know is that whatever I heard about how big Kentucky basketball is, was wrong. . . . It's bigger."

In 1986, led by a Hall-constructed roster that included Kenny Walker, Sutton posted a 32–4 mark and guided the 'Cats to the latest in their seemingly endless pile of league titles. Unfortunately, Kentucky was unable to beat Alabama for a *fourth time* that season and lost in the Elite Eight, 68–63.

Eddie Sutton was named the National Coach of the Year. Then things started to slip, if only a little.

In 1987, a young roster led by Rex Chapman finished fourth in the league, and UK missed the tournament with an 18–11 record (10–8 in the SEC). Chapman was named SEC Freshman of the Year. He would return though, and Kentucky was recruiting two elite high-school talents: an LA kid and another from Elkhart, Indiana.

Chapman upped his scoring to nineteen per contest in 1988. The Wildcats won the SEC for the thirty-seventh time. In the Elite Eight, Chapman, a Western Kentucky native who had become popular enough with the fans to earn the moniker "King Rex," tallied a career-high thirty points. The only problem was that Chapman didn't get much help, as all five opposing Villanova starters finished in double figures, and the Wildcats from Kentucky were upset, 80–74.

Then, things started to tumble down a ravine.

Chapman bolted for the NBA after his sophomore year. The recruitment of Chris Mills, the kid from Los Angeles, blew up like a Molotov cocktail. A cash-filled envelope from UK assistant Dwayne Casey airmailed to Mills's father somehow opened on an Emery cargo plane, sparking an NCAA investigation.

Maybe Shawn Kemp would help fix the problem.

Yes, that Shawn Kemp, whom you might remember as a ferocious dunker and later a six-time NBA All-Star, three-time All-NBA selection, and leader on the Seattle SuperSonics squad that gave Michael Jordan and the Bulls a run for their money in 1996.

As you might also recall, Kemp, a prized recruit, never played for Kentucky, although he was on campus for a little while.

After starring in the 1988 McDonald's All-American game, his test scores weren't high enough to gain eligibility. In Lexington, with too much time on his hands, Kemp stole two gold necklaces and pawned them. The jewelry belonged to teammate Sean Sutton, son of head coach Eddie. Kemp was not charged but promptly kicked out of school, and thus, not part of any basketball solution.

To make matters worse, NCAA investigators were now looking into $1,000 payments made to Kemp's mother. The probe was expanding, and the subsequent year in Lexington was a dark one.

With the young Mills on the roster, and not much else, UK went 8–10 in conference and 13–19 overall in the 1989 season. It was the first outright losing campaign for the 'Cats in sixty-two years.

Then came the dreaded NCAA findings: a bevy of recruiting violations and academic fraud. The punishment: Kentucky was placed on three years' probation, prohibited from participating in the postseason for two years, and banned from television for the upcoming season. The program further incurred a reduction of scholarships and had to return revenue from the 1988 NCAA tournament. And that thirty-seventh SEC title was vacated.

Yet, they still had a pulse!

Sports Illustrated summarized a key passage in the findings: "Because of the nature of the violations," reads the report, ". . . the committee seriously considered whether the regular-season schedule for the men's basketball program should be curtailed in whole or in part for one or two seasons of competition. In the judgment of the committee . . . the violations found would justify such a penalty."

In other words, no death penalty.

Citing the Kentucky Athletic Department's cooperation in the investigation, the NCAA did not deliver Big Blue a so-called death sentence that would prohibit them from play the next season. The assistant coach who made the payments, Casey, was handed five years' probation.

Notably, he sued the company handling the envelope—the one with the cash that sparked the whole brouhaha—and settled for nearly $7 million.

As for Eddie Sutton, he was done in Kentucky.

If Adolf Rupp was the Baron of Bluegrass who built Kentucky basketball, then Rick Pitino was the city slicker who resurrected it.

In 1989, the Long Island native couldn't seem to sit still. It was like Pitino was always looking for the next thing. After a twenty-one-win campaign at Boston University in 1983—and a trip to the NCAAs—he departed for an assistant post with the New York Knicks. Two years after that, it was back to the college ranks at Providence College, where he quickly built a Big East power.

A couple years later, Pitino led the Friars to the 1987 Final Four, at which point he swiftly left Rhode Island and headed back to Midtown Manhattan to replace the interim HC Bob Hill, who had replaced the fired Hubie Brown earlier in the season.

Well, you can probably guess how long Pitino lasted in New York this time: two years!

Meanwhile in Lexington, changes were aplenty following the investigation.

Sent packing, along with Sutton, was Kentucky AD Cliff Hagan, who was replaced by a former teammate, C. M. Newton. For his part, Newton publicly declared Pitino as his guy. A five-year pact was placed on the proverbial table, and after MJ and the Bulls ousted Pitino's Knicks in the Eastern Conference semis, he was college-bound once again.

This stop would last longer than two years.

"I'm a college basketball coach, and I think that's where my heart is," Pitino said at his exit Madison Square Garden press conference.

"And I think that's in the best interest of everyone." (For the record, Pitino made it six years in the college ranks before again returning to the NBA.)

Pitino was just thirty-six when he arrived in Lexington, where he was handed the controls to the Gulfstream and given years to take-off.

Year one saw a .500 record and a winning mark in the conference. In year two the curtain went up on a talented Big Apple kid named Jamal

Mashburn, and Kentucky, still ineligible for the Dance, finished atop the league.

Year three, now 1992, brought on a 29–7 mark, a first-place finish in the SEC, and an Elite Eight appearance. It was there that the Wildcats *almost* dethroned the defending champs. Instead, Grant Hill found Christian Laettner, and the Blue Devils sent Pitino back to the recruiting trail.

THE UNTOUCHABLES

Pitino has long been an excellent recruiter. There is no better example of his ability to piece together a nearly unbeatable group than in the mid-1990s when he built the Untouchables.

It began in 1995 with seven future pros. Kentucky was still a year away from pure domination, and the initial run ended against UNC with a trip to the Final Four on the line. Jerry Stackhouse (eighteen points, twelve boards) and '93 champ Donald Williams (eighteen points) manhandled the young 'Cats. It was a defeat they would hear and think about often.

That fall, Pitino picked up a couple more soon-to-be NBA performers for—yes, your math is accurate—*nine* future pros. Kentucky's toughest opponent was, well, itself.

"Man, it was brutal," says Derek Anderson, a junior on the 1996 team. "We would take naps before practice because we knew how hard it was. I got out of class at 12:50. I'd get back to the dorm, and it would be as quiet as a mouse.

"We were fighting for minutes," Anderson explains.

A junior transfer from Ohio State, he was battling Ron Mercer. Starting point guard Tony Delk faced Jeff Shepard and Wayne Turner, who all tussled for playing time. Senior Mark Pope (currently UK head coach) would get challenges from freshman Nazr Mohammed. And Antoine Walker would mix it up in the paint with Walter McCarty.

That makes nine. Really, ten future pros were on the practice floor.

Scott Padgett was a peripheral member of the 1996 Untouchables. The future all-league selection, who spent eight years in the pros, was academically ineligible but still able to participate.

"We practiced hard," Anderson continues. "From start to finish, guys are diving for loose balls, and this was like the first ten minutes of practice, so imagine what the next hour and a half is like.

"Every day was like a job interview. You had to earn it."

Coach P, as his players referred to him, was at the center of it. Individual time, then team drills, "going a hundred miles an hour," according to Anderson.

The Wildcats began the year, reasonably, as the preseason overall number one. After an early loss to Marcus Camby-led UMass, the Untouchables racked up twenty-seven consecutive wins before a loss to Mississippi State in the SEC tournament finale. That Bulldog team was no slouch, and weeks later, they advanced to the Final Four, where Kentucky was waiting.

The Untouchables burned through their first four tournament games—beating San Jose State by 38, Virginia Tech by 24, Utah by 31, and a Tim Duncan-anchored Wake Forest by a measly 20.

In the Final Four, the Wildcats exacted retribution against the Minutemen (and John Calipari), with an 81–74 win, their narrowest margin of victory in three months.

The finale against Syracuse was somewhat competitive. Jim Boeheim's bunch initially rattled UK's inside attack with its 2–3 zone. Pitino and company pivoted outside of the paint, attempting twenty-seven threes on the night (a lot back then), draining twelve of them.

Anderson (eleven points, three steals) and his defensive mates forced twenty-four turnovers by the Orangemen to claim the school's sixth national crown with a 76–67 triumph.

"I think we're national champions because of the North Carolina game," Pitino told the *Lexington Herald Leader*, referencing the '95 regional final loss. "I brought that game up to the team five hundred times."

The ten future pros didn't hurt either.

The quasi-dynasty continued in 1997.

Despite Antoine Walker, Tony Delk, and Walter McCarty all departing in the first round of the NBA draft, as well as Mark Pope in the second, Pitino was left with another ridiculously good squad that picked up right where it had left off the previous spring, by wreaking havoc on just about everyone.

After losing their opener, in overtime, to Clemson, Kentucky throttled Syracuse by thirty-four in a rematch—that was anything but—before it proceeded to run off fourteen straight wins.

Firmly positioned at third in the polls, Kentucky rolled Auburn at home on January 18. But Anderson, now a senior and the team's second-leading scorer (seventeen ppg) behind Mercer, suffered a devastating injury, tearing his ACL.

If he hadn't, Kentucky may very well have won back-to-back-to-back national championships.

Stick with us for a moment.

In 1997, the loaded 'Cats went to the title game, where they lost to Arizona, 84–79, in overtime.

In 1998, Kentucky—now coached by Tubby Smith, following Pitino's departure to the Boston Celtics—went 35–4, and Scott Padgett (academically eligible!) scored a game-high seventeen to cap off a fourteen-game winning streak and a victory over Utah in the national title game.

That's two banners in three years.

Now back to '97: What if Anderson had been healthy? Well, what if we told you that he was?

"I had been cleared," begins Anderson, who was as much the heart and soul of the '97 team as any other name on the roster. Anderson says surgeons used a piece of tendon from a cadaver, which speeded up the healing process.

"I just rehab, rehab, rehab. Then we got to the Final Four and the doctors said, 'Hey, he's fine.'

"So, I went to practice. He practiced me full-bore, for like an hour and a half. And I really went full-steam—I was knocking over people, shooting well, driving. Everybody was so excited."

An assistant signaled to Anderson to be patient. Then Pitino refused to play one of his best players in the Final Four.

"I understood what he did," notes Anderson. "He said he wanted me to have an NBA career."

The coach and player never discussed the decision. Anderson's reaction to Pitino's choice is paradoxical.

"I won't question it. I never have, but to this day, I wish I played. I don't care how much money—I would have traded that championship for whatever the future held."

Anderson says he thinks about three in a row every time he goes to Lexington.

His amazing story is about much more than a knee, though.

Born in 1973, his dad walked out when he was ten. His mom, an alcoholic, left him two years later, after which he lived on his own until he was fifteen and cut grass to make money. Fifteen is also when Anderson became a father to Derek Jr.

That little boy was seven when he first met Rick Pitino. And it's only natural to wonder how much the future Anderson, and an opportunity to break a cycle, factored into the coach's decision to hold him out of a game.

COACH CAL

After Rupp, no Kentucky coach won more games, went to more Final Fours, or had anywhere near as many first-round draft picks as did John Calipari.

Coach Cal had more NBA first round selections in 2010 (five) than Rupp had in his four decades at the helm. Calipari had two other individual seasons—2012 and 2014—in which four players were chosen in the first round, exactly as many as Rupp had—total—in forty-two years.

OK, sure, so the NBA wasn't founded until 1947, seventeen years after Rupp's arrival. Still, the steady production line of professional talent from 2009 to 2022 in Lexington demonstrated a never-before-seen efficiency in the sport.

To put a finer point on it, Calipari's selections in those mere fourteen seasons started to close in on the total allotment of first-round picks Mike Krzyzewski had across his entire career at Duke (forty-two).

When Calipari arrived from Memphis in 2009, the money was monumental and the expectations gargantuan, and, for a while, Cal lived up to it all.

His first season ended in the regional final when a loaded roster that included DeMarcus Cousins and John Wall was ousted by West Virginia. Wall would emerge as the top overall draft pick, but Cousins considered sticking around.

At their end-of-the-year meeting, Cousins got some frank advice from his head coach:

"The conversation lasted about three minutes," Cousins later told Kevin Garnett on the *KG Certified* podcast.

"He [Calipari] said, 'If you want to take care of your family, you're going to leave. If you want to take care of my family, you're going to stay.'"

Coach Cal went to four Final Fours in his first six years and won a national championship in 2012—Kentucky's eighth and Calipari's first. There was a 38–0 start to the 2015 season that ended at the hands of Wisconsin in the NCAA semifinal.

After all that smashing success, Calipari and Kentucky incurred a decrescendo, much like what went down in the last couple of years of Tubby Smith's ten-year tenure.

During the first eight of those ten, Smith won the 1998 title, along with three trips to the Elite Eight and a pair of Sweet Sixteens. But his last two campaigns in Lexington consisted of two second-round NCAA losses and mediocre in-conference results.

Multiple factors were at work in Cal's case: an improved conference, the churn of one-and-done stars getting outmuscled and outsmarted by more experienced collegians, and a delay in adjusting to some staples of the modern game.

After that 38–0 start in 2015, Calipari's teams proceeded to go 10–7 in the Dance across the next decade. For five years, Kentucky failed to get out of the first weekend and had memorable losses to St. Peter's and Oakland.

Ultimately, things ran their course. In April 2024, Calipari departed for a fresh start—and the major NIL resources—of Arkansas.

Big Blue Nation had effectively run off another coach. Maybe it doesn't happen if Kentucky runs the table in 2015. Or if Cal manages another, more recent, Final Four.

Still, an acrimonious departure—at least on some level—seemed inevitable. After all, it's what had happened with just about every one of Cal's predecessors.

Or perhaps better described: every Rupp successor.

If all this sounds familiar, as in, say, all the coaches who succeeded John Wooden and Bobby Knight, that's because this sort of thing has happened before in other college basketball hotspots.

Calipari wasn't the first coach in Lexington to fall out of favor with the rabid fan base. And it's unlikely that he will be the last.

An overarching question surrounding the future of Kentucky basketball presents a question of when—not if—the 'Cats will one day win a ninth national championship. And when they do, just how much grace, deference, and patience will those Wildcats fans muster?

The nation of Big Blue has no time for disappointment.

CHAPTER 6

University of North Carolina

The University of the People

NCAA Titles (6)—1957, 1982, 1993, 2005, 2009, 2017
Final Fours (21)—1946, 1957, 1967, 1968, 1969, 1972, 1977, 1981, 1982, 1991, 1993, 1995, 1997, 1998, 2000, 2005, 2008, 2009, 2016, 2017, 2022
Elite Eights—29
NCAA tournament appearances—53
Conference regular season titles—42
Conference tournament championships—26

SITUATED ROUGHLY HALFWAY BETWEEN WASHINGTON, D.C., AND Atlanta, on the fringe of the Deep South, squarely within the Bible Belt, and on top of fertile soil and red clay, sits one of the most quintessential, bucolic, and picturesque college towns in America: Chapel Hill.

The University of North Carolina at Chapel Hill is the oldest public university in the country. It has been called the crown jewel of the UNC system, a public ivy, and the most important institution in what is today the nation's ninth-largest state.

Founded in 1789, the campus is dotted with centuries-old poplars, pines, and post oaks. UNC produced a president—James K. Polk, America's eleventh. An eight-foot bronze statue honoring the North Carolina native looms inside the Morehead Planetarium. That planetarium served as a training ground for Neil Armstrong, Buzz Aldrin, and most every NASA astronaut from 1959 until 1975.

Yet for all the accolades, postcard vignettes lurking around eighteenth-century buildings, *U.S. News and World Report* rankings, graduate turned inhabitant of the White House, or even connections to those who walked on the moon, Chapel Hill is best known for something else:

The basketball team.

> I'm the luckiest guy in the world and I've said that. To be in Chapel Hill. To be at the University of North Carolina. I arrived in August of '58. Thanks to Frank McGuire—a great friend—I was able to come. Thanks to my players, I was able to stay. They didn't fire me. What loyalty I've had.—Dean Smith, at his retirement press conference, October 9, 1997

North Carolina has played for the national championship in nine straight decades. No other school boasts a tally beyond six.

The last time UNC posted back-to-back losing seasons, Harry Truman occupied the White House. Carolina has more Final Fours than any other school, the most NCAA tournament wins of any program, and—much to the chagrin of most every fan visiting the Dean E. Smith Center—more banners than, well, anybody.

Precisely 143 banners are hanging from the Smith Center rafters. That figure is greater than the number of *seasons*—114—in Carolina basketball history.

Seven massive symbols of excellence hang high behind one hoop—each representing a national championship. Twenty-one banners honor the Final Four teams, along with a seemingly endless collection of ACC regular season and ACC tournament markers. And then, opposite the title flags, dangle the fifty-three retired and honored jerseys. For the innumerable legends who made it all happen. From Lennie Rosenbluth to Tyler Hansbrough.

"The University of national champions," offers Bobby Frasor, a UNC graduate and a 2009 National title winner himself.

"There's just a lot of different unique things that make Carolina stand out. It's an amazing, beautiful campus. On the basketball side—the banners, the tradition, the history with Michael Jordan—the greatest player of all time; the Jumpman logo. It's a place that people are passionate and prideful about, and rightfully so."

It's also a place that boasts a deep familial construct that runs back generations.

More on that later.

Carolina Rising

For many children who grew up in the Old North State, Carolina basketball resembles something of a higher power. Perhaps it is all that heavenly blue. Or the way in which fans pilgrimage to Chapel Hill every winter. Then again, one might not really need to look any further than the fatherly figure who guided the program for thirty-six years, Dean Smith.

"You have to understand, Carolina was bigger than God," David Lewis reflected in his office at the North Carolina General Assembly in 2019. Lewis, then a powerful Republican in the North Carolina House, hailed from rural Harnett County, about seventy miles southeast of Chapel Hill. Born in 1971, his youth coincided with one of the greatest stretches ever produced by one of the greatest programs.

From Phil Ford to James Worthy, to three-time All-American Sam Perkins, to Mike Jordan. By the time Lewis was heading to middle school, Carolina had won a national championship, played in the Monday night finale two other times, and was well into a streak of consecutive Sweet Sixteen appearances that would extend across thirteen years, culminating with another banner season in 1993.

If you've pegged Lewis as some fanatic, turned UNC graduate, who today wears the part-time ambassador polo for the school he grew up idolizing, try again.

These days, David Lewis is an NC State fan.

As for the Wolfpack—one of only fifteen programs with multiple NCAA tournament titles—NC State is no schlub. It's just a far cry from its nearby neighbors to the west, adorned in blue. Although, that hasn't always been the case.

The painful irony, which is not lost on Lewis or many other well-read and sometimes wrinkled basketball fans in the state of North Carolina, is the fact that long ago, before Dean and Mike and Lenny, there was a period during which Carolina (as in UNC) was running second in the state, without answers for its nearby foe, hoping to one day surpass its counterpart from Raleigh.

Indeed, the Wolfpack, well prior to its two national championship banners, was the marquee basketball program in North Carolina. The mightiest on Tobacco Road.

Now briefly, we must salute the 1924 edition of Carolina hoops, a roster that ran the table with a 26–0 mark. Long before the days of shot clocks, televisions, or plane travel, not to mention a three-point arc, those Tar Heels beat such dignitaries as the Charlotte YMCA and the Durham Elks. To be fair, UNC also beat Kentucky during the Southern Conference tournament, in what was the first-ever match-up between the two blue-blood schools. During this decade, Carolina played its home games in a structure called the Tin Can, which aptly provided all sorts of heating challenges. But with all due respect to the '24 squad, we have a lot more to get to.

OVERCOMING THY NEIGHBOR

To best understand how Carolina eventually came to be the basketball powerhouse it is today, one must appreciate the in-state rival that came, conquered, and menaced UNC; a nemesis that first established a bar of basketball excellence in North Carolina.

During the first half of the twentieth century, Carolina played its home games in Woollen Gymnasium, which capped out at about six thousand spectators. It was hardly a standing-room-only kind of joint, and the Tar Heels found limited success as they were nowhere near as consistent or dominant as the iterations of rosters in the decades since.

Although it is worth noting that Carolina—playing under future Hall of Fame inductee Ben Carnevale—did go 30–5 in the 1946 season when it lost in the national championship game to a Henry Iba-coached Oklahoma A&M team, 43–40.

It was the first tournament played after the conclusion of World War II, and in the subsequent summer of settling tumult, several notable basketball dominoes would fall.

Carnevale's stint in Chapel Hill was short—just two seasons—which resulted in the near natty and an overall mark of 52–11.

Born in 1915, in Raritan, New Jersey, Bernard Louis Carnevale graduated from Somerville High School (New Jersey) before attending New York University, where he was a member of the 1935 national championship team and a participant in the first-ever National Invitational Tournament at Madison Square Garden in 1938.

After graduating, Carnevale served as a gunnery officer in the navy where, in December 1942, he was torpedoed and spent several days in an open lifeboat before he was rescued. Carnevale was later honored with the Purple Heart. This all is prior to his time guiding the Tar Heels.

So, with this as his professional backdrop, and the yet-to-materialize pedigree of the Carolina basketball program, it is not hard to understand Carnevale's answer when the Naval Academy called with an offer in 1946. Why, of course, he would return to Annapolis to coach.

In his first season, Carnevale was named National Coach of the Year. Across twenty campaigns presiding over the midshipmen, he won 257 games opposite 160 losses, earned six postseason appearances, and became the winningest coach in school history.

Navy would trend upward while Carolina fell like a leaking submarine—bottoming out similar to a sunken U-boat off the coast of North Carolina's Outer Banks—as the Tar Heels posted—gasp!—consecutive losing seasons in the 1951 and 1952 seasons. That futility hasn't found air in the more than seventy years since.

At the same time that Carnevale was departing the national runner-up Tar Heels for more familiar footing in Maryland in the spring of 1946, another coach was departing the navy, heading south, to North Carolina.

Except, Everett Case wasn't going to North Carolina. He was going to the state of North Carolina, or maybe described more accurately—North Carolina State.

"Carolina beat State fifteen consecutive times," Lou Pucillo ('59) told the ACC Network more than half a century later, "so the administration launched a national search for a basketball coach."

When he arrived at NC State, Case was in his mid forties and already boasted a résumé that would make plenty of coaches envious.

Two years after graduating from the University of Wisconsin, Case claimed the first of what would be four Indiana State championships at Frankfurt High School. In a wonderful gift from the basketball gods that foreshadowed later successes, Case had multiple clashes with a young opponent. That opponent, first as a player, helped end one tournament run for Frankfurt. Later, Case got some retribution against that gentleman, by then a coach, in the state quarterfinals.

The gentleman in question was John Wooden.

Case amassed 726 wins at Frankfurt—a town barely an hour north of Indianapolis, with a population just over twelve thousand.

After the Japanese bombed Pearl Harbor, Case enlisted in the navy in 1941, at the age of forty-one, and was commissioned as a senior-grade lieutenant.

When the war ceased, Case was ready to coach again full-time. And in 1946 he landed in Raleigh, at North Carolina State University, then a member of the Southern Conference.

During Case's first decade in North Carolina's capital city, he elevated NC State to nationally elite status. Each of his first ten teams won a minimum of twenty-four games, and across ten years posted an aggregate mark of 265–60.

In year one under Case, the Pack made the NIT semifinal, and in season four a trip to the Final Four, where his team fell to eventual champ CCNY. Beyond the regular and postseason success, the program began to have an impact that extended beyond line scores in a newspaper.

"Was he a great coach?" Bucky Waters, who played for Case in the 1950s, asks rhetorically.

"Well, that depends on how you define coaching. Did he call time-outs and come up with a miraculous play at a critical time? No. He hired a coalition—Vic Bubas [the future coach at Duke] and other guys, and he let them do their job."

The legend of Coach Case includes introducing his players to the tradition of cutting down the nets after championship wins; and, introducing the players themselves—literally—with a spotlight, in front of a packed, smoky arena.

"Everything was about promotion," recalls Waters. "He could have been in Hollywood. You got so many promotional things; it was like going to a Broadway show."

As for the home venue, it became almost as central a program asset as the coach himself. In addition to claiming on-court superiority over nearby Carolina, Case helped to usher in an advantage in facilities.

Carolina called Woollen Gymnasium home. Duke opened Cameron Indoor Stadium—today the mecca, or co-mecca (along with Allen Fieldhouse) of college basketball. And in 1942, NC State broke ground on a new gym, but wartime delays (actually, a work stoppage) followed. The delay proved fruitful.

"It was part-way up. It was going to be identical to the Palestra with about eight thousand seats. The iron was already down. And Case said you got to make it bigger," Waters says.

Coach Case successfully persuaded university leaders to increase the seating capacity of the building.

When the 12,400-seat Reynolds Coliseum finally opened in 1949, it was the largest arena in the Southeast. The Atlantic Coast Conference was founded four years later, and the beautiful new venue was selected to host the first ACC tournament, which NC State won.

Reynolds hosted the next twelve conference spectacles. Case went on to win 73 percent of his games during an eighteen-year tenure and to this day outpaces every other coach in NC State history by more than one hundred victories.

UNC was simply not the preeminent program in the state. School leaders were displeased when Case rattled off fifteen consecutive wins against UNC during a six-year run.

But in the mid-1950s, that all began to change.

Enter Frank McGuire, head coach of the St. John's Redmen. These days it may not be hard to imagine a sideline sergeant leaving Queens for a promotion in Chapel Hill. However, back in 1952, this scenario bordered on preposterous.

Just consider McGuire's path.

He was a New York City native and 1936 St. John's graduate. After a brief professional basketball career and a stop in the navy—consistent with the narrative of many coaches during this time—McGuire landed back with the Johnnies, er, Redmen.

His teams twice finished third in the NIT, before hometown crowds at Madison Square Garden. Then, McGuire made it all the way to the 1952 national championship game.

There, St. John's was outmatched, succumbing to Clyde Lovellette and Phog Allen-coached Kansas, 80–63.

"After the gun went off, everybody mobbed the Kansas players and there we were—me and the basketball players," McGuire told the *New York Times*.

"We were second in the United States. But we might as well have been fiftieth. It was a lesson."

Indeed, it was. Finishing second is no prize.

But McGuire would return to the final a few years later with another team, and this time he'd be a winner.

Impressed with the job that McGuire had done in Queens, Carolina hired him after the '52 season. UNC was looking for an ascending coach who could match up with the legend of Everett Case.

UNC did just barely OK in its first three winters under McGuire—38–31 overall—and NC State retained the upper hand. After the ACC was formed in 1953, State won the first three league tournaments.

At home, of course.

But by year four, the basketball winds were shifting like a late afternoon breeze in the Appalachian Mountains.

Years earlier, Case had passed on a tall, gangly recruit from New York City. McGuire didn't make the same mistake. And Lenny Rosenbluth emerged as the first certifiable legend in Carolina history.

After NC State passed on recruiting Lenny Rosenbluth, the New York City native became a legend in Chapel Hill, leading the 1957 Tar Heels to a 32–0 record and the 1957 National Championship.

Rosenbluth was among the first in a long line of New York City talents who landed in the Old Confederacy. Known initially as McGuire's New York City to Chapel Hill "underground railroad," the pipeline still exists today and has included—among *many* others—Billy "The Kid" Cunningham, Charlie Scott, and Kenny Smith.

After sitting out his freshman year, as was mandated at that time, Rosenbluth earned Third-Team All-America honors as a sophomore, averaging twenty-five points and eleven rebounds per outing.

Nevertheless, Carolina struggled and finished only 10–11 in 1955. As a junior, the six-foot-five Rosenbluth offered similar production on a much-improved team. Carolina went 18–5 and sputtered out in the ACC tournament semifinal.

In Rosenbluth's senior year of 1957, he and a fine supporting cast led by Tommy Kearns, Pete Brennan, and Joe Quigg really started winning.

And as it turned out, they never stopped. Carolina beat everyone in 1957. They made their first Final Four in eleven years—and the only one under McGuire.

In the semis, Carolina beat Michigan State, 74–70, thanks to a game-high thirty-one points from Rosenbluth, who managed to hit twelve of his *forty-three* shots. Two nights later UNC somehow topped a Wilt Chamberlain-led Kansas squad in triple overtime, 54–53, in one of the greatest college basketball games ever.

Rosenbluth (twenty points on an improved eight-for-fifteen shooting) was one of the five starters—all of whom had arrived on McGuire's train from New York City.

"Basketball didn't really start taking off in North Carolina until Carolina won in '57," explains Barry Jacobs, a longtime writer at *The News & Observer* who covered the ACC for decades.

"It's when kids started playing in the yard. Started playing basketball. That was when the ACC as we know it started, and other teams hired coaches to compete with Frank McGuire."

Although some children, such as the former state representative Lewis, pivoted away from Carolina and *all* its successes, most younger fans—some of whom inherited Carolina in the gene pool—stayed put.

Plenty more pass the Tar Heel DNA on to their next of kin. Others are unsurprisingly intoxicated by the national branding. All the winning makes climbing aboard the bandwagon an easy exercise.

General widespread reverence, though certainly not uniform, extends across the 503-mile state to Carolinians past, present, and future. At times, it's an overwhelming presence of a fan base. It is believed that more Tar Heel fans are in Winston-Salem, home to Wake Forest University, than there are Demon Deacon graduates on the planet.

And then there's Durham, home to rival Duke. But even there, the Tar Heel fanatics outnumber the Blue Devil followers, comfortably. Carolina fans are *almost* like compound interest—a wonder of the world and hard to outpace.

Frank McGuire's tenure in Chapel Hill peaked in 1957. He spent four more years guiding the program, but those seasons were a relative disappointment. He managed only one more tournament appearance.

In 1961, it went from bad to worse when an investigation revealed that Carolina basketball players had been bribed to shave points during games.

Doug Moe, who arrived a year after the triple-overtime win against Kansas, and would later become a two-time All-American, took a bribe.

UNC-Chapel Hill chancellor Charles Aycock suspended Moe, and McGuire stepped down as head coach.

In the on-deck circle was a glorious future.

THE DEAN'S LIST

Chancellor Aycock could have cast a wide net, sought the Next Big Thing from the Big Apple, or pursued another head coach from, well, anywhere really, as he navigated the aftermath of the bribery scandal. Instead, he opted for a closer connection, hoping for some stability.

He made the right choice.

Dean Smith was an assistant for UNC beginning in 1958. Prior to that, he was best known as a *Jayhawk*. Born on the last day of February in 1931, Dean Edwards Smith was raised by two public school teachers in Emporia, Kansas. He played for Phog Allen and was a member of the KU 1952 title team—the one that beat St. John's and Frank McGuire.

After a stint on Allen's bench, Smith was onboard as an assistant at Air Force for a couple of years. That's where he was when UNC beat his alma mater—in that '57 triple-OT game—and when future boss McGuire asked for a celebratory restaurant recommendation, a perturbed Smith suggested McGuire check out the most expensive restaurant in Kansas City.

At that point, McGuire already had respect for the young coach, and shortly after consuming the overpriced short ribs, added him to the Carolina staff. In the years that followed, the two men grew closer.

From the outside, the Carolina basketball program has a religious-like quality. From the inside, the social fabric is that of a family.

In 1961, the thirty-year-old Smith was installed as the McGuire replacement with a simple edict from the chancellor who was left cleaning up a mess:

Don't worry about wins and losses, just run a clean program.

Smith did both.

"If he were alive, he'd never take credit for it, but it all starts at the top and all started with Coach Smith," says Scott Cherry, a reserve on Smith's second national championship team in 1993.

Dean Smith became the patriarch of Carolina—and just maybe the most important figure in the history of college basketball. Smith won 879 games across thirty-six seasons—breaking the then record for wins previously held by Adolph Rupp.

He won two titles, went to eleven Final Fours, had twenty-five first-round NBA draft picks, and graduated 96 percent of his players. He oversaw twenty-seven consecutive twenty-win seasons, his teams made every Sweet Sixteen in the 1980s, and in the final thirty-one years of his reign Carolina never finished worse than third in the mighty ACC.

Whew!

Now, all that quantitative undeniably puts him in the conversation with Rupp, Wooden, Bobby Knight, and Mike Krzyzewski. The qualitative is what puts him in a class of his own.

Smith gave us the fist bump, the point (to the assisting player), the four corners, the integration of the Carolina Athletic Department, and the conscientious positions as civil rights advocate.

There was his endless humility and a coaching tree that extends like a live oak. Prominent branches include the only man to win both a national championship and an NBA title (Larry Brown) and a coach who surpassed Smith in national championships and career wins (Roy Williams, with 3 and 903, respectively).

Maybe more than anything, it was Smith who constructed the Carolina family.

"I would argue that he was, and is, the GOAT," adds Jacobs, the sportswriter who, for whatever it's worth, went to Duke.

"I think he was way more innovative in how he utilized or manipulated things. He was methodical and calculated. He once had Bill Guthridge go to the ACC office, when there was a coin toss to see the order of seeds in the ACC tournament, to make sure that it was done properly. He took nothing for granted."

Wayne Norman, UConn's longtime radio guy, recalls interviewing Smith before a game in Carolina. Smith had allotted Norman four minutes to complete the interview.

With precisely a single second left on the clock, Smith, without having looked once at a timepiece during the entire interview, simply got out of his seat without saying a word and walked away.

"I'd never seen anything like it," says Norman. "To have that level of control over his time. This was a gift, time management at its absolute finest."

Smith built the family through traditions, big and small. He would begin each practice with a thought of the day. They had to be memorized. Quotes and lessons. Grammar and history. Hundreds of lessons across his time.

"Coach Smith was a tremendous person," Cherry says. "The lessons of humility were so important, because when you're at a place like that—you're kind of put on a pedestal. You walk down the street, and you can very easily become very intoxicated with all the attention. He wanted you to value what you were being given."

Smith was a principled competitor who sincerely viewed his role as part coach and part educator. His central tenets included valuing other people, and he wanted the philosophy emulated in perpetuity.

"Coach Smith, when I played here, never let us look at the stat sheet," 1991 UNC graduate Hubert Davis recalls, sitting at his desk inside the building named for his former coach, in 2023.

"He believed in focusing on the preparation and the process. And at the end of the day, the play will take care of itself. I really believe that if we prepare and we practice up to our capabilities, I think the play will take care of itself. And at the end of the year, we'll be happy with what we've achieved."

Carolina didn't achieve much during Smith's first five years overseeing the program. No postseason berths, conference titles, or twenty-win seasons. Smith was even hanged in effigy after a blowout loss at Wake Forest. Smith would later write, "I could tell it was me because of its long nose."

Dean Smith turned the corner in year six. Led by Larry Miller, the ACC Player of the Year, Carolina went 12–2 in league play to win the conference for the first time in a decade. Smith and Miller clipped the nets at the conference tournament and then advanced to the first of Smith's eleven Final Four appearances.

Charlie Scott, a rising sophomore, gained eligibility that fall.

"He's one of the great, underappreciated players in ACC history," Barry Jacobs surmises. "Partially because of the way he played—pardon the expression—above the rim.

"He just could do everything. And he was an incredible clutch player. He was just a galvanizing player, and he's one of the few of that group that could not only play around the rim, but he could shoot from distance."

In that sixth season, 1968, Scott teamed up with Miller to claim the conference title at 12–2, win the ACC tournament, and move on to the Final Four. That's *three* Smith Center banners for those of you scoring at home.

The season ended in defeat when UCLA pulverized the Heels, 78–55, in the finale for their second of seven straight titles.

And although UNC might have failed to get yet another banner out of that campaign, 1968 was about more than basketball. You see, it was again the qualitative as much as the quantitative.

Charlie Scott had broken the color barrier in the South.

"On my official recruiting visit to Chapel Hill, coach took me to his church to worship," Scott wrote in Dean Smith's 2004 book, *The Carolina Way.*

"It might not sound like a big deal today, but in the mid-1960s not many white men were taking African Americans to church with them in the south. I visited many schools including Duke, NC State and Davidson, and Coach Smith was the only coach who asked me to go to church with him."

Coach Smith and Scott would later dine together, a symbolic—if not still uncomfortable table setting for many to view—in transitioning away from the segregated, Jim Crow South.

Then there were the road trips, about which Scott was unsurprisingly apprehensive.

"It was usually quite an adventure, let's put it that way," he reflected.

Yet, like so many other facets of the program, it was the preparation, consistency, and fundamental respect that ushered Scott into a place of comfortability and historical significance.

"When we went into hostile environments to play," Scott wrote, "Coach Smith helped me greatly by treating me like everyone else on our team. If he had singled me out and prepared me in a special way, it would have stayed on my mind all the time.

"Respect is a very big thing with coach. He taught us to respect every opponent and never sell anyone short."

Charles Scott—Coach Smith didn't refer to him as Charlie—did for Smith and Carolina what most other schools scattered across the South had continuously failed to do: integrate. Everett Case had evidently wanted to do so but faced internal pressures. Ditto for Bones McKinney at Wake Forest.

For good measure, Scott was also a member of the 1968 gold medal-winning Olympic basketball team, an American teammate of John Carlos and Tommy Smith, in a summer of change.

In the late 1960s, Miller and Scott, along with Bill Bunting, Dick Grubar, and Eddie Fogler, won three straight ACC titles, arrived at the Final Four three years in a row, and elevated Smith and the Carolina program to a newfound level of success from which they have never looked back.

Scott thrust open a door that had been prejudicially bolted down and in doing so began to normalize a long-overdue acceptance. He allowed young black boys to see themselves on Carolina's basketball team. Among those taking stock of the new-look Tar Heels was a rising high-school star in the small suburban Charlotte town of Pineville, situated on the South Carolina border.

Without Charlie Scott, the Tar Heels might not have welcomed Walter Davis. That would have meant no fan favorite from the 1970s, no miraculous shot against Duke in the 1974 regular season finale. And without Uncle Walter, it is objectively unclear who would be coaching the Tar Heels today.

We'll get to his nephew a little later.

Also, please excuse—or at least try—the brevity with which we must chart through *all* these Carolina legends.

The youngest of thirteen children, Walter Davis arrived on campus in the fall of 1973. Beloved by the crowds and known by the simple moniker "Sweet D," Davis linked up with Phil Ford to help North Carolina sustain a place among the upper echelon of vaunted programs.

He was selected as an All-American, an All-ACC performer, and played for Smith at the 1976 Olympics when the United States rebounded from the travesty of '72 to win a gold medal. Phil Ford was on that Montreal Olympic team. So, too, were Carolina teammates Mitch Kupchak and Tommy LaGarde.

The most legendary moment in the career of Walter Davis came on March 2, 1974. Carolina's regular-season slate concluded with a home date against Duke. Down eight points with seventeen seconds remaining, it was a done deal.

Until it wasn't.

First a score. Down six. Then a steal and score, another defensive swipe and bucket followed. The eight-point lead was cut to two. Carolina then fouled, and Duke went to the line for a one-and-one with a chance to put it away. (Remember, no three-point line for another decade.) But

Duke clanged the freebie, and after Coach Smith called a time-out, but three seconds lingered in a very, very quiet Carmichael Auditorium.

Kupchak, who went on to win three NBA championships with the Lakers before blossoming into a stout NBA executive—a career stop that produced another seven rings—was the inbounder. Duke dropped off the freshman (now eligible) from Pineville, so Kupchak flipped Davis the rock, Sweet D took three quick bounces and let it fly. The release looked more like that of a shot put than a basketball. Regardless, it caromed off the backboard and in.

The roar of the surprised, hysterical crowd—some of whom had departed when Carolina trailed by eight with less than twenty seconds remaining—echoes half a century later. The cheers can easily be heard on YouTube, and with a little more searching, there may just be crevices in the aging Carmichael gym where the heroics of Walter Davis resonate like roaring waves inside a seashell.

Freshman Walter Davis tied the game. UNC won in overtime, 96–92.

The legacy of Davis is alive and well within the Carolina program through another Davis.

"I'm here today because of Uncle Walt," says nephew Hubert, hired to lead the program in 2021. "You know, when I was four years old, I came up here to watch him play. And that was a birth of, for me, where I wanted to go to school and where I wanted to be. And I didn't want to be Uncle Walt. But I wanted to be where he was and what he experienced. And I wanted to go to school here. I wanted to play here for Coach Smith and Coach Guthridge. I wanted to put on that uniform, play in front of that crowd, and play on that floor.

"I wanted to experience what my uncle experienced," continues Hubert, "and you know, the things that I've experienced today as a result of being a part of this program, and this university, is because of my uncle."

Dave Colescott saw the regulation-tying buzzer-beating southern prayer that Davis drained in 1974. He looked up to Sweet D. An Indiana high-school star, the son of a legendary high-school coach, Colescott was named Indiana's Mr. Basketball in 1976 and was a stellar baseball player as well.

For a time, Colescott considered a two-sport college path. Bob Knight recruited him, but Purdue was—for a while—his dream school. Then, Colescott paid a visit to Walter Davis and his Tar Heel teammates.

The recruiting trip took place in 1975, and the prospect didn't see much of the iconic coach, then in his mid forties, beyond a pickup from the airport.

"He said, 'There's two things that I will promise you. Number one, we will be loyal to our returning lettermen first. And number two, the players will vote on you,'" Colescott remembers.

"'After the weekend they will meet with us, and if they don't feel like you're a good fit, we will respectfully not offer you a scholarship.'

"I thought that was real cool."

Colescott was enamored with the reasonably sized campus and his future teammates. He was all in. A four-year letterman and member of the 1977 runner-up team (Marquette), Colescott overcame injuries, backed up Phil Ford, and never materialized as an elite college player, before having a cup of coffee in the NBA.

His position on the hierarchy or the pecking order was irrelevant, because at Carolina, the coach did what he could do to diminish, if not eliminate, it.

Upperclassmen were given deference and agency; freshmen carried the bags and waited their turn. Even number 23 hauled duffle bags, although he did start. Everyone wore a shirt and tie when traveling—commercially in those days.

"Coach Smith always wanted a sense of family," Colescott explains. "When we traveled, he always wanted us to eat one meal, wherever we were, together as family. We'd go to New York, he would pick out a restaurant, and we have our pregame meal there."

Across the 1970s the Carolina family grew, with more graduating classes, additional fans, and dinners. Many, many dinners. What was also expanding, in conversation, during this period was a simple query:

Can Dean win the big one?

The Big One in the Big Easy

In 1968, Carolina lost in the title game to a superior UCLA. Nine years later Al McGuire prevented pandemonium on Franklin Street. And in 1981, it was Coach Knight, armed with a ferocious little point guard from the West Side of Chicago named Isiah Thomas, who clipped the nylon.

Smith was zero-for-three in the Big One, and the noise from his critics was increasing.

As you already know, the narrative was upended on a March night in New Orleans, 1982. It was arguably the most talented roster of all the Tar Heel teams that ever took the floor. It was led by junior All-American James Worthy and three-time All-American Sam Perkins. Roy Williams was an assistant on that team.

This time, Georgetown—coached by Big John Thompson, and featuring All-American Eric "Sleepy" Floyd and freshman Patrick Ewing—stood in Smith's way.

Seventeen million people watched the Monday night affair, which proved to be a back-and-forth drama toward the finish line. After Floyd vaulted the Hoyas to a 62–61 advantage, Smith called a time-out and, recognizing that Georgetown would target Worthy, drew up a play in which the ball would skip to the corner.

The nineteen-year-old freshman from Wilmington—Michael Jeffrey Jordan—was open.

Bang.

Jordan hit the baseline jumper with fifteen seconds remaining. Georgetown's Fred Brown then—promptly and accidentally—mistook Worthy for a teammate and passed him the ball.

UNC 63, Georgetown 62.

It ended Carolina basketball's twenty-five-year championship drought and got Coach Smith off the schneid.

"I don't believe that 'winning the big one' says all there is to say about you," Smith told *Sports Illustrated* after the win in the Bayou, which came in his seventh trip to the Final Four.

"You win big ones to get to the Final Four, or even just to get into the tournament. The method we have for picking a national champion—one loss, and you're out—certainly creates a lot of interest. But you and I know that the NCAA tournament doesn't always produce the best team as its champion."

The 1924 title team played in the Tin Can. Woollen Gymnasium was home for much of the first half of the twentieth century, before Carmichael Auditorium provided home-cooking beginning in 1965.

"I love playing at Carmichael," says Jay Bilas, 1986 Duke graduate turned ESPN broadcaster. Bilas played three games in the former gym, as well as pickup games there against his rivals.

"It had a lot of elements that Cameron does. It was smaller, it was really loud, packed all the time. And you'd go to the locker room and smell the chlorine from the swimming pool," adds Bilas.

"It was a really, really cool place that had a ton of character. And you know, whether it was Carmichael or Cole Field House or Reynolds Coliseum at NC State, you know, progress. Progress comes, so you know that everybody moved to bigger arenas, but that was a great time, playing in the league in those iconic venues."

By the time Coach Smith silenced the doubters in 1982, conversations were already afoot about *the next* facility. And although it's reasonable to think that a desire for increased seating capacity and modern amenities were what led university officials to upgrade facilities, it's also natural to wonder if they just needed more room for all those banners.

A site was identified on the south side of campus. A new basketball cathedral would be erected. It would dwarf the capacity of the building Everett Case ushered in four decades earlier. And it needed a name.

Coach Smith was adamant, initially, that his name would *not* adorn the side of his team's future home. It struck him as hardly having a chord of humility. But begrudgingly—convinced in no small part by the power of his name when it came to fund-raising efforts necessary to provide all that concrete—Smith acquiesced.

The Smith Center was to open in 1985.

Well, it didn't open in 1985.

Construction delays. New Year's Day 1986 came and went. Turns out not even the patriarch of Carolina basketball can overcome the speed of construction. The grand opening was delayed, it just so happened, until Bilas and his Duke teammates made the eleven-mile trek from Durham.

"It was the first game there," Bilas recalls. "We played the first game there in the middle of January, I think it was like January 16th, 1986, something like that . . . Carolina was ranked number one, and we were ranked number three, and both teams were unbeaten. And, you know, Carolina had multiple lottery picks on their team.

"Great, great team, and we had a great team, and you know, there's no three-point shot back then. That was the last year before the three came along in college basketball, and still the score was like 95–92, or something like that."

Something like that. Don't let the casual nature of his delivery fool you.

The grand opening of the Dean E. Smith Center was January 18, 1986. Top-ranked Carolina opposite number three Duke. Both were undefeated. Among the six future NBA players on the UNC side were Kenny Smith, who would establish a new career assist mark before leaving Chapel Hill; and Brad Daugherty, another top overall pick (Cleveland, 1986).

Meanwhile, the Blue Devils had five future NBAers, in addition to Quinn Snyder, Tommy Amaker, and Jay Bilas. Coach Krzyzewski's 1986 team went all the way to the title game, where it fell to Louisville.

The final score, without a three-point line and in regulation, was indeed 95–92, as Jay Bilas remembered.

The only detail he forgot to mention explicitly was that Carolina prevailed.

The rivalry between Carolina and Duke was in full swing at this juncture of Tobacco Road history. The elder statesman and the younger, former army cadet, trying to out-prepare one another, trading quotes in the press and vying for many of the same prized recruits. Had Christian Laettner not gone to Duke, he almost assuredly would have worn a different shade of blue.

Just think about that for a moment.

The 1986 grand opening of the Smith Center is but one in a seemingly endless list of bitter clashes, occasionally blood-soaked, in which one—if not both—of the rivals was vying for a top ranking, a top seed, or the next top high-school player.

UNC and Duke had been playing for decades, sure. But it was in the 1980s, with Carolina perennially at the top of the sport and Duke seeking to join them—a proliferation of television cameras following along—when the greatest rivalry in college ball took off like a Richard Petty stock car down the homestretch.

Duke played for the title in 1986. A year later Coach K, the understudy, lost to his mentor in the Sweet Sixteen. Bob Knight and Indiana were propelled to a championship a week later when Keith Smart hit a Syracuse-crushing baseline jumper to give Knight his third—and final—ring.

For Krzyzewski, it was a momentary, if not acutely painful, setback. Beginning in the autumn of 1987, Duke would commence a streak of five consecutive Final Fours, culminating in two national championships, a sustained five-year plan of winning that no one—not even Coach Smith—had put together since the Wizard of Westwood.

Which brings us to 1993.

THE TIME-OUT CHINA DIDN'T SEE

If 1982 was the star-studded ensemble of future Naismith Hall of Fame inductees that provided Smith and Carolina with their first trip to the mountaintop in a quarter century, the 1993 rendition of Carolina was something much different. To be clear, it was a collection of damn good basketball players but with a different cachet than the Worthy-Perkins-Jordan squad.

Whatever the unit eleven years later might have lacked in terms of a star-studded cast, it made up for with a deep sense of team.

"It wasn't roses all the time," explains Scott Cherry, a senior reserve on the '93 roster. "We had disagreements and fights. But to this day, we love one another. And I don't know that we realized that at the time. I don't think we were the best team in terms of talent. But we were the best team. There was no one that pouted, sulked, didn't show up, or practice hard every day. No one complained about the coaches. I've been a part of a lot of teams—and that's rare."

Cherry, who was initially choosing between Holy Cross and Fairleigh Dickinson—until a scholarship came available after J. R. Reid turned pro and Kenny Anderson committed to Georgia Tech—was as much a part of the *team* as future first-round selections George Lynch or the late Eric Montross.

Carolina won its first eight games before losing to Michigan, 79–78, in a sign of things to come. Conference play was a relative breeze, as UNC won fourteen of sixteen for another league title. The Heels were also unbeaten at home that season.

Cherry recalls team meetings during which Coach Smith "would work you through the truth, even if it was hard to hear. You didn't want to let him down—or just do something that would cause us to fail. You wanted to try to be the best you can be every day, so you were valued in what you did every day."

In the postseason, UNC narrowly lost to Georgia Tech in the conference tournament final, 77–75, and then set its sights on The Dance.

Carolina needed overtime to slip past Bob Huggins, Nick Van Exel, and Cincinnati, to qualify for another Final Four—Smith's ninth.

Once there, Carolina comfortably defeated Kansas and Smith protégé Roy Williams, avenging a loss to the Jayhawks in the national semifinal two years earlier, a defeat that also denied Carolina a chance to play Duke for a national championship. The Blue Devils claimed their first title that year.

Cherry and company held onto the missed opportunity from 1991— it left them angry. By the time the last Monday night of the '93 season rolled around, the pressure had mounted. And prior to the title game, to be played in New Orleans just like the '82 final, Smith delivered one of his aphorisms. It wasn't the first time he uttered it, or the last.

"There's a billion people in China that don't even know this game is being played," Smith said.

"Yeah, all those people in China," chuckles Cherry. "Coach said, 'They don't care who wins this game,' so the message was: don't get nervous. It's not that important."

In the locker room of the Superdome, Smith sought to recalibrate the energy. He used the reference to China during time-outs as well, a regular reminder that although basketball is big, it isn't everything.

Donald Williams boosted Carolina that night. The sophomore had the performance of his life, hitting five three-pointers and leading all players with twenty-five points. Forging the way for the Wolverines was Chris Webber, who paced the Fab Five with a magnificent-until-forgotten, eleven-for-seventeen, twenty-three-point performance.

UNC led by a point when Michigan fouled Pat Sullivan, an 80 percent free-throw shooter. The Tar Heel made the front end of a one-and-one but missed the second. Webber hauled in his eleventh rebound of the evening, and Michigan could tie or take it all. Webber promptly traveled ("Oh, he walked, and the referee missed it," Bill Packer told CBS viewers), dribbled into the frontcourt before promptly calling the most famous time-out this side of James Naismith's birth. But Michigan didn't have any time-outs remaining. The game would end with four UNC free throws and perpetual heartache in Ann Arbor.

UNC 77, Michigan 71.

Two brief '93 postscripts:

First, there is a fantastic joint in Chapel Hill on the corner of East Franklin and Henderson Streets. They serve the most delectably greasy cheeseburgers and as scrumptious a chicken biscuit as you can find nearby. It's tasty, cheap fare. It's called TimeOut. A painfully appropriate homage to Webber. The restaurant's logo is a set of hands forming a "T" for the time-out that never existed, and the walls are lined with pictures of former Carolina players and fans making the signal.

Second, the game of basketball has grown to almost every reach of the globe since the early 1990s. Carolina gave us MJ, and MJ starred on the Dream Team, and the Dream Team opened the doors to an abundance of European players in the NBA. Then Yao Ming. Then—have you figured out where this is headed yet?—popularity swept across the country with the Great Wall. Today it's only natural to wonder: Are there still a billion people in China who don't care about Carolina?

The morning after Webber's costly blunder, and Smith's second title, the bonfires had been extinguished on Franklin Street in Chapel Hill, and preparation for the *next* season, the 1994 campaign, was already well underway.

In Philadelphia, one of the nation's top high-school prospects watched the Carolina-Michigan game, went to school on Tuesday morning and then bopped into his mama's house that afternoon.

Something slipped into the corner of his eye, and he turned, slid off his headphones, and was surprised to see Dean Smith and Phil Ford sitting on the couch.

"Coach, what y'all doin' here?" Rasheed Wallace recalled asking the future Hall of Famer and his assistant during an episode of the *All the Smoke* podcast.

"Y'all supposed to be celebrating; you just won the national championship?"

Then 'Sheed shared Smith's reply.

"Oh, no, it's back to business—we let the kids celebrate. It's back to business."

"That right there showed me a lot," Wallace said.

Dean Smith was sixty-two at this point and still, clearly, had plenty in the tank. Although it's important to acknowledge that the game was changing, the money was increasing exponentially, and more than thirty years since he had taken over, the coaching-teaching dynamic was in transition.

Two years later Wallace, along with Jerry Stackhouse, helped carry Carolina to the Final Four, where they fell to the defending national champ Arkansas, 75–68.

Two months later Stackhouse and Wallace were selected third and fourth, respectively, in the NBA draft. Both would retire from the association eighteen years later.

After their departure, UNC suffered a *relative* downturn—a 21–11 season in 1996 that saw the Heels bounced by Texas Tech in the round of thirty-two. Unworthy of a banner, two freshmen by the name of Vince Carter and Antawn Jamison made significant strides that summer. In 1997, Carolina won the ACC Tournament and in doing so logged career win 875 for Smith, one away from the record established twenty-five years earlier by Adolph Rupp.

Carolina beat Fairfield in the 1–16 game of that year's tournament, although it was hardly a romp. The Stags kept it close in the second half before the Heels pulled away to help Smith pull even with Rupp.

The win came on Tobacco Road, in Winston-Salem to be precise, and set up a round of thirty-two matchup against the one and only Bob Kni--- Oh, wait, that's what the selection committee had in mind, but the actual story didn't have Smith poetically going through Bobby for the record.

No, you see, a young point guard from Denver had other visions of the bracket.

Colorado sophomore Chauncey Billups had a game-high twenty-four points as the Buffaloes disposed of the Hoosiers in the 8–9 game. Naturally, Knight verbally unloaded on his team and then walked the three miles back to the hotel with a police cruiser following shortly behind him.

On second thought, that is kind of poetic.

Smith's final team had little trouble with Billups and company two nights later, logging a 73–56 win that handed Dean the all-time win record. UNC advanced to beat California, then Louisville, before losing to eventual champ Arizona in the Final Four.

It was Smith's eleventh trip to the national semifinals. And his last.

From 1961 until his retirement in the fall of 1997, the Carolina Way was cemented under Dean Smith. From the outside, it became a quasi-religious institution. From the inside, it ostensibly became a family. With Coach Smith as the patriarch at the top, loyalty (with but a few exceptions) began to root. His impact extends across seven decades, firmly anchoring today's program.

Frank McGuire called him "the most loyal man in the world." James Worthy opined that Coach was "the greatest man he has ever known," and Michael Jordan called him a second father.

Roy Williams, who later received the torch Coach Smith carried for thirty-six years, and eventually surpassed his mentor in one revered department (national championships, with three) said the driving force that fueled his decision to return to Chapel Hill in the spring of 2003 was to simply make Coach Smith proud.

Dean Smith died on February 7, 2015. It was a Saturday.

The coach had long been a remnant of his former self—the leader so widely revered. His memory slipped away in the final years, what his family called a "progressive neurocognitive disorder," a particularly harsh illness for a man who had had such a sharp intellect and memory.

Weeks after his departure, following the public memorials, in true Coach Smith fashion, a final lesson of humility arrived in the mail.

"I almost threw it in the trash," admits Colescott (class of '80). "You know, we get all kinds of letters from the university. They want things."

This letter was different. Coach Smith had left every one of his former lettermen $200. It arrived in the form of a check, with the aim of a meal.

"I couldn't think of a better thing to do. His legacy is that he basically said, have one of our pregame meals, have a dinner out, you know, with each other."

Colescott went out with three of his former teammates—on his own dime.

"I never spent it; I have it in a case. I framed it," Colescott says of the check.

"What he wanted for all of his players, just like with the pickup games, he wanted to break bread with family. And that's what he was teaching us; he was basically giving us this gift of breaking bread with our family."

Pickup

Family dinners are a throughline for Carolina basketball, and the pickup games constitute the annual summer reunion.

From Harlem's Rucker Park to the Pacific-adjacent Venice Beach, America is home to many renowned blacktop courts, where trash talk flows, games are to eleven, win by two, and a steady stream of fivesomes await, having already declared, "We got next."

Chapel Hill has long been a premiere destination for summer runs, a stretch during which it is common for NBA All-Stars to put the young bucks in their place before offering them some tricks of the basketball trade.

The pickup runs remain part of Carolina lore to this day. Upperclassmen depart, handing the program to the once-younger recruits, only to return and remind them of a generational hierarchy.

"In the summer we always had great pickup games," Wallace said. "We had two courts going. It was always the old heads versus the young ones. It was that brotherhood that kept that going."

"We came back and beat Vince [Carter] and Antawn [Jamison], and then when they left, they would come back and beat whoever was there. It's still like that to this day."

Scott Cherry remembers a particular story about His Airness, from the summer of '90.

"He was in his prime, right there on the cusp of winning all the championships. He told you exactly what he was going to do. And then he just went and did it.

"I'll never forget a play when he went backdoor for an alley-oop. George Lynch was guarding him. George was just finishing his freshman year, and King Rice was trying to hype George up. King was not bashful in his trash talk or the way he played.

"George was doing pretty well, you know, in terms of trying to guard the best player on the planet. And then they throw Jordan an alley-oop. It was a little short, and George went up and caught it, with two hands."

Unfortunately for George Lynch, MJ was timing it all.

"Jordan jumped over him, snatched it out of his hands, and dunked it—all in the same motion."

These summer runs are known to include Blue Devils from time to time, and long ago, a former UNC linebacker.

"Lawrence Taylor is the toughest guy I ever faced in pickup," remembers Colescott.

The six-foot-three, 240-pound Taylor was an unsurprising terror on the summer court.

"I mean, you just had to be careful; he was, you know, on another level."

From Taylor and Jordan to Rasheed, Vince, Julius Peppers, Ty Lawson, Hansbrough, and a cast of more contemporary players, the games persist.

"The real benefit is when you see knowledge being passed down," says Jones Angell, play-by-play voice of the Carolina team.

"I remember watching Tyler Zeller, who was ACC Player of the Year in 2009, and played in the [NBA] for multiple years, going against Armando Bacot. There was a break, and Tyler pulls Armando over to the side, and they talk a little bit. . . . Hey, here's what you did here. Here's what you could maybe do better. Here's what I did to get the better of you. The competition is fierce.

"Nobody's given anything when they are playing. But then I think there's also that moment of, hey, let me help you and show you, using my experience."

The summer reunion runs are part of the aura of the Carolina program, and it is not unnoticed by other legends from other marquee teams.

"I'm envious of that, of how close they are, and all of the camaraderie. It's unique," says Dan Issel, a three-time All-American at *Kentucky*.

Following any legend is not easy. The man after *the* man seldom matches the previous accomplishments. To be fair, it's nearly impossible. And the result is more often an unmemorable encore than sustained success. Who replaced Bobby Knight at Indiana? Or Wooden in Westwood? Who *is* the coach who followed Jay Wright? You're likely a Tuesday trivia whiz at the local pub if you know all three answers.

Do you remember who came immediately after Dean? It *wasn't* Matt Doherty (we'll breeze through those dark days soon). It was Bill Guthridge, Smith's longtime top lieutenant. And Guthridge was simply fantastic.

In three seasons at the helm. Guthridge, who was almost as beloved, at least internally, as Smith, provided a stable, short-term succession model. In those campaigns Carolina went 80–28, 32–16 in the ACC, won the conference tournament in year one, and reached the 1998 and 2000 Final Fours.

In the first Final Four, a season in which Carolina set a school record with thirty-four wins, Utah got the best of UNC—before losing in the title game; two years later came a sort of Cinderella run (UNC was an 8-seed), which ended at the hands of soon-to-be champ Michigan State.

In June of 2000 the sixty-three-year-old Guthridge, exhausted from the endless recruiting demands, not to mention a coaching career that ran without a break for forty years, retired.

And that's when the trouble began.

There was a long, impressive, list of names, and surely one well-established Carolina graduate would return home.

Larry Brown, Eddie Fogler, George Karl, Phil Ford, Roy Williams.

No, no, no, no, and *no!*

Brown initially wanted the job but did not click with UNC Athletic Director Dick Baddour. So, he remained with the 76ers and would oversee his team in the NBA Finals less than a year later.

Fogler, only fifty-two at the time, was a former player under Smith and a fifteen-year assistant on his staff. The then-Gamecocks coach took himself out of the running, posted a second straight losing season in Columbia, South Carolina, and was out of coaching for good. Karl, happy in a lucrative NBA role that didn't require dizzying recruiting travel, passed as well. His Milwaukee Bucks lost to Brown and Philadelphia in the Eastern Conference Finals the following spring.

Phil Ford would have made a wonderful replacement. However, months earlier he was arrested for driving while under the influence, and concerns about his drinking persisted. It was not the only DUI Ford would incur.

And then there was Williams, who we should note, had replaced Brown in Lawrence twelve years earlier. The pressure of the vacancy gnawed at his core. And it wasn't anything new.

"In April 1997, Coach Smith, Coach Guthridge, Coach Fogler and I met in Fort Myers, Florida, for a two-day golf vacation," Williams wrote in his book, *Hard Work: A Life On and Off the Court.*

Smith told his disciples he was mulling retirement, and the possibility of Williams taking over came up.

"Somebody tell me what I would tell my players," Williams posed.

Williams was a Carolina man who had become a Kansas man. He passed in 1997, though he remained in close contact with Guthridge. By the spring of 2000, Guthridge told Williams he didn't think he would return. Williams writes that he tried to convince Guthridge to stick it out and return for another winter, so that he wouldn't be faced with the decision *again*.

It didn't work; and after Guthridge resigned, Williams found himself in an unenviable position. He was offered the Carolina job, returned to campus, and took an early morning walk with his wife, Wanda. She said, "How are you going to feel if you don't go to North Carolina, and they win the national championship?"

His retort: "How would I feel if I left Kansas, and they won the national championship?"

It was there on campus, by the centuries-old Davie Poplar, when Williams conceded his mind-set was changing.

"I began to think, *you're happy at Kansas. It's your program. It has your fingerprints all over it. You've been there twelve years, your whole career, and you've always admired a coach that stays at one school his entire career.*"

Beyond that, there was Nick Collison. What was he supposed to tell Collison, who he had pledged to stick around for his entire collegiate career. Never mind that Collison, a rising sophomore who had just started every game but one in his rookie campaign at Kansas, was really good. Williams had given him his word.

Williams passed, and on July 14 Matt Doherty was introduced as the next coach in Chapel Hill. He was thirty-eight years old and had precisely one season of coaching experience following a career in finance. That season bore out a 22–15 record for Notre Dame.

"He is a great choice for this program because I think he maintains the same character, quality, and integrity that has always marked Carolina. He is the right person to keep this program number one in the country," Chancellor James Moeser said at the introductory press conference.

Moeser was very much mistaken.

The Doherty years, although dotted with some success—an ACC championship in 2001, and the recruits for the next great team—were mostly a disaster. Carolina went 8–20 in 2002 and would have posted another losing season in 2003 were it not for a run to the NIT quarterfinals.

Making it all worse was what happened off the court, away from the abysmal play. Doherty was a Jekyll and Hyde leader—some days a comrade, others a tyrant. He cleared out longtime basketball staffers. And most of his players couldn't stand him.

His 23–25 mark in ACC play shouldn't ever have happened. Carolina shouldn't have dipped the way it did at the beginning of the century. As it turns out, though, without the bungled stretch of Doherty, the timing might not ever have been right for Williams.

ROY'S RETURN

Roy Williams coached Kansas for the final time on April 7, 2003. Syracuse—aided by Gerry McNamara's six first-half threes, Carmelo Anthony's game-high twenty, and Hakeem Warrick's Gumby impersonation (see block on Michael Lee in the waning seconds)—defeated Kansas, 81–78, in, where else, the Superdome. As an aside, outside the state of North Carolina, the Tar Heels have played more historic games in the Crescent City than just about anywhere else.

Ol' Roy was still without a natty.

After the game, when Bonnie Bernstein asked Williams to address the rumors about his interest in filling the coaching vacancy in Chapel Hill, he said unforgettably, "I could give a shit about Carolina."

It was the most perfectly uncomfortable moment. There's no way that Bernstein can't ask that question, and there's no way that Roy can't give that answer. Moreover, there's no way that Jayhawks fans weren't left with a nausea-inducing truth:

Roy Williams was going home.

Williams had honored his pledge to Collison. He had won 418 games throughout his fifteen years in Kansas. His teams went to four Final Fours and lost in the national title game twice. He had done everything except for you know what.

When Williams and his wife, Wanda, returned to Chapel Hill—and all those old trees—in the summer of 2003, he left the near-misses behind. What followed was an eighteen-year run unprecedented in Carolina history.

Aided by Doherty's recruiting class of Raymond Felton, Sean May, and Rashad McCants, Carolina won the league in 2005 with a 16–2 mark, went a near untouchable 33–4, and gave Williams his third chance at capturing Monday night.

Before the title game against Illinois, he told his team, in part, "Phil Ford and Michael Jordan and Dean Smith are North Carolina basketball, but if we play our butts off tonight, you'll be North Carolina basketball forever."

Freshman Marvin Williams put back an errant McCants heave with just more than a minute remaining to give UNC a lead it didn't hand back.

UNC won 75–70, and Roy Williams didn't go to sleep that night.

Shortly after Williams got his first title, he refocused on the next one. A freshman from Poplar Bluff, Missouri, arrived that summer. And he would embark on as good a college career as we've witnessed in the past thirty years.

Tyler Hansbrough became the first player to earn first-team All-ACC honors four times. He was named an All-American four times, as well, the latter three selections consensus first-team picks.

Hansbrough improved upon Ford's thirty-year school scoring mark and finished his college career with 2,872 points. Hansbrough also left as the program's all-time leading rebounder. And he never lost a game in Cameron.

Known by the faithful as "Psycho T," Hansbrough brought an intensity that carried Williams and the Heels to another storied season in '09. Coming off a Final Four campaign, UNC was bestowed a preseason number one ranking. Then, after unceremoniously dropping its first two in league play, went on to claim its third-straight ACC regular season title. Carolina went 34–4, beat every NCAA tournament opponent by double digits, and sat at the top of the mountain again.

Williams told his champion group afterward, "Fifty years from now, when they have another reunion in 2059, that night when you go out on the court, at seventy-two years old, you go out there and remember one thing, that no coach has ever felt more privileged, no coach has ever felt more proud of a team that handled things like you did. The adversity, the injuries, other people's expectations. I honestly feel like I'm the luckiest coach that has ever lived . . . I love you."

"I loved playing for him," recalls Bobby Frasor, a senior reserve on that team. "I'd say he was extremely intense, an unbelievable motivator. I think a lot of people ridicule Coach Williams and kind of knock his record just because he went from Kansas to North Carolina. And everyone says, oh, anybody can win at those places. Well, it's like, you still have to do it.

"Everybody knew what he was going to run. Everybody knew our secondary breaks. He was stubborn to a fault. But it worked."

Frasor also points out that Williams's mastery, his extended coaching prime, went well beyond diagramming inbounds plays.

"I think so many people just get bogged down in Xs and Os. He knew how to handle media, how to handle donors, how to handle recruiting, who to hire—all of it. And I think that's a very underrated value that people don't realize outside of the basketball world.

"All they do is look at wins and losses on the court. [They don't look at] what he is doing as far as running a program, his ability to walk into any room at any event and just be able to control the room.

"He was an artist at that."

The artist was far from complete with his masterpiece. Williams coached for eleven more years in Chapel Hill. The floor inside the Smith Center was named for him in 2018. He perpetually infuriated many fans with his stubborn approach to not calling time-outs when opposing teams went on big runs, but he was quickly forgiven.

There were five more ACC regular-season titles. There was a trip to the 2016 title game where, after Marcus Paige's foolish double-clutch three pointer to force overtime, Villanova rejected overtime. Kris Jenkins hit an uncontested buzzer-beating three to win the championship.

Then, a year later, there was redemption. Paige wasn't around for it, but Joel Berry, Justin Jackson, and Luke Maye—among others—were.

Carolina beat Kentucky in the Elite Eight and downed Gonzaga for the school's sixth national championship.

Williams had surpassed his mentor, in one important, though not all-encompassing factor: national titles.

The historic ceiling laundry is one of the most prominent, and perhaps the lone quiet reminder, of a program that is to be feared and respected; inspiring jealousy, and, if we're being blunt about it, annoyance.

Since the Smith Center opened nearly four decades ago, Carolina has won 85 percent of the games beneath those banners. On relatively mild winter nights, in the American South, it is common to see fans—adorned in blue, or of the opposing persuasion—with necks craned upward. Counting or squinting. Trying to make out a jersey number. When did *he* play again . . . ?

Fans from small hamlets across the state and big cities across the country dart in on the Interstate or disembark at the Raleigh-Durham International Airport.

There are the regulars, of course. And then there are the regular out-of-towners, who come early for a visit to the Carolina Basketball Museum and stay late for the experience of Franklin Street. It's a place of charm, legends, and basketball folklore.

And above all, *family*.

UCLA

Bright Lights, Big City

NCAA Titles (11)—1964, 1965, 1967, 1968, 1969, 1970, 1971, 1972, 1973, 1975, 1995
Final Fours (19)—1962, 1964, 1965, 1967, 1968, 1969, 1970, 1971, 1972, 1973, 1974, 1975, 1976, 1980, 1995, 2006, 2007, 2008, 2021
Elite Eights (22)—1962, 1964, 1965, 1967, 1968, 1969, 1970, 1971, 1972, 1973, 1974, 1975, 1976, 1979, 1980, 1992, 1995, 1997, 2006, 2007, 2008, 2009
NCAA tournament appearances—52* (1980 vacated)
Conference regular season titles—38
Conference tournament championships—4

IN THE IMMEDIATE AFTERGLOW OF THE REALIZATION OF HIS ULTIMATE basketball dream—the 1983 NCAA championship—Jimmy Valvano of North Carolina State was already looking ahead to the next big challenge.

The challenge he craved the most, according to confidants, was the UCLA head coaching job, eight years after John Wooden's magical victory tour had concluded.

For whatever reasons, he and UCLA didn't happen to connect back then. But five years later, following the firing of Walt Hazzard, the fifth in a long line of Wooden successors, Valvano and his wife, Pam, made the trip across the country for an interview.

According to Mark Heisler's book, *They Shoot Coaches, Don't They?*, Valvano's interest in the job cooled considerably when he got a look at those tony housing prices in Beverly Hills and Bel Air. Many times that of similar homes in Raleigh, North Carolina.

Unlike John Wooden, Valvano wasn't about to settle for a modest two-bedroom condo in the San Fernando Valley. And whatever UCLA was going to pay him would not come close to making up the difference, as the school was well-known for skimping on coaching salaries.

Anyway, this matchup never transpired, and Valvano's all-too-brief life journey would take him in a radically different direction; to places in the heart far removed from a basketball court.

But it's an intriguing scenario to ponder. What astonishing alchemy might have emerged had Valvano landed in La La Land?

Most likely, a stint as Bruins head man would have yielded another kind of life lesson for the irrepressible young coach:

Be careful what you wish for.

FOR WANT OF A PHONE LINE

In answer to a question that no one is asking:

Yes, Virginia, they did play college basketball at UCLA before Santa Claus arrived in the guise of a thirty-eight-year-old, soft-spoken Midwestern hoop genius named John Wooden.

But it was, shall we say, basketball lite.

UCLA was relatively late to the dance, establishing its first basketball program in 1919. The first coach of any consequence was an attorney named Caddy Works. You might have wanted him beside you on a golf course, but he was largely ineffectual on the sidelines of a basketball court, given that he practiced law full-time by day and only coached his teams during the evening hours.

According to one of his players, a future Olympian named Frank Lubin, Works was "more of an honorary coach" whose basketball knowledge and coaching skills were probably above average for an attorney but well below that for even a part-time college basketball coach.

Nevertheless, he must have had some pretty good players, and probably a few fine bench coaches, because his teams posted a winning record (173–159) over his eighteen after-hours years at UCLA.

Succeeding Works was a gentleman named Wilbur Johns, who coached from 1939 until the arrival of John Wooden in 1948. He left behind an undistinguished W-L record of 93–120 but made a more lasting contribution to UCLA as athletic director during Wooden's first fifteen years on the job.

By 1948, management at UCLA decided they needed to significantly upgrade their basketball program, reaching all the way to Indiana, where they attempted to recruit IU's highly successful head man, Branch McCracken.

As noted in the IU chapter, Branch had a good thing going in Bloomington and had no desire to relocate his family and take on a huge, highly risky turnaround project. He suggested to UCLA that they speak with his close friend and fellow WWII naval officer John Wooden.

It is truly extraordinary how many major inflection points in American history hinge on the smallest things, like, say, a nonworking phone line.

Wooden, who was coaching at the time at Indiana State Teachers College, was, like his buddy Branch, a Midwestern kind of guy who had no desire for big-city life among the coastal elites.

He was ambitious, however, and he was looking for a step up in pedigree from his current job. When the UCLA offer came, Wooden was engaged in serious negotiations for the head coaching job at the University of Minnesota.

The two sides had a tentative agreement, pending the Minnesota AD getting approval from the school president to allow Wooden to hire his own assistants. This would have entailed extra costs on the part of the university.

Anyway, Frank McCormick, the Gopher's AD, got the necessary approval and arranged to call back Wooden at 6 p.m. on that appointed day. However, bad weather in Minnesota knocked out the phone lines, and when the call from McCormick didn't come through as scheduled,

Wooden assumed that the Gophers were no longer interested in him and accepted the offer from UCLA that was already on the table.

Being John Wooden, and a man of his word, when he learned otherwise—that Minnesota had, indeed, agreed to his terms and wanted him very badly—he would not go back on his commitment to UCLA.

So, the ultimate result of some bad weather leading to a downed phone line: ten national championships for the Bruins of UCLA and ten fewer championships for the Golden Gophers of Minnesota.

Such are basketball dynasties created and lost.

That's history for you.

STRANGER IN TOWN

John and Nell Wooden and the kids headed west in the summer of '48, stopping along the way to marvel at the Grand Canyon and Carlsbad Caverns.

In Westwood, California, Wooden found himself at a commuter school where football and men's track were the big-time sports and basketball was, at best, an afterthought. The new coach was not encouraged to find such a lack of interest in basketball, coming from the hoops hotbed of Indiana.

Moreover, the facilities were subpar. The old men's gym where his teams practiced was dusty and in constant need of dampening down and sweeping. The dressing rooms and showers were also nothing to crow about.

But the up-tempo style of play he brought from Indiana yielded immediate results on the hardwood. Wooden took a team that had finished 12–13 the previous year to a school record twenty-two wins and a Pacific Coast Conference Southern Division championship in year one.

He bettered that the following year with twenty-four wins and the school's first trip to the NCAAs.

A very promising start.

But although things on the court were certainly looking up, the faster-track LA lifestyle wasn't sitting well with the Wooden family, especially Nell, who missed her old life back in the Midwest. After year two, Wooden was leaning toward taking the open coaching job at Purdue but reconsidered when UCLA officials reminded him that he had signed a three-year contract. And, once again, being John Wooden, he was loath to walk out on a previous commitment, written or verbal.

The early- to mid-1950s produced some pretty solid results—a second NCAA bid in 1952, a Sweet Sixteen run in 1956, and four division championships—especially considering Wooden's absolute refusal to recruit outside the immediate Southern California area.

"My family comes first," he stated. "I would not go away to scout. I would not be away from home . . . and I didn't have assistants do that [for me]."

Wooden's philosophy back then was simple: take in some local kids with raw athletic ability—kids who really wanted to share in his vision for the program—and coach them up to be the best team they could be.

The overwhelming emphasis on practice, rather than on in-game strategizing, would characterize Wooden's coaching approach throughout his time at UCLA.

Things inevitably got worse for the program as the decade came to an end, given the lack of talent and the dominance of the Pete Newell-coached California teams in the conference. And then a scandal that involved illegal payments to football players from several conference teams, including UCLA, wound up imposing probation on all Bruin sports.

The 1959–1960 team finished 14–12, Wooden's worst-ever season record. Something had to be done, and that meant UCLA coming out of its shell and going after great athletes from both near and far away.

Camelot was on the horizon.

WALT AND LOOIE LONGLEGS
The turnaround began like many turnarounds do—with a greater emphasis on recruiting better athletes.

UCLA hired Jerry Norman, a recruiting specialist, as a full-time assistant, and he began venturing forth into the wider universe of high-school basketball in search of higher-quality players.

In 1961, UCLA hit pay dirt in the form of Walt Hazzard, a six-foot-two guard out of Overbrook High School in Philadelphia, which had produced Wilt Chamberlain several years earlier. Hazzard's team featured two other future pro stars, Wali Jones and Wayne Hightower.

The young Philadelphian's grades weren't good enough for a scholarship offer, but Hazzard was keen enough on attending UCLA that he did a stint at a local community college to get himself scholarship eligible.

In Hazzard's sophomore season at UCLA, the team went to its first NCAA Final Four.

"Walt Hazzard was the difference, the guy who made it all possible," says Gary Cunningham, a California kid and a teammate on that 1962 Final Four team. "Walt could pass you the ball; he was quick and could defend all over the court. He just brought a whole different dimension to the program."

Gail Goodrich, a chunky five-foot-eight shooting guard from LA (he later grew to six feet one) who came in a year after Hazzard and became his backcourt mate on UCLA's first championship team in 1964, agrees that Hazzard was the first straw to stir the drink.

"Now, it was possible for [Wooden] to put in the 2-2-1 full-court zone press. Along with Keith Erickson [a six-foot-five forward], we had the people who could play in an up-tempo style for ninety-four feet . . ."

The famed UCLA zone press was one of John Wooden's major strategic contributions to the game of basketball (along with his renowned high-post offense). Up to that time, a full-court press was something coaches would call up in desperate catch-up situations at the end of games.

Wooden, on the other hand, would whip out the press at any point in the game, confusing and disorienting the competition. Today, every team has been drilled ad nauseum on all the ways of beating a zone press, but back then, that pesky press was a real backbreaker.

Walt Hazzard was, and remained, a big admirer of John Wooden, but he didn't particularly cotton to his esteemed coach trying to rein in his excesses, like behind-the-back passes.

He got benched a few times for his overimaginative play; at one point, he even considered walking away and returning to Philly until his dad set him straight on the meaning of commitment. By his senior year, he and Goodrich comprised one of the most cohesive and effective backcourt duos in college basketball history.

With Hazzard gone, Goodrich and company won the title again in 1965.

Those first two championships would forever hold a special place in the coach's heart, coming as they did with a group of undersized, under-rated athletes playing in a dusty two-thousand-seat multipurpose gym.

Wooden had now set the agenda for another eight championship seasons to come. And it centered around his ironclad belief that a team plays like it practices. "Failing to practice is practicing to fail" is a mantra shared by every major D1 program, but to Wooden this was precept.

The practice court was a stage upon which the "Wizard of West-wood" performed his wizardry. His highly choreographed practice sessions featured an overriding focus on fundamentals, endlessly repeating drills, and a bit of scrimmaging at the close. Full attention was paid to the minutest details, such as teaching players how to tie their sneakers correctly to avoid bunions.

In his mapped-out daily practice routine, notes Larry Farmer, a former Wooden player and later a UCLA head coach, everything was timed out to the minute. Wooden carried a 3x5 index card with the daily schedule on it, and he brooked no "frivolity."

Somehow, he managed to build team stamina without putting players through suicide drills and related afflictions common among coaches of his era. He got his teams into tip-top physical condition without running them into the ground.

It was on the practice court where the man did nearly all his coaching, given that he was not much of an in-game strategist, rarely calling time-outs during games to diagram plays. Nor did he go in for scouting other teams pregame.

"Coach taught us the same way my dad taught me," sums up Gail Goodrich. "Fundamentals. Nothing fancy; just a lot of effort."

His method of communicating all this to his players befit a church deacon, a conservative-minded family man, and a role-model of gentle-manly behavior.

Goodrich says one "Goodness gracious, sakes alive" from John Wooden could curdle a player's insides as effectively as a string of f-bombs from a more bombastic coach. Ralph Drollinger, a member of two Wooden championship teams in the '70s, says the coach didn't even need to speak most of the time to make known his extreme displeasure and get his wishes obeyed. A stern glance usually did the trick.

Nevertheless, neither his professorial manner, nor temperate disposition, nor attention to minutiae, masked a fiercely competitive spirit. One that often showed up in his disagreeable dealings with those referees he deemed incompetent.

These hallmarks of a Wooden regime, now augmented by two national titles, were firmly in place by the spring of 1965. What was required to elevate his tightly knit program to true legend status was a major jolt of superior talent.

That would come very soon.

The seven-foot-two Lew Alcindor, or "Looie Longlegs" as he was known in the upper Manhattan projects where he was raised, in the winter of 1965 was lusted after by virtually every major basketball program in America. Offers came from some sixty schools, including Michigan and his hometown St. John's, Columbia, and NYU.

After a visit to the UCLA campus in early April and a meeting with Coach Wooden, Alcindor held a press conference in his Power Memorial High School gym a month later to announce that he had chosen UCLA "because it has the atmosphere I wanted and because the people out there were nice to me."

And that is undeniably true, as far as it goes. Alcindor was most certainly impressed by the look and feel of the UCLA campus and the new Pauley Pavilion athletic facility. And everybody on campus, especially the UCLA players who accompanied him on his tour, including Edgar Lacy and Mike Warren, treated him as they would a visiting dignitary.

The common belief back then, and one that still haunts fans of St. John's, is that the final choice came down to UCLA and the Redmen (now the Red Storm). The decades-long lamentation emanating from Jamaica, Queens, stems from the belief that Big Lew would have stayed home had not the legendary St. John's coach Joe Lapchick retired after winning the 1965 NIT.

That is bushwa, according to Gary Cunningham, who, as a Wooden assistant and freshmen team coach, was involved in the effort to recruit Alcindor. Cunningham says St. John's was never really in the running. He adds that the sensitive, thoughtful young man, by the end of the nerve-racking recruiting process, had narrowed his decision to UCLA and Michigan. And he was leaning strongly in the direction of Ann Arbor.

What ultimately drew him to UCLA, insists Cunningham, was a meeting with Ralph Bunche, a brilliant Nobel Prize-winning scholar and diplomat, who had studied international relations on a basketball scholarship at UCLA. Bunche had graduated at the top of his class in 1927, and his professional and personal accomplishments in the making of the modern world would fill this entire book.

There could be no better role model for a young Lew Alcindor (later Kareem Abdul-Jabbar). As a teenager, he may not have had his life all figured out, but he was, even at his impressionable age, fully cognizant of the fact that his future would revolve around more than a basketball court.

Just being in the presence of a man such as Ralph Bunche—and such a UCLA man—reportedly shifted his interest west of Ann Arbor and all the way to Westwood, California.

Whatever had influenced his monumental decision, the stage was set with an incoming freshman recruiting class the likes of which had never been assembled on any campus and likely never will again. In addition to Alcindor, it featured another big out-of-state catch, six-foot-two guard Lucius Allen, from Kansas City, Kansas, who would have been a megastar on any team that didn't have Lew Alcindor on it. Forward Lynn Shackelford and guard Kenny Heitz, both Southern Californians, were also key pieces of the class that would forever transform UCLA basketball.

Gary Cunningham had the pleasure of coaching that freshmen team and watching them take apart the varsity in a now-famous scrimmage.

Apart from talent, "those guys had great on-court chemistry," says Cunningham.

The following year, the four freshmen moved up to starting roles on the varsity, joined by junior guard Mike Warren, another major out-of-state recruit from South Bend, Indiana. Warren, a fine college player, would go on to entertain millions of TV viewers as Officer Bobby Hill on the cop drama series *Hill Street Blues*.

Although the UCLA fan base was delighted beyond measure at having Lew Alcindor anchoring this powerhouse unit, a bit of skepticism was expressed as to whether his game would mesh smoothly with Wooden's classic high-post offense. This "continuity offense" generally began with the center flashing from the low to high post to pull man-to-man defenders away from the basket. In this scenario, the center functions primarily as a passer or screener, not necessarily Alcindor's strongest suits.

However, flexibility was yet another of John Wooden's manifold coaching gifts, and with Alcindor out there, he tweaked the high post to get the most out of his natural talents, the most obvious of which was scoring a whole lot of points via his patented "sky hook," taught to Looie Longlegs back in the sixth grade by a man named George Hejduk at St. Jude's Parish.

"I owe this man everything," Alcindor (by then Kareem Jabbar) told a reporter in 2019.

Anyway, the rejiggered high-low post offense, with a forward manning the high post and Alcindor posting down low and doing his thing, worked extremely well. When the NCAA banned the dunk in '67, the big man just dipped into his bag of nifty low-post moves and came up with a few more.

The end result of all this:

Three consecutive NCAA titles and an 88–2 record over those years (one 30–0 and a pair of 29–1s), cementing the dynasty that had been inaugurated by Hazzard and Goodrich and others. Alcindor averaged 26.4 points per game in the eighty-eight games he played in his varsity career.

Of those two lonesome losses, one was to USC's "stall ball" offense in a game best described as the basketball equivalent of Ambien. The other loss could well be termed a sort of victory in defeat, as it came at the hands of Houston in a nationally televised, prime-time "Game of the

Century" extravaganza that helped put college basketball on the path to March Madness.

In this battle of unbeatens, Houston's Elvin Hayes had thirty-nine points and fifteen rebounds while Alcindor had the worst performance of his college career, playing with an eye injury that limited his vision.

UCLA, and Alcindor in particular, didn't view this game as a great step forward for college basketball but, rather, as a stinging loss that needed to be avenged. And when the two teams met up again that season in the NCAA semifinal, UCLA demolished the Cougars, 101–69.

A sidelight to the game of the century was the benching of starting forward Edgar Lacy eleven minutes in. Lacy never got back in the game and quit the team soon after, upset about Wooden's comments that suggested he had wanted out of the game.

"I never enjoyed playing for that man," Lacy said. Forty years later, Wooden apologized for his hurtful comments.

This incident did highlight another aspect of the Wooden persona, which was that he could sometimes come off as insensitive, or opaque, in dealing with his non-star players.

In any case, much bigger problems were bubbling beneath the serene surface of an 88–2 run.

First, in converting from Catholicism to Islam in 1968 (Alcindor publicly changed his name three years later, reflecting this conversion), he had kicked up a storm within the American public, which responded as one might expect—with acrimony and resentment. The young man, still coming to grips with his identity, was now seen less as the consummate jock than as a highly controversial symbol of black activism. To a large segment, if not most Americans, this was not a good look.

The counterculture was also taking root within the UCLA program. Alcindor was experimenting with psychedelics; and Wooden's other star, Lucius Allen, was getting busted for pot. Players were enjoying the fruits of the sexual revolution and testing the limits of their coach's tolerance, which were surely stretched but not nearly to the point of anarchy.

Meanwhile, Alcindor was being stressed-out from all over. His parents were not happy about his conversion; his teammates were feeling confused and, in some cases, deceived; the media were being most uncharitable, and the fans were writing hateful, threatening letters.

In a 1969 op-ed piece in *Sports Illustrated*, Alcindor reported feeling "trapped" after his sophomore year, being among "cracker kids" at UCLA. He added that he and Lucius Allen had discussed transferring to another school, which Allen confirmed to a reporter years later, noting that he and Alcindor had a deal with boosters to move together to Michigan State.

However, none of these tentative plans came to fruition, and Lew Alcindor would get no closer to attending Michigan State than he was to attending Michigan. And the three 1967–1969 championship teams would go on to become enshrined in college basketball history.

"Our loyalty to John Wooden and UCLA overcame our momentary petulance," Kareem Jabbar would explain many years later.

No doubt, America has long forgiven him for his petulance and his dalliance with the counterculture.

As for becoming a Muslim, refusing to play on the 1968 Olympic team, and morphing into a dedicated, outspoken advocate for a fair and just society, that would largely depend on who you ask.

PAPA AND THE WIZ

Sam Gilbert, a successful LA businessman, devoted UCLA benefactor, and reputed Mob associate, was a BMOC (Big Man off Campus) during the Wooden years and beyond.

For nearly twenty years, "Papa Sam" freely spread his beneficence among a sizable number of grateful UCLA players. A series of articles in the *Los Angeles Times*, which eventually led to NCAA sanctions in 1981, explored the magnitude of Gilbert's largesse, which was stunning in its excessiveness: cash for their game tickets; substantial discounts for cars, stereos, meals, and clothing; cash to pay for an abortion for a player's girlfriend.

And none of this was done in the shadows. Gilbert was about as open as open could be, viewing NCAA rules as outdated relics of an innocent time that had long passed. He looked on the players as his surrogate

Lew Alcindor gives the boys from Stanford a bit of that old razzle-dazzle, in the form of a reverse slam-dunk. *New York World-Telegram and the Sun* staff photographer. Public domain, via Wikimedia Commons

offspring and gave them not only material things, but someone close to the program with whom they could share their feelings and get some empathy. In short, he gave them a friend and confidant.

Their head coach, by contrast, was more inclined at that time to exhibit a chilly detachment toward his players' personal concerns.

Anyway, nobody seemed to be in a hurry to confront the Gilbert situation—not the UCLA administration, the NCAA, or the press. Indeed, both the school and the media treated Sam Gilbert more as a quasi-school official than a rogue booster running roughshod over the myth of UCLA as a "clean program."

Coaches across the country, similarly, were well-aware of these goings-on in Westwood, which was one major reason why the cynics among them took to referring derisively to Coach Wooden as "St. John."

Mark Heisler, in his aforementioned book, recounts a story about a speech Wooden gave at one of his clinics. In that "homily," the coach brought up the two words that to his mind characterized his program: "respect" and "balance."

"A USC assistant leaned over to the coach sitting next to him and whispered, 'I'll tell you what the two words are: Sam Gilbert,'" Heisler wrote.

Indeed, those coaches who viewed Wooden as an A-1 hypocrite tended to voice that view softly and quietly.

Except, of course, Bobby Knight, who made no bones about his negative feelings toward John Wooden.

"I have a lot of respect for him as a coach," said Knight in an interview. "But I don't mind saying I don't respect Wooden [himself], because he allowed Sam Gilbert to do whatever it took to recruit kids."

Knight added that Wooden once told him he didn't know how to deal with the guy.

"And I'm saying to myself, 'I damn sure could have dealt with him.'"

John Matthew Smith, in his book *The Sons of Westwood: John Wooden, UCLA and the Dynasty That Changed College Basketball*, says Wooden never got over having knowingly allowed an outsider to besmirch his name and tarnish the reputation of his beloved program.

Smith argues that the way in which Wooden cracked down on rules violations with his final 1975 championship team—enforcing more rigid dress codes, for example—was a reaction to the indignity of the Gilbert affair.

Nevertheless, the narrative that Wooden was oblivious to Gilbert's shenanigans, or reluctant to rock the boat, is open to some debate.

Wooden reportedly made more than a fleeting pass at keeping his program aboveboard.

Two sources close to Wooden say that he was deeply distressed about the situation and approached J. D. Morgan, the athletic director at the time, to urge him to bar Gilbert from contact with the players, or to at least take forceful action to restore the program's integrity.

According to one of those stories, Morgan responded that although he understood Wooden's concerns and concurred with his opinion that something ought to be done, Gilbert was simply too valuable a program asset to be messed with.

The other version, which hews fairly closely to the one above, has Morgan listening sympathetically to Wooden's plea to get rid of Gilbert and assuring the coach that he would "take care of it."

Which, of course, he didn't. Nor did anyone else, for that matter.

The truth may well be that John Wooden, as powerful a presence as he was within the UCLA hierarchy, did not possess the authority or the political clout necessary to keep his program as clean as he was.

Which is not to say that he deserves a pass on this. Only that judging people by their worst actions, or inactions, is not a very sporting thing to do.

The Next Five

After the departures of Alcindor, Lucius Allen (who left for the NBA following his junior year), and other stalwarts of the late 1960s, the mantle of success was passed to a new group, led by Sidney Wicks and Curtis Rowe, arguably the two best forwards in the nation. They were ably abetted by two fine guards, Henry Bibby and John Vallely, and a six-foot-nine center, Steve Patterson, who did a pretty solid job filling some very big shoes.

By this point, the dynasty, now five championships in, was an inviolable fact of life among the players, coaches, boosters, and fans. Anything less than a title was unacceptable, if not unthinkable.

And the new group, which was in some significant ways closer and more selfless than its predecessor, did not disappoint, taking no prisoners on their way to two more championships (making it seven, in total) while compiling an impressive record of 57–3.

Nevertheless, the pressures were building throughout those years. A referee who worked one of those championship games recalls how the members of the team out on the floor were talking among themselves about their fear of failing to defend Wooden's winning streak.

In his autobiography, Larry Farmer recalls coming into the locker room after the 1971 final win over Villanova and expecting a lot of jumping up and down and carrying on. Instead of exuberance, he found the senior starters sitting back and smiling, "looking more relieved than happy."

Everyone knew what was next on tap, as they had seen the six-foot-eleven Bill Walton and his freshmen team.

"Walton was incredible," says Farmer. "He was quick and graceful and was already being compared to Kareem."

And not just for his immense basketball skills and his deep passion for the game. Walton, who passed away in 2024, was also an outspoken, polarizing political figure, vehemently protesting the Vietnam War and calling upon Americans to cease cooperating with an "inherently evil" government.

His tie-dyed musical tastes, however, diverged markedly from Kareem's, as Walton was a lifelong "deadhead" (fanatical lover of the Grateful Dead).

And unlike Kareem's rather dour countenance, Walton went about all of this with a wide smile.

Coach Wooden, as would be expected, was less than comfortable with Walton's radicalism, as well as his modes of dress—long hair and flip-flops.

But again, as he managed to do with previous players who pushed the envelope, Wooden withstood the test, maintaining control of the "Walton Gang" via a modest amount of discipline and a lot of grudging acceptance.

Walton, for his part, absolutely loved his coach—his humility, his practices, his offensive and defensive philosophies, all of it.

Walton says Wooden had an open-door policy toward him, and the two chatted in the coach's office every morning. This was contrary to Wooden's general attitude toward his less-influential players, who did not have the luxury of strolling into his office for a morning schmooze.

Pete Trgovich, a member of the Gang and a starter on Wooden's final championship team of 1975, was, during his first couple of years in the program, one of those "marginal" players who didn't get a lot of hand holding from the coach. Trgovich says he has always had enormous admiration and respect for Wooden but chafed at the coach's unwillingness to be upfront with him as to his status on the team and his playing time.

"I don't feel like he always treated me right," says Trgovich. "I worked my butt off, and he'd sit me down and bury me on the bench, telling me it was my attitude.

"Maybe I was somewhat immature back then," acknowledges Trgovich, "but I still felt like I deserved answers I never got."

The Walton Gang, which also featured the formidable talents of Jamaal Wilkes, Greg Lee, and backup center Swen Nater (who made it all the way to the NBA despite logging scant minutes as a Bruin), went 60–0 in its first two years, stretching the championship streak to seven (nine, overall).

Walton's final year was, to say the least, a disappointment; 26–4, ending in an NCAA semifinal loss to David "Skywalker" Thompson and North Carolina State.

Trgovich says it was after the crushing loss to Carolina State that Walton demonstrated one of his finest attributes, as a ballplayer and a man.

"Back in the locker room, we're all feeling really bad. Andre [McCarter, a sophomore guard] was falling apart. Walton goes over and helps him up. He says to Andre, 'It's OK; you'll get this one back next year.' That's what a leader does, even when he's down himself."

As it turned out, Walton's prediction was spot-on. UCLA returned to championship form in 1975, winning its tenth title and sending its coach into retirement on the highest of notes.

Andre McCarter played one of the best games of his life in that final against an excellent Kentucky team, racking up fourteen assists—ten in the first half—while Trgovich, his backcourt mate, registered sixteen points and four assists. Together, they controlled the tempo and took away Kentucky's press.

After that game, Wooden was approached by an alumnus who only half-jokingly suggested that the coach "owed" them this one for not having won the previous year.

It was the utter exhaustion that came from dealing with that absurd level of expectation, combined with the pressures he put on himself, the death of his beloved Nell, and the impact of a heart attack he had experienced two years earlier that prompted Wooden's retirement announcement prior to the NCAA final.

Although he had told his assistant, Gary Cunningham, and others of his decision to retire early in the 1974–1975 season, it was the manner in which he announced it—right after the semifinal win over Louisville—that shocked the basketball world and discombobulated the Wildcats.

To Joe B. Hall, Kentucky's head coach, it was another example of John Wooden being John Wooden, using his entitled position as a living legend to get an edge on the competition; knowing that the whole world, which includes the referees, would be inclined to give the venerated old coach a break in his final farewell dance.

After it was over, Wooden eased gracefully into retirement, which in his case lasted another thirty-five years. He was an avid Bruins basketball fan until the end, and years after his death, his spirit still resides in Pauley Pavilion.

"You just have to look up at his yellow chair in the stands, and his pyramid of success, and you know you're in a place where the expectations are sky-high," says Thomas Welsh, who played at UCLA from 2014 to 2018 and currently plays pro ball in Japan.

Welsh's major claim to fame is being the third leading rebounder in UCLA history, behind the two greatest players to have ever played college ball, Kareem Abdul-Jabbar and Bill Walton.

Someday, says Welsh, he'll tell his grandchildren all about the legend of John Wooden and the only two men to have outrebounded their grandfather.

Two, Two, and Two

If John Wooden himself, after winning ten titles in twelve years, was feeling the heat from a fickle fan base for not winning every single year, you knew it would not be easy to find a replacement who could handle that level of stress.

Nevertheless, J. D. Morgan was sure he had his man. Gene Bartow, or "Clean Gene," as he was known (for the cleanliness of his programs), was about as close to a Wooden clone as there was out there in D1 basketball land. Bartow was a gentlemanly figure, a small-town Midwesterner, and a devoted family man with a respectable record of success.

Most notably, Bartow coached the 1972–1973 Memphis State Tigers all the way to the NCAA final, where they ran smack up against Bill Walton's twenty-one for twenty-two shooting performance in an 87–66 blowout.

"My dad absolutely loved coaching," says his son, Murry, who became a college coach himself and would one day serve as an interim head coach at UCLA.

"It was always fun for him, and he was excited to be at UCLA."

He understood that he was replacing an irreplaceable figure and that it would take some time—maybe as long as a year or so—before "nostalgia" for the former coach would fade. As long as we keep winning, he said shortly before the kickoff to his debut season, all would turn out just fine.

By the end of his first game as UCLA coach, whatever fun and excitement there was had come to a crashing halt, and it was abundantly clear that Gene Bartow had seriously miscalculated the degree of nostalgia for John Wooden.

In that opening game against Indiana, which had gone 31–1 the previous year and watched UCLA snatch the crown that they felt was rightfully theirs, the Hoosiers exacted revenge on the Bruins, to the tune of a twenty-point rout.

UCLA won its next eleven games on the way to a 28–4 season and a trip to the Final Four (where they were again the victims of an undefeated Indiana team in the semi). But an impressive Final Four finish wasn't nearly enough for the fans or the boosters. The die had been cast back in late November.

Perhaps the only way the whole experience could have been any worse for Gene Bartow at UCLA would have been if the internet had been around in 1976.

Murry, who was a teenager during this period, says there were lots and lots of hate letters, nasty call-in talk shows, and "mean-spirited" newspaper columns. Some of Bartow's players—by no means all—mocked his country manners; and as for the general reaction from the alumni community, well, that would be just shy of shopping for a rope.

"My father never brought any of this home to his family," says his son. "That was the kind of person he was. I was about fifteen, hanging around the locker room, and I never picked up on [the vitriol]. It was years later when he confided to me that this was the first time in his life that he felt no joy in coaching."

Gary Cunningham, who had left for grad school after the '75 season and would succeed Bartow upon his resignation two years later, says Clean Gene simply wasn't cut out for big-city life, let alone the challenge of taking on an impossible job in a no-win situation.

"He called people in LA 'the kooks,' and he became paranoid about certain things that he believed were going on," adds Cunningham. In 1993, Bartow publicly thanked the NCAA for not investigating Sam Gilbert, as he felt this unsavory character had literally threatened his life.

In addition, the new head coach may have made some mistakes in trying too soon to roll out new policies, which were roundly criticized for not being Wooden policies.

"I believe that had Gene stayed at UCLA any longer than he did, he would have had a full-scale mental breakdown," says another colleague.

Bartow's parting words upon leaving Westwood were that in all his time in this hellish situation, he never worried about getting fired.

"But assassinated," he added, "that's a different thing."

It is worth noting that Gene Bartow's two-year record at UCLA would have sufficed quite nicely at any other college in the country—52–9, with a trip to the Final Four and the NCAA second round (fifth ranked in the final AP poll in year one and second in year two).

After his unfortunate stay in California, Bartow moved on to a more tranquil and congenial spot at the University of Alabama at Birmingham. There, he served as the school's first head basketball coach and athletic director and remained in those positions for eighteen years, taking the Blazers to nine NCAAs and five NITs.

The fun hadn't really died. It had just taken a couple of years off.

Gary Cunningham's two-year coaching stint at UCLA was likewise very successful, record-wise—50–8 with an Elite Eight and a Sweet Sixteen finish. But being a Wooden protégé and more comfortable in the surrealistic hothouse of UCLA basketball made his time as head coach more palatable than Bartow's. That, and the fact that two years later, the ridiculous expectations had been toned down ever so slightly.

"I have to say, that in terms of coaching, I really didn't feel pressure there," he insists.

Where the pressure came from in Cunningham's case was in house hunting. J. D. Morgan was long of the strong belief that coaching at UCLA is a privilege and that to pay coaches a reasonable wage for that awesome privilege was unseemly.

"Truth is I couldn't afford a decent house anywhere in the area," laments Cunningham. "At the time, I remember Cal State Fullerton was paying more money than UCLA. But Morgan wouldn't budge on this point. I had no choice [but to move on]."

The next coach to stay the normal two years was none other than Larry Brown, who, as noted in the Kansas chapter, was a true basketball nomad. Brown was making his fourth stop on the coaching carousel in Southern California, after a wrenching stay with the Denver Nuggets, which reached a chaotic crescendo during the 1978 playoffs.

Brown was said to have lost control of his emotions at the end of the regular season—screaming at his players, instituting last-minute lineup changes, and putting in new plays willy-nilly.

"He became like a madman," Nuggets guard Mack Calvin told *Sports Illustrated*.

Brown left the Nuggets in midseason the following year and shortly thereafter got a call from his buddy, J. D. Morgan. For Brown, the perfect antidote to the NBA was a job teaching college kids, eager to soak up his knowledge and willing to follow his instructions for "playing the right way."

His general demeanor and behavior were more or less the same at UCLA as they would be in Kansas a few years later, only he had less time to strike up a love affair with Westwood.

As always, he was ultra-passionate about coaching basketball but inclined to pull his team out of practice to see a movie or cheer for another UCLA team. And as at Kansas, people were always swirling about him—basketball friends, family, players, and student admirers.

"Larry was the birth of cool here," notes Larry Farmer, whom Brown hired as an assistant in his first season. Farmer says when Brown first encountered two hundred enthusiastic students camped out the night before a game to get good seats, he walked out among them, breezily chatting and shaking hands. And the following morning he returned with dozens of donuts to pass around to the hungry throng.

"I'd seen students lining up for games since I was a player," Farmer wrote in his book, *Role of a Lifetime*.

"But it never crossed my mind to do something that thoughtful. The overnighters loved him. That was cool!"

Yes, just about everyone loved the cool guy, just as they later did in Kansas. And as always, the time for loving was all too short.

"We all hated to see him go," says Farmer.

In his first season, Brown took his team, which featured Kiki Vandeweghe, Rod Foster, and Mike Sanders (Gary Cunningham's sole big-time recruit, out of Louisiana) on an improbable run to the NCAA final. There they lost to the Louisville "Doctors of Dunk," coached by Denny Crum, a devout John Wooden acolyte.

In true UCLA fashion, after that loss an alumnus pointed out to Brown that he had just become the "first UCLA coach ever to lose a final."

Welcome to town, Mr. Brown.

Year two in the brief UCLA/Brown saga was considerably less enjoyable. His team finished 20–7 but got bashed by Brigham Young in the first round of the NCAAs.

Brown resented the omnipresent influence of Sam Gilbert on his program and received a death threat before a game at Stanford, according to *Sports Illustrated*.

Brown also ran into the same problem that Gary Cunningham had faced: a salary insufficient to buy a home. On top of that, the guy who hired him, J. D. Morgan, had passed away; Brown's office was cramped and airless; and some of those old insecurities may have popped up, making Brown more susceptible to fears of being fired.

"Who knows with this guy?" says an old coaching colleague. "It could have been all of those things or none of them. I'm not at all sure that even Larry Brown really knows why he can't just stay in one place."

Brown, as was his wont, left them all wanting more and with sanctions nipping at his heels, which reflected the investigation into Sam Gilbert's activities.

The NCAA voided the 1980 postseason and slapped the university with a two-year probation, which included a ban from postseason play in 1982. Four freshmen on the '79–'80 team were cited as having received late-model automobiles, and there was a slew of related violations.

After another NBA pit-stop in New Jersey, Larry Brown would be off again, to the University of Kansas. There he would come to feel more at home, away from fickle Bruins fans and their bodily threats, safe in the bosom of basketball's founding spirits.

THREE, FOUR

After eleven years at UCLA—three as a varsity ballplayer and eight as an assistant under four head coaches—Larry Farmer got his role of a lifetime, being named head coach prior to the 1981–'82 season.

After the tumult of the Brown regime, UCLA wanted a UCLA guy. No matter that he had no head coaching experience and at thirty years of age would be the youngest man to coach at UCLA. He had the right lineage and was, to everyone in the UCLA community, an admirable, friendly, thoroughly decent fellow.

Having been around to witness the toll that the job could take on a normal human being, Farmer fortified himself by eschewing any reading material, television, or radio transmissions related to UCLA basketball.

"Watching Gene Bartow go through that kind of brutal treatment, I told myself that if I ever became a head coach anywhere, I was never going to pick up a newspaper and read an article about me," he says.

Farmer looked to model his coaching on the man who had coached him a decade before, all the way from running Wooden's classic high-post offense and his meticulous practices, to carrying a rolled-up program on the sidelines.

But emulating Wooden and being Wooden were two very different things, which Larry Farmer would soon discover, along with the realization that you can ignore all the nasty voices out there, but you can't escape them.

Farmer's first major challenge would be dealing with all the fallout from the Sam Gilbert investigation, which would have been much easier if not for Farmer's extremely close relationship with the booster. UCLA had been ordered to "dissociate" Gilbert from the basketball program, and enforcing that provision took an emotional toll of its own on the new coach.

And then, there was the postseason ban. Farmer's first team, loaded with NBA-quality talent—Mike Sanders, Stuart Gray, Rod Foster, Darren Daye, and Kenny Fields, among others—went 21–6 (second in the conference) but had to sit out the tournament.

The next year, with much the same cast of talented upperclassmen, the Bruins finished 23–6 and won the Pac-10.

But a dismal loss to tenth-seeded Utah in the opening round of the NCAAs brought on the full wrath of the alumni base, and things went straight downhill from there.

In his third year, with several key players gone but a freshmen Reggie Miller seeing limited playing time, UCLA went 17–11 and declined an invitation to the NIT. It was their worst record in twenty-four years.

What happened after that was confusing, to say the very least.

A great deal of back-and-forth discussion ensued over the closing days of March, some of it related to the firing of Farmer's two assistants, Craig Impelman and Kevin O'Connor, to be replaced by former UCLA jocks Walt Hazzard and Jack Hirsch. Farmer was unhappy about the firings, as he was close to his assistants and grateful for their help in keeping players on the academic path to four-year degrees.

But Farmer says his biggest and most immediate concern about his future at UCLA—that is, should the chancellor and AD elect not to fire him—was a change in recruiting policy that would prevent UCLA coaches from making use of "special action" admissions.

"I knew that given this academic restriction on our recruiting, there was no way I was going to be able to do what they expected from me," explains Farmer. "I was basically setting myself up for failure."

Through all this hubbub, added to a disappointing third year on the job, Farmer says he came to truly understand what Gene Bartow meant about coaching not being fun anymore. He had already reached his initial goal of lasting three years—a year longer than his last three predecessors. So, he drafted a resignation letter.

After more conflicting statements, hand-wringing, and assorted craziness, a question posed at an impromptu press conference led to the chancellor announcing that Farmer would be given a two-year contract extension.

Farmer was both dazed and confused. He says he tried to put on a good face, knowing that his situation was untenable. He told the media he'd been "burned out" but was ready to march forward into a better tomorrow.

Four days later, Larry Farmer abruptly resigned, a decision he has not regretted.

Nevertheless, he says now, "This was not the way I would have liked to go out. I shouldn't have gone along with that press conference. My mistake was getting swept up in the moment."

None of what happened toward the end, insists Farmer, can detract from all those years, especially those "magical" John Wooden years.

"But at some point," he concludes, "you do grow up."

Farmer's successor, Walt Hazzard, had a solid UCLA background like Farmer's but with a certain toughness and fiery nature that Farmer did not possess. Plus, the guy was already in the building. Indeed, his hiring and Farmer's resignation occurred the same day.

Hazzard had proven his ferocity as a ballplayer, at Overbrook High and UCLA, and over a ten-year NBA career. Although his coaching résumé was sparse—a couple of years at a community college and two at Division II Chapman University—his combined W-L record at those two schools was an impressive 97–23. But his conversion to Islam during his NBA career did nothing to advance his coaching career.

At UCLA, his ferocity was matched by his volatility, which included a dust-up with a reporter at a press conference after UCLA won the 1985 NIT and numerous arguments with referees and others. Hazzard's countenance—an occasional scowl and a raspy voice that could frighten small children—added to his image as a tough guy.

In reality, he was usually warm and friendly, and his players responded to his warmth and tolerated the outbursts.

On the court, Hazzard's tenure did not go at all well.

After the first disappointing year, which yielded the NIT title, the 1985–'86 season came in at 15–14, including a first-round NIT loss to UC-Irvine. As expected, there were lots of unhappy players and reports that some had lost interest in competing.

Things turned sharply the other way in Hazzard's third year, as a new recruiting class—headed by six-foot-seven forward Trevor Wilson and seven-foot Greg Foster—meshed with Reggie Miller, Pooh Richardson, and Jack Haley to deliver a 25–7, conference-winning season. They won UCLA's first NCAA tournament game in seven years but were bounced out by Wyoming in round two.

And then, the roof caved in yet again in year four—a 16–14 record and a demoralizing first-round knockout in the conference tournament.

All the bad vibes from two years before had returned, along with another NCAA investigation—also relating to Sam Gilbert—and attendance at Pauley falling to historic lows.

Walt Hazzard thus became the first UCLA coach to get fired.

This was a big, historic thing at the time.

It would later become a trend.

4.8 SECONDS TO GLORY

At this point, not a lot of top coaches wanted the UCLA job, given what they'd witnessed during the long parade of two, three, four years and out. Jim Harrick, a former assistant under Gary Cunningham, wanted the job, although he knew very well what it entailed.

In the end, he not only broke that unfortunate string of short-lived coaching stints but added to Wooden's vast treasure trove an eleventh national title.

His ties to UCLA ran pretty deep.

"I became a director at John Wooden's basketball camp while I was still in high school," relates Harrick by way of introduction. "I started coaching at Morningside High [number one-ranked nationally in 1973] right behind the Forum. I went to every [UCLA] clinic. This was my dream job."

Harrick signed on to UCLA after nine years at Pepperdine, where he took his teams to four NCAAs and a couple of NITs. Things took an upswing immediately upon his arrival. He brought in Don McLean, UCLA's most highly touted recruit in years, prior to coaching his first game.

Other high-school hotshots followed: by 1992 he had eight future NBAer's on his roster, including Ed O'Bannon, Gerald Madkins, Tracy Murray, Mitchell Butler, and Derrick Martin.

All eight of Harrick's teams reached the NCAAs, with the '90 squad going to the Sweet Sixteen, the 1992 team to the Elite Eight, and the '95 team all the way to the championship.

There was the usual griping along the way from boosters (you know, the ones who thought Wooden owed them another title) and impatient fans. Harrick wasn't tough enough with his prima donna players, they said. His teams were undisciplined, and weren't regularly going deep into the tournament, and so on.

On the flip side, it was hard not to like the guy. His players recognized how much he cared about them.

To take a prominent example: after Gerald Madkins sustained an injury while riding his moped, Harrick brought him into his house, where he stayed for two weeks in his son's bedroom during his recuperation.

Madkins and Harrick have been friends ever since.

On the basketball side, Harrick brought a few new wrinkles to the court, including a one-on-one full-court defensive drill and a so-called six-second drill—now the stuff of legend—that he ran once a week with his fleet guard, Tyus Edney.

The drill called for Edney to receive an inbounds pass from the baseline and take it end-to-end in six seconds or less.

"Edney was a road runner," says Harrick. "He'd score almost all the time in practice."

With 4.8 seconds to go in the second round of the 1995 NCAA tournament, trailing Missouri 74–73 with the ball under the UCLA basket, it was time to see if practice would make perfect.

Ignoring a suggestion that UCLA throw a long pass to half-court, he called on his man, Edney, to do his thing. Edney took the pass, brought it about halfway up court, veered slightly to his right and took it the rest of the way to the hoop for the winning bucket as time expired.

Edney's mad dash was madly celebrated by his teammates, who used it as fuel for their eventual run to the title.

Both Harrick and Edney say they never doubted that the play would work.

Harrick's final season, by contrast, ended with a whimper: a listless 43–41 first-round loss to Princeton in the 1996 NCAAs. The Tigers were coached by Pete Carril, whose specialty was lulling opponents to sleep and back-dooring them to death. Harrick has never forgiven him.

Two weeks before the start of the next season, Jim Harrick became the second coach in team history to be fired, over accusations involving a student-athlete recruiting dinner.

Harrick was alleged to have falsified receipts from the dinner after two of his current players joined the table. Because Harrick had paid for the entire meal, this constituted an improper benefit to the two players. Harrick attempted to cover up this minor offense by putting his wife and the wife of Michael Holton, his assistant, on his expense report.

Picking up the tab for the two players would have likely resulted in a gentle slap on the wrist. But to Athletic Director Pete Dalis and the UCLA administration, the lie was an unconscionable breach of ethics.

Harrick at the time did not deny the allegations but noted that the AD had had it in for him for some time. And there is more than a little truth in that.

"I never felt supported by him," laments Harrick. "I got my eyes opened at UCLA."

All in all, a sad ending for the only man not named John Wooden to have hoisted a UCLA championship trophy.

Steve Lavin, the longest-serving assistant to Harrick, stepped into the job. He was, personality-wise, the un-Harrick.

The former coach was a fast-talking West Virginian who had come up the career ladder the hard way, through a string of nowhere jobs including night work in an assembly plant.

In other words, a grunt.

Lavin, on the other hand, was a handsome, smooth-talking thirty-two-year-old from suburban Marin County with a load of charm. Or as one of his many UCLA detractors put it, a guy with "cool hair" who put in a minimal effort when it came to all facets of the job—recruiting, teaching, scouting.

Baron Davis, one of Lavin's most consequential recruits, offered this brutal assessment of his former coach while looking up at the eleven UCLA championship banners: "We should have a banner up there—the only team to make the [NCAA] tournament without a coach."

Harsh words, which perhaps should be taken with a chaser of skepticism, because Baron Davis is the same guy who noted back in 2023 that winning championships was not at the top of his priority list back in college.

Sure, he said, I wanted to win, but the major aim was putting on a show.

"Let's send it up. Crosses, dunks, all that. . . . No matter what, we gonna create some entertainment. I gotta make sure I get my highlights. It was more so like they have to remember me."

Anyway, for a guy who allegedly couldn't coach his way out of a paper bag, Lavin's credits weren't half bad. In his first six years at UCLA, his teams made six trips to the tournament, including four Sweet Sixteens and an Elite Eight. Twice he had the number one recruiting class in the country, and fourteen of his recruits played in the NBA.

But none of that meant a thing, once it all came a-tumblin' down with a vengeance in year seven—a 10–19 record, the first losing season at UCLA since Wilbur Johns's final go-round in 1947–1948, and a low-point in the program's history.

Lavin was let go immediately after season's end, the third straight UCLA coach to get the heave-ho.

Next up was Ben Howland, who had rebuilt a faltering program at the University of Pittsburgh into a top Big East contender. And he had done it the Big East way, with fierce defense, strong rebounding, and a deliberately paced offense. Just the way John Thompson, Rollie Massimino, and Jim Boeheim had constructed their championship Big East programs.

Howland noted at the time that the only job that would get him to leave Pittsburgh was the UCLA job, but once he got there, it took some time to get used to the Southern California culture.

"It was very different, more transitory," he says. "LA's a pro town, like New York. You had the Lakers and the Dodgers you were competing with, [as well as] other colleges."

Coaching at any major D1 program is a tough job by its very nature, adds Howland, but the expectations at UCLA made that job especially difficult. Howland points to Matt Painter, the highly successful coach at Purdue, who went through a stretch of early-round losses to lightly regarded teams in the NCAAs.

"He wouldn't still be coaching if he was at UCLA," says Howland.

Howland's first order of business was bringing to the program a "physical brand of basketball with tough players who wanted to play defense and rebound and give maximum effort."

Although he declines to denigrate the Lavin players he inherited in year one (which ended at 11–17, 7–11 in conference), they were not players who fit his brand of basketball. His early recruits, including Jordan Farmar and Arron Afflalo, were more suited to the Big East style of play, and the results backed that up: a trip back to the tournament in year two (first round exit), followed by a trip all the way to the NCAA final (a loss to Florida) and two more consecutive Final Four appearances.

Unfortunately, those three straight Final Fours would be the highlights of Howland's UCLA career.

It was reported that one of his players, Reeves Nelson, was a "bully" on and off the court, to the point of deliberately trying to injure teammates. Reports also surfaced that Howland had allowed the situation to fester for more than two years.

Howland denied the allegations, but the damage was done—multiple players left the program, including Nelson, who was dismissed in December 2011.

There were other problems involving other players, and a feeling among the UCLA administration and fan base that Howland's brand of physical, defense-oriented basketball was becoming "boring."

After the last appearance at the Final Four in 2008, Howland's teams failed to get past the second round in any of his last five seasons, and he was let go immediately after a twenty-point, second-round blowout by Minnesota in the 2013 tournament. He was the fourth consecutive coach to exit via that route.

Howland calls his time at UCLA "a terrific experience," which it was. Until it wasn't.

The UCLA experience of Steve Alford, who would be the last of the fired five (as of this writing), got off to a shaky start before he even arrived in town.

There was the major blowback from Alford's time as Iowa head coach regarding his defense of Pierre Pierce, a star player accused of sexual assault of another student. Many fans, and not only female fans, were inclined to view Alford negatively based on this issue alone.

Then there was the charge of nepotism that came from playing his son, Bryce, over Zach LaVine, who left UCLA after one season and found his way to the NBA. And Alford's close connection to Bobby Knight similarly sat poorly with many in the base, given that Knight, as previously noted, was an outspoken critic of the venerated John Wooden.

And then there was that full-blown international incident in China, stemming from the shoplifting arrests of three UCLA freshmen players, including LiAngelo Ball.

If it had only been those off-court distractions, Alford's problems at UCLA probably would have sorted themselves out.

But there was also the matter of his team's performance on the court.

Alford had been hired to reinvigorate Howland's sagging offense, and to an extent, he accomplished that.

"Our goal was to outscore the opponent," says Thomas Welsh. "Run and gun, lots of motion on offense. That was the game we played."

The trouble was at the other end of the court. Alford's team played defense like France did in the early stages of WWII—in other words, barely at all.

Alford's first two teams managed to run and gun their way to the Sweet Sixteen, but a 15–17 record in his third year dampened enthusiasm even further. After another Sweet Sixteen finish the following year, the team just squeaked by into the tournament's "First Four" and lost that play-in game.

The coach did not make it all the way through his sixth campaign.

Murry Bartow, whose ties to UCLA dated back more than forty years, had been brought in to help establish some semblance of defense, but by then, even Alford's high-octane offense was stalling out.

With a record standing at 7–6, following a dreadful loss at home to Liberty University, Alford was canned, becoming the first coach ever to be fired mid-season.

"It's a tough town," says Alford, echoing the spirits of all his predecessors who failed to measure up to expectations in the post-Wooden era.

Alford, his staff, and at least some of his players took the firing hard. Although firing coaches had become commonplace, if not almost de rigueur at UCLA, such a thing had never occurred in the middle of a season and with this much rancor.

"I hated the way that it happened, the way it went down all of a sudden," says Bartow, who was named interim head coach. "I think, in terms of personnel, UCLA has created a monster."

Under Bartow, the team went 10–10 down the stretch and finished at 17–16. Bartow says he knew that he was not a candidate for permanent head coach, and it is doubtful he'd have accepted even if offered.

That spot went to UCLA's next hire, and, as of this writing, its last.

Mick Cronin, who'd done yeoman's work at Cincinnati for thirteen years—nine straight NCAA appearances—became the fourteenth coach in UCLA history on April 9, 2019.

COVID ended his first season, pre-tournament. In 2020–2021, after a disappointing regular season capped by selection to the NCAA First Four, UCLA made it as far as the Final Four. The 2021–2022 team got to the Sweet Sixteen and, as Pac-12 regular-season champs, they returned to the Sweet Sixteen the next year.

With a freshmen-laden squad in 2023–2024 (seven in total), the team finished at 16–17.

Mick Cronin did not get fired.

"Mick gets it," says one of those UCLA coaches who came before. "He understands what it takes to coach here. You need to win, and you need to entertain, in that order."

There are plenty of reasons to agree that Mick Cronin gets it. But so did others who thought they'd had coaching in this frazzling environment all figured out.

Just be careful what you wish for, is all we're saying.

Epilogue

The Light Blue Bloods

A FAIR NUMBER OF ELITE COLLEGE BASKETBALL PROGRAMS FELL SHORT, but not too short, of our blue-blood cutoff, which was at least four NCAA titles gathered over a course of at least three decades. Anyway, we felt that these five programs were worth a few words of recognition.

VILLANOVA

Three championships—1985, 2016, 2018
Four additional Final Fours—1939, 1971* (vacated), 2009, 2022
Elite Eights—15
Tournament appearances—41

Any team whose head coach inspires them to victory in a regional final by invoking the spirits of spaghetti and clam sauce belongs somewhere in this volume.

Rollie Massimino, a man who loved pasta almost as much as he loved concocting abstruse defensive schemes that mystified his opponents, was the architect of 'Nova's first NCAA title in 1985.

The final game, a stunning 66–64 win over defending champion Georgetown, has been dubbed the "perfect game," given that the Wildcats hit nearly 79 percent of their shots while constricting John Thompson's potent offense by controlling the pace and tempo.

In 2016, Rollie and some of his '85 players were in the stands to cheer on the 'Cats in their title game, which featured arguably the most amazing finish in NCAA finals history: a three-pointer at the buzzer by 'Nova's Kris Jenkins.

That game-winning shot came right after an even more amazing double-pump, three-pointer by North Carolina's Marcus Paige that tied the game at 74 with less than five seconds on the clock.

Villanova's last title in 2018 was nowhere near as nerve-racking—a seventeen-point win over Michigan—but it cemented Coach Jay Wright's position in the college coaching pantheon.

One more Villanova title, in another decade, and we'd have had a Magnificent Eight.

LOUISVILLE
Three championships—1980, 1986, 2013*
Seven additional Final Fours—1959, 1972, 1975, 1982, 1983, 2005, 2012*
Elite Eights—14
Tournament appearances—43

Let's begin with the title that had to be the most fun: 1980.

That team was known as the "Doctors of Dunk," and they rocked the college basketball world. Coached by the John Wooden disciple Denny Crum, the doctors—Darrell Griffith, the national player of the year; Derek Smith, Rodney McCray, and their associates—took full advantage of a rule change that allowed slam dunking.

Griffith, aka "Dr. Dunkenstein," had twenty-three points in the final win over UCLA.

"I have to admit it, I loved it," Crum told a local radio station.

Crum won his second title in 1986 with a less high-flying but supremely talented group led by Pervis Ellison, Milt Wagner, and Billy Thompson. Ellison had twenty-five points in Louisville's 72–69 win over Duke in the final.

Twenty-seven years later, then under the direction of the always fascinating Rick Pitino, Louisville won its third title, but that championship season was tainted two years later by tales of lurid sex scandals dating back to 2010. Sanctions, self-imposed and otherwise, invariably followed.

The Louisville program has undergone some good times and bad times since then, but that's college basketball.

Michigan State
Two championships—1979, 2000
Eight additional Final Fours—1957, 1999, 2001, 2005, 2009, 2010, 2015, 2019
Elite Eights—14
NCAA appearances—37

Magic/Bird: That's the 1979 final game that got the whole March Madness thing started.

The winners, of course, were Magic Johnson's Spartans. It wasn't a particularly memorable game, basketball-wise—MSU won by eleven and was never seriously threatened by Larry Bird's Indiana State Sycamores. Nevertheless, the impact of that contest has reverberated across college and professional sports, and the world at large, for the past forty-six years.

Forty-million sets of eyeballs witnessed a white man and a black man, the two dominating players of their era, go head-to-head for the first time. This set the stage not only for all the collegiate madness to come, but for a deep and lasting friendship, a lot of books, a Broadway drama, and a rebirth of the dormant National Basketball Association.

Oh, yeah, Michigan State did win another title in 2000, coached by Tom Izzo, whose brand of basketball is—how to put this gently?—a tad rough around the edges. Still, Izzo has been to the Final Four eight times in the past thirty years and has won more than seven hundred games.

So, that's pretty cool, too.

North Carolina State
Two championships—1974, 1983
Two additional Final Fours—1950, 2024
Elite Eights—7
NCAA appearances—29

The saga of the 1983 NC State Wolfpack is, at its very heart, a love story between Jim Valvano and his guys. No team in college basketball history—at least none that we can recall—embraced its coach and his vision with more passion and with more belief in both.

The result was a highly improbable, bordering on impossible, championship run.

But Valvano's kids imagined it from the very start. And, in the end, they all lived his dream.

The 1974 championship was another story entirely.

As opposed to the '83 underdog "Cardiac Pack," the '74 Wolfpack rolled through the entire season like a land-based leviathan, losing only one game to UCLA in mid-December. Led by "Skywalker" David Thompson, a supernatural talent; seven-foot-two center Tom Burleson; and the diminutive Monte Towe, they put a dramatic stop to UCLA's seven-year championship streak.

Only two titles to their name, but the Wolfpack sure made them count.

CINCINNATI
Two championships—1961, 1962
Four additional Final Fours—1959, 1960, 1963, 1992
Elite Eights—8
NCAA appearances—33

For the Bearcats, that five-year span of greatness (1959–1963) merits a special mention here.

It all began with the "Big O," Oscar Robertson, who played there from '57 to '59. There has never been a guard who could rack up triple-doubles (double-figure points, rebounds, and assists) more airily than did the Big O. Long after his career ended, he told a friend that if he knew how much importance the basketball world was going to place on that one statistic in the modern era, he'd have actually given some thought to posting more triple-doubles back when he was playing.

It has always puzzled fans that Cincy didn't win its two titles until Oscar was already gone.

The coach of those two championship squads, Ed Jucker, generally has been overlooked in discussions about legendary coaches, perhaps because he seemed "remote" to his colleagues and in a perpetual state of anxiety. Moreover, his immersion in the details of coaching did not allow him much time for self-promotion.

Still, had it not been for a frantic, last-second overtime loss to Loyola of Chicago in the 1963 final, Jucker eventually would have joined John Wooden as the only coaches to have copped three titles in a row. It might also have led to Jucker being named to coach the 1964 United States Olympic team.

How all this would have impacted the coach's anxiety level is an open question.

ACKNOWLEDGMENTS

From Mark: To my wife, Phyllis, whose patience in allowing me to commandeer her study to write this book will be rewarded.

To my coauthor, Jeff, whose passion for college basketball is inspirationally contagious.

To our editor, Ken Samelson, with whom it is always a pleasure to work.

To my late friend, Jay Blickstein, a fellow St. John's fan, who is out there somewhere waiting for Rick Pitino to turn the ship around.

And, finally, to my dad and all the forgotten "gypsies" of the 147th Army Infantry Regiment (Iwo Jima, Guadalcanal, Okinawa, Saipan).

From Jeff: To Mom, my biggest fan and original editor; Dad, for instilling a work ethic and love of people; Blair, for the unwavering support; Milo and Auri—the two greatest gifts I will ever receive; and Mark, for the opportunity to make a childhood dream come true.

SOURCES

UCONN
Kevin Freeman, Tom Penders, Steve Pikiell—former players
Dom Perno—former player and head coach
Jim Calhoun—former head coach
Dom Perno Jr.—former team manager
Andy Baylock—UConn sports oral historian
Wayne Norman—UConn radio broadcaster
Greg Ashford—former assistant coach

DUKE
Mike Gminski, Jay Bilas, Steve Vacendak, Jeff Mullins—former players
Bucky Waters—former head coach
Dave Colescott—former UNC player

INDIANA
Tom Van Arsdale, John McGlocklin, Steve Alford, Steve Ahlfeld, Adam
Ahlfeld, Kory Barnett, Collin Hartman—former players
Jordan Hulls—former player and current assistant coach
Mike Davis—former head coach
Jim Sherman—IU psychology professor and friend of Bobby Knight
Bob Starkey—current assistant coach in the LSU women's program
Tom Penders and Gary Cunningham—friends of Bobby Knight

KANSAS
Jeff Guiot, Dale Greenlee, Greg Gurley, Tad Boyle—former players

Ted Owens—former head coach
Jerrance Howard—former assistant coach
Carmaletta Williams—Kansas historian
Andrew Milward—memoirist and KU basketball fan
Steve Singular—writer and KU fan

KENTUCKY
Derek Anderson, Dan Issel, Jack Givens—former players
Mike Gminski—former Duke player
Oscar Combs—UK resident basketball historian

UNC
Hubert Davis—former player and current head coach
Scott Cherry, Dave Colescott, Bobby Frasor—former players
Bucky Waters—former Duke coach and NC State player
Barry Jacobs—sportswriter
Jones Angell—UNC broadcaster
Wayne Norman—UConn broadcaster
Jay Bilas—former Duke player and current ESPN analyst
Dan Issel—former Kentucky player

UCLA
Gail Goodrich, Pete Trgovich, Thomas Welsh, Tyus Edney, Ralph Drollinger—former players
Gary Cunningham, Larry Farmer—former players and head coaches
Jim Harrick, Ben Howland, Steve Alford—former head coaches
Murry Bartow—former interim head coach

Index

Barker, Cliff, 134–38
Barnett, Kory, 94
Barnhardt, Mitch, 153
Barnstable, Dale, 136, 138
Barry, Scooter, 118
Bartow, Gene, 217–19
Bartow, Murry, 217–18, 230–31
basketball, history of, ix–x, 67–68, 101–3
Bassett, Armon, 92
Battier, Shane, 62
Baylock, Andy, 11
Baylor, Elgin, 142
Bayno, Bill, 118
Bearcats. *See* Cincinnati Bearcats
Beard, Ralph, 134–38
Beck, Ed, 141
Benson, Kent, 85–87
Berger, Cliff, 143
Bernstein, Bonnie, 194
Berry, Joel, 197
Bialosuknia, Wes, 8
Bibby, Henry, 213
Big Blue. *See* Kentucky, University of
Big East Conference, 10–13, 26–27
Bilas, Jay, 46, 50, 56–58, 62, 64–65, 182–73
Billups, Chauncey, 68, 188
Bing, Dave, 45
Bird, Larry, 235
Blab, Uwe, 78
black athletes: Duke and, 51; Kentucky and, 148–49;

Southeastern Conference and, 143; Texas Western and, 143–44; UConn and, 3–5
blue bloods, vii–xv; characteristics of, viii–xv
Blue Devils. *See* Duke University
Boatright, Ryan, 27, 28*f*
Boeheim, Jim, 45, 123, 158
Boone, Josh, 21
Boston College, 12
Boston University, 155
Bowie, Sam, 151–52
Boyle, Tad, 100, 114, 116
Bradley, Bill, 6, 43
Bradley, Harold, 36
Brennan, Pete, 172
Brown, Hubie, 156
Brown, Larry, 120*f*; character of, 117; and KU, 59, 100, 114, 116–19; record of, 119; and Self, 124; and Smith, 175; and UCLA, 219–21; and UNC, 40–41, 192
Bryant, Paul "Bear," 136–37
Bubas, Vic, 6–8, 36–37, 41–46, 168
Buckley, Jeff, 44
Buckner, Quinn, 85, 87
Buford, R. C., 118
Bunche, Ralph, 207
Bunting, Bill, 178
Burrell, Scott, 20
Butler, Caron, 22–23
Butler, Mitchell, 225
Butters, Tom, 54–56

Moncrief, Sidney, 150
Montross, Eric, 185
Morgan, J. D., 213, 217, 219–21
Morgan, Rex, 145
motion offense, 80–83
Mullins, Jeff, 41–44, 46–47, 50
Murray, Tracy, 225
music, locker room/hype, 44,
    48, 59

Naismith, James, 3, 67, 100–102,
    104–5, 132
Naismith College Players of
    the Year: Duke and, 33, 58;
    Kentucky and, 129
Naismith Hall of Fame, 121, 184
Napier, Shabazz, 21–22, 23f, 27
Nater, Swen, 215
National Invitational Tournament
    (NIT): Carnevale and, 167;
    UConn and, 17–18
Naval Academy, 167
NCAA Runners-Up: Duke and,
    33; Kentucky and, 129
NCAA titles: Cincinnati and,
    236; Duke and, 33; Indiana
    and, 67, 87; Kentucky and, 129;
    KU and, 97; Louisville and,
    234; Michigan State and, 235;
    NC State and, 235; UCLA
    and, 199; UConn and, 1; UNC
    and, 163, 181–84; Villanova
    and, 233
NCAA tournament appear-
    ances: Cincinnati and, 236;

Duke and, 33; Indiana and,
67; Kentucky and, 129; KU
and, 97; Louisville and, 234;
Michigan State and, 235; NC
State and, 235; UCLA and,
199; UConn and, 1; UNC and,
163; Villanova and, 233
Nelson, Reeves, 229
Newell, Pete, 80, 203
Newton, C. M., 156
Newton, Tristen, 31
Norman, Jerry, 203–4
Norman, Wayne, 15–16, 175
North Carolina, University of
    (Chapel Hill; UNC), 37, 41, 53,
    89, 111, 149, 163–97; record of,
    163–64
North Carolina State University,
    36–37, 165–70, 215, 235–36;
    record of, 235
Northeastern University, 14
Northington, Nate, 143

O'Bannon, Ed, 225
O'Brien, Jim, 16
O'Connor, Kevin, 223
Okafor, Emeka, 21
Oklahoma A&M, 166
O'Koren, Mike, 48
Oladipo, Victor, 94
Oliver, Jerry, 84–85
Ollie, Kevin, 16, 20, 26–27
Olsen, Harold, 60
Olsen, Jack, 112

Williams, Roy, 60, 72, 121–23,
181; and KU, 100; record of,
122; and Smith, 121–22, 175,
185, 189, 193; and UNC,
192–83, 194–97
Williams, Wanda, 193, 195
Wilson, Trevor, 224
Wittman, Randy, 87
Wojciechowski, Steve, xi
Wolfpack. *See* North Carolina
State University
Wooden, John, 44, 168, 199–217;
character of, 205–6, 209; and
Farmer, 222; and Harrick, 225;
and McCracken, 70; record of,
202, 208
Wooden, Nell, 202, 216

Woodson, Mike, 87, 89, 96
Woollen Gymnasium, 169
Works, Caddy, 200–201
World War I, 3
World War II, 3, 35, 69, 129–30,
135, 137, 167–68
Worthy, James, 51, 181, 188
Wright, Jay, 234

Yankee Conference, 4, 12
Yonakor, Rich, 48

Zeller, Cody, 94
Zeller, Tyler, 191
zone defense, 83
zone press, 204

www.ingramcontent.com/pod-product-compliance
Lightning Source LLC
Chambersburg PA
CBHW071631270125
20780CB00002B/2

* 9 7 8 1 4 9 3 0 8 4 4 7 0 *